碁

EZ-GO

— *Oriental Strategy in a Nutshell*

Written by:
Bruce Wilcox
Sue Wilcox

Illustrated by:
Sue Wilcox

Ki Press
Redwood City, CA

Library of Congress Catalog Card Number: 96-76041

ISBN 0-9652235-4-X

Ki Press
P.O. Box 5558
Redwood City, CA 94063-0558

Contents

◆◆◆Overview◆◆◆

Metaphorical Go

The Dinosaur's Hind Brain

The Wolf Pack

ESP

Call of the Wild

Alerts you to the dangers of enclosure and shows how sector-lines are an early warning system for groups and define potential territories. **page 37**

Danger — Radiation Area

Examines the dangerous influence of stones on nearby intersections and the use of walls for territory or attack. **page 49**

4,3,2,1, Contact

Teaches finding one's balance, advantage, and purpose while next to enemy stones. **page 67**

Group Defense

Darwinian Evolution

Lays out fundamental shapes and how to evolve them. Covers the basics of survival with two eyes. **page 81**

Flight and Fight

Extols the virtues of running and explains its interdependence with counterattack. **page 91**

The Great Escape

Provides a no-lookahead formula for trying to break out of containment. *page 99*

Group Attack

Buy Wholesale, Sell Retail

Reveals a simple secret for better strategic play by showing you when not to attack or defend. *page 113*

Rampant Machiavelliism

Educates you in the sophisticated pleasures of attacking enemy groups without trying to kill them. *page 119*

The Dark Side

Explains the magical techniques for finishing off enemy groups. *page 133*

Territory

Fools Rush In

Addresses the attack and defense of large potential territories, including reductions and invasions. *page 147*

Quibbling

Discusses the final moves of the game and how to adroitly shift the balance of territory in your favor.
page 163

High Concepts

Yin & Yang

Describes the dynamics between strategy and tactics and provides some meta-rules about both.   **page 175**

A Question of Balance

Compares American and Oriental traditions of fighting and competition. Considers balance and consistency, looking at styles. Uses 'The Great Wall' opening as an example of how to disconcert established players with the psycho style.   **page 187**

Winds of Change

Considers the need for anticipation when riding an elemental force, while discussing issues of sente and gote.
page 199

Sacrificial Lamb

Tells when to abandon stones and shows how some Go board entities can be traded away for greater value.
page 209

GO

Curios

The Road Less Traveled

Catalogs the rare and not-so-rare Go board phenomena of ko and seki.

Go Sharping

Treats the subjects of board assessment, local expectation, and exploiting your opponent's human weaknesses.

Variations on a Theme

Uncovers merits in games closely related to normal Go.

You Rang?

Who Was That Masked Man?

Glamorizes the histories of the authors.

Want More?

Good methods for tracking us down or joining our mailing list.

What Does It Mean?

Translates Japanese Go jargon.

Where Was That Bit About...?

Indexes concepts.

Parenthetical Pages

Acknowledgements

We would like to acknowledge that we are standing on the shoulders of giants, and quite a few ordinary people as well. As with a shopping list we're sure to have left off someone vital and have to go back for them next time.

This book was printed with the financial assistance of Paul Margetts, philanthropist extraordinaire.

Robert A. Chapnick: illustration of a Magic card.
Roland Crowl: alpha testing, general debugging of concepts and a critical eye.
Jean De Maiffe: proof reading and an attempt to get the authors to write more clearly
while avoiding insulting the many feminists in the American Go community.
Toby Hecht: he got Bruce into business metaphoring.
Duncan Hines: physical nourishment and mental inspiration.
Hubble Space Telescope: for cosmic backgrounds, distorted for the cover art:
Photo# STSci-PRC95-11, Jeff Hester and NASA
Photo# STSci-PF95-13, Jon Morse and NASA.
Paul Margetts: long distance scanning.
Bill Taylor: his posting of Deadly Sins to rec.games.go inspired our Go & Sin page.
Roger White and the AGF: for going where no sponsor has gone before.
Kian and Christie Wilcox: inspiration for Kids' Go.

All the writers on our booklist, and all those who colored our backgrounds.
The movie directors who kept our imaginations alive with the wonders of tomorrow.
And the Sci-Fi TV shows that provided recreational quibbling.

> *Humor is the only test of gravity, and gravity of humor. For a subject which will not bear raillery is suspicious; and a jest which will not bear a serious examination is certainly false wit.*
> Aristotle

Who this book is for

This book is primarily intended to help mid-range kyu players and low-range dan players play a game that means more to them. It has discarded the Oriental and traditional approach of teaching by repetition. Instead we aim to teach by entertaining and making your moves meaningful to you. The first three chapters have an additional function as a stand-alone introduction to Go theory for relative beginners. We do assume you know what a board looks like and what Go stones are. One thing that does seem lacking in the world of Go is something to help established players teach others the game. Hence the starter chapters. We know *you* know this stuff but it enables you to establish a framework for a newcomer to the game. To this end we permit you to photocopy **Section 1: Overview** exactly as is and distribute it free of charge as a teaching aid. Pages of this book are not to be reproduced otherwise without our written permission.

What our goals are

We would like to see Go become more popular in the West. Not just to make it easier to get a game ourselves but because we feel that Western society has a lot to learn from the Oriental approach to competition, strategy and planning. Throughout the book there are examples of how Go can be applied to business as a way to reexamine your approach to the long term strategy of your company and to the tactics of daily interaction. This integration of Go theory and business application is a topic that has already been found invaluable by many top managers and salespeople — we hope to expand its distribution more widely.

How this book is organized

Overview: These chapters provide an overview for the game. They define the language with which we discuss Go and explain the ways the game can be understood using metaphor.

ESP: These chapters cover the extra sensory perceptions you need to acquire to detect the dangerous situations you will encounter on the Go board. These are the street-sense instincts that will keep you out of trouble without your having to think about it.

Group Defense: Then it's time for the blunt practicalities of defending yourself while under attack. We look at when discretion should be the better part of valor and when a fight is in order, what to do when there seems to be no escape and how to evolve your way out of a bad situation.

Group Attack: Now it's time to become more aggressive. The next three chapters look at how to attack your opponent's groups. We look at the relative merits of large scale and small scale attacks, then turn to an examination of the politics of the Go board. Is death and destruction the best path to take or can you come up with a better way? If a final termination is what you want, then techniques that seem like magic are available to help you.

Territory: Once the main sketching out of the board is complete you need to know how to handle the territory you have acquired, or how to deal with that which lies in your opponent's hands. The use of metaphor comes to assist you in the perception of complex formations as part of the scenery and those minor endgame points as debates in the halls of justice.

High Concepts: Next comes a series of chapters on the higher level concepts involved in Go. Here are the philosophical perspectives to give you a grasp of what is really happening on the board and help you relate it to parallels in day-to-day existence.

Curios: If you feel you can take it all in your stride, there is the expert's delight still to come. *The Road Less Travelled* takes you to the complex world of bluff and counterbluff known as a ko fight. Then, just when you thought you knew it all, we have to reveal that all is not necessarily as it seems and you could be subject to the ruthless maneuvers of a Go sharper. Even worse, we then change the rules on you to demonstrate that you can learn more from Go than strategy and tactics.

You Rang? Finally, you learn who the authors were, what their products are, what strange Japanese words mean, and where you can find things in the book.

Who Said It

We have written this book together, yet some stories and attributes are Bruce's and some are Sue's. Faced with the possible task of attributing a name to every "I" in the book we finally decided you the reader could distinguish the authority of a dan player from the need for explanation of a kyu player. The threats to do awful things to you on the Go board, if you dare to diverge from EZ-GO theory, are Bruce's; but we think you'll be able to spot that for yourself.

Diagram Notation

In addition to the usual diagram notation used in other Go books, we sometimes add the following (as exemplified in Diagram 1):

1. A captured stone in a diagram is shown as a numbered or unnumbered box. This allows you to know which stones in some confusing mass have been captured and which still remain at the end of the diagram. White 1 was captured by Black 2.

2. When a play is suggested at a point but the play hasn't been made yet, it is shown with a letter inside a box of the color expected to play it. Black might play *a*.

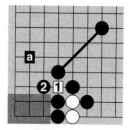

Diagram 1

3. Sometimes we shade territory and/or add sector-lines. Black owns six points of territory and has a sector-line showing. The board is always shaded, to help make the White stones appear clearer. Black shading is then darker, and White shading is lighter.

4. Empty intersections with minuscule dark circles on them occurring on nine points of the board on the fourth line and center are handicap dots. They are where you place handicap stones in Japanese rules, and aid in knowing where you are on the board relative to the edge and the corners. They are easily distinguished from the small (but much bigger) boxes used as marks to highlight an intersection on a link path.

Overview

Metaphorical Go

Philosophy and Go

The Dinosaur's Hindbrain

Ranks & Handicaps

The Wolf Pack

Go on the Information Superhighway

To order, send US $25* + $3.50 shipping or
18 pounds Sterling + 2 pounds shipping
For overseas air mail add extra:
Europe = 4.50 Sterling or $6.50   Asia = $8.50
* CA residents add $2.25 sales tax

Make checks payable to:
Bruce & Sue Wilcox
PO Box 5558
Redwood City, CA 94063-0558

Metaphorical Go

T*he sheriff stepped out onto the dusty street. The sun burned directly overhead, blinding him for a second. Facing the sheriff, the outlaw tensed his hands over his holsters. The outlaw began to reach for his gun, and, with a loud crack, it was all over. The outlaw, in disbelief, fell to the ground.*

Bobby Fisher hunched over the chess board, gazing sightlessly at the hand-carved wooden pieces. One could almost see the wheels turning in his head, looking at sequence after sequence, trying to find a way to save his beleaguered king. There! Was that it? His mind reviewed the sequence of moves he had just imagined. If Black plays here, then White plays here, then Black plays here, checkmate. Yes! Swiftly he moved his pawn ahead one square. Check, and mate in two. The game was his.

These scenes are Western metaphors. We tend to imagine confrontations as one-on-one, hero versus villain, relatively simple encounters. In each confrontation there is some climactic moment when the hero takes sudden skillful action and immediately vanquishes the opponent. These metaphors govern our actions in real life. In business we seek a monopoly— the total destruction of our competitors. In war we try to crush our enemy in a big battle, being "firstest with the mostest." In science we initiate the big crash project, aiming for the breakthrough that magically solves some problem. In diplomacy we adopt "saber rattling" confrontation. In life we think hard work at a single goal and commitment to the company way will yield the good life. Competitive, fast, direct, short-term, extreme, one-shot. These are adjectives that describe our Western style.

But the world has become complex, cutthroat, and interdependent. Our Western metaphors haven't been working as well as they used to. Many people have begun seeking answers from the Orient, be it divining the future with the *I Ching*, avoiding the material world through the philosophy of Zen Buddhism, trying to understand nature and human behavior with *The Way of the Tao*, or applying Chinese military strategy from the *Art of War*.

Go (*Baduck* in Korea, *We'i Ch'i* in China, *Igo* in Japan) is a four-thousand-year-old game. Before that, it was a means of divination. Go is the Orient's metaphor for war and business and a Rorschach test for judging character. The CEO of Nintendo plays Go to "size-up" competitors before negotiating a contract. Mao Tse-tung compared his guerrilla war approach in taking over China to the game of We'i Ch'i. What happens when their metaphor meets our metaphor? The quagmire of Vietnam. Oriental dominance in consumer electronics and memory chips. The acquisition in bulk of major American companies and real estate. That is why an editorial in the New York Times admonished then President Bush to learn Go before going to Japan.

Cooperative, competitive, eternal, subtle, balanced, flavorful. These are adjectives that describe Oriental style and the style of Go. Go is a positional game, a game of delicate balance and coordination of planning and execution. Miura Yasuyuki, head of Japan Airlines Development Company and Nikko Hotels wrote: *The study of Go can reveal how the Japanese businessman thinks and develops business strategy.* Go is a valuable metaphor.

Just as Go is a metaphor for teaching other lessons, other metaphors can be used to teach Go. I use metaphors freely throughout this book. When I teach Go to children, I use a metaphor to convey the goal of Go. They get the point right away. You will too. Pretend you are a five-year-old. (I don't teach them any younger lest they try to eat the stones themselves.)

The Goal of Go: Imagine a freshly-baked square pan of brownies. Smell the aroma wafting through the air toward your nose. See the chocolate icing spread over the top. Savor how it would taste in your mouth. Now, imagine you have a friend with you. Naturally you want all of the brownie for yourself. However, your mom is standing nearby, so you know you can't get away with it. Instead you are supposed to cut the brownie fairly, in half. Will you? Or will you wiggle the blade to get a slightly bigger half? Or cut the brownie so that the best frosted bits are on your side? In other words, you will want to get something better than your friend, but not enough so that Mom will notice and take the brownie away from you and divide it evenly.

Christie and Kian Wilcox with their brownie Go board.

OK. Back to being an adult. The Go board is like the brownie. You want it all. But you don't deserve it all and you won't get it all. If you try to get it all, you will surely get less than you could otherwise. It's the nature of the game. So you must aim to share. Cooperate, but be greedy. Aim for a little bit more than your opponent. Something almost unnoticeable. That is your goal.

The Play of Go: Go is a two-player game between Black and White. The Go board is typically a 19x19 square grid, but it can be smaller, like the 9x9 board shown below. The board will be entirely empty at the start. You place stones of your color, one per turn, on any empty intersection, trying to enclose regions of empty intersections touched only by your stones. These regions are *territory*. Black always plays first. Diagram 1 shows Black and White alternating six moves each on a 9x9 board. Small boards are good for beginners because the games end quickly, providing fast feedback. The numbers on the stones indicate the order in which they were played. Once played, stones don't move from their original spot. Whoever controls more territory when the game ends, even if only slightly more, wins.

In Diagram 1, Black has built a complete wall around ten points of shaded territory in the bottom left corner. (Shading is used to show territories in our diagrams, but exists only in your imagination in a real game.) Diagonal stones are an acceptable solid boundary. White has claimed eighteen points, but there are three holes in White's boundary. By the end of the game, White will need to fill them in. Currently in Diagram 1, neither player has yet grabbed any territory in the lower right corner.

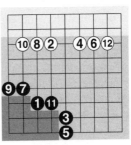

Diagram 1

5

Expect that the two of you, Black and White, will divide the board into several small territories, some yours and some your opponent's. Your job is to be slightly more efficient than your opponent, to get slightly bigger territories or slightly more territories. Placing your stones is like alternately carving the brownie with your friend. For each move/ slice you make, your opponent/friend makes a move. Expect to share most of the board/ brownie and subtly try for that extra point/frosting.

In the Beginning...

The board is empty. It stares at you like an empty canvas, daring you to touch it with your paintbrush. Wherever you touch, the paint will stick permanently, so you fear even getting close. Where should you start? Dare you spoil the center? Will you dribble here and there, make a bold splash across the canvas, or try to recreate the Mona Lisa in a small corner?

Sketching: It is a common mistake of the fledgling artist to take a single spot of canvas and flesh out every last detail of the picture there, neglecting the canvas as a whole. In Go, the novice Black player often begins by placing stones in a line, then using that line to solidly surround a piece of territory. This is as wrong in Go as it is in painting. Instead you must paint your stones in broad brush strokes — sketch a rough outline of your intended picture and fill in the technical details later.

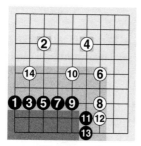
Diagram 2

In Diagram 2, Black seals the corner doggedly while White sketches out the rest of the board. White's claim of forty-four points has weaknesses, but even if Black can destroy half of White's claims, White will still have far more than Black's claim of ten points.

Of course, in Go, you have a competing artist, so your intended outline is likely to become distorted beyond recognition. That's OK. Pretend you are going to create an abstract masterpiece using your opponent as a random influence on your brush.

Corners then Sides: Traditional military or chess theory says take the center first to dominate the landscape. That's great in a game where the pieces move. In Go, however, you rope off regions without moving pieces. Traditional Go theory dictates playing in the corners first, taking advantage of the two intersecting board edges as preexisting fences around your territory. After taking the corners in a full size 19x19 game, players then spread out to the adjoining sides, where a single board edge can still be used profitably. The center acts like a big theater in the round; anyone can get in easily, so no one can really control it. It is not used in the opening. Early moves there would allow the opponent to gain much more potential territory along the sides.

Corner Moves: Go, like chess, has evolved a large number of standard opening sequences that start both players off on roughly equal footing. These moves are called *joseki*. In chess the openings use the entire board, but in Go they cover only part of the board. It is possible to pick joseki that interact badly with other stones on the board, even though locally they are perfect. As a beginner, you don't have to master any joseki right now. The following simplistic approach will work for your next hundred games or so.

Opening play is usually on *a*, *b*, or *c* of Diagram 3 or on one of the marked intersections. The lettered intersections are on the third and/or fourth line from both edges. You will learn about the value of playing on these lines shortly. The marked intersections, being on the third or fourth line from only one edge, represent uncommon play. They aim more for control of the corresponding side and less for control of the corner.

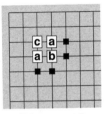

Diagram 3

A corner move on a symmetrically positioned intersection (*b* or *c*) does not immediately require further attack or defense of the corner. If your first corner move is not on a symmetrically positioned intersection (not on *b* or *c* of Diagram 3), your opponent will usually quickly respond, since your corner is not secure.

In Diagrams 4, 5, and 6, either player would like to take one of the indicated points. *a* is the most popular and common point, followed by *b*, *c*, and *d*. In Diagrams 4 and 5, *a* is more common because it is harder to enclose (therefore it is safer). In Diagram 6, *a* is safer because it is closer to the corner than the other choices and closer to the edge than Black's stone. This may allow it to "steal" some of the corner territory.

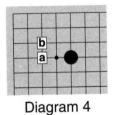

Diagram 4

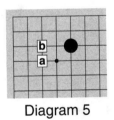

Diagram 5

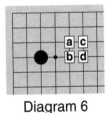

Diagram 6

Side Extensions: Once you have built your fortress in the corner, it is time to spread out and pacify adjoining unclaimed countryside along the side. This takes advantage of your nearby corner strength and allows you to use your corner stone(s) to fortify the area quickly when that becomes necessary. When extending along the sides, look for the widest unclaimed area between your stone and an opponent's stone. Don't play in this area unless it is at least three points wide. (To measure the width, count the empty perpendicular lines between the stones.) Anything smaller than three lines wide is unimportant until the endgame.

The first sixteen unnumbered moves in Diagram 7 were joseki. The players then began staking out the unclaimed sides. Black 17 claimed the largest one (nine lines wide prior to Black 17). White 18 took the next largest (seven lines). Black 19 took the next (six lines). White 20 took the last unclaimed side (three lines).

All remaining unclaimed side areas between Black and White are fewer than three lines wide. Wide areas between stones of the same color (e.g., between *a* and Black 17) are potential territory for that color. Playing

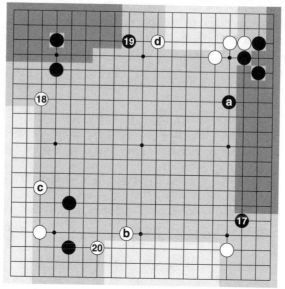

Diagram 7

in those areas is a midgame activity, not an opening game one. These twenty stones completed the opening. The corners and sides are now sketched. Black claims 63; White claims 62.

Third and Fourth Lines: To take advantage of the edges, I've already said to begin sketching in the corners, then expand to the sides. But where should you play? The third and fourth lines from the edge represent the most efficient play, so they are equivalently good places to play. This is where corner moves were played in Diagram 3, or side extension moves were played in Diagram 7.

Diagram 8 suggests why this is so. Black uses 52 stones on the third line to control the outer territory (140 empty points). That's about 2.7 points per stone played. White uses 44 stones on the fourth line to surround the inner

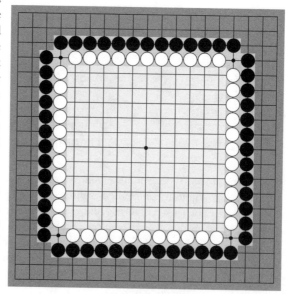

Diagram 8

territory (121 empty points). That's exactly 2.75 points per stone. The point-per-stone ratios are similar on the third and fourth lines.

All other lines diminish in value rapidly. On the second line the point-per-stone ratio is 1.125 points per stone, while on the fifth line it is 2.25 points per stone. On the first line it's 0 points per stone. You don't play there to make territory.

Balance Third and Fourth Lines: As you stake your claims to the biggest areas first, you must consider the impact of the third and fourth line at each move. The third line is the line of territory. A third-line stone makes secure territory efficiently but can be threatened from above. If you put all your stones on the third line, you are vulnerable to being threatened from above and kept out of the center.

The fourth line is good for fighting. Being close to the center, a fourth-line stone lends a supporting hand throughout the board but is weak at holding territory it bounds. If you put all your stones on the fourth line, you make territories that are vulnerable to invasion, so you may later lose much of what you have claimed.

You should seek balance, a mixture of third and fourth line moves overall. If one end of your area is on the third line, try to put the other end on the fourth line. In politics this might seem wishy-washy, but politicians don't want to lock themselves into extreme positions. Neither should you.

In Diagram 7, Black 17 on the third line balances from the fourth-line stone (*a*) above it. White 20 balances the nearby fourth-line stone *b*. White 18 is questionable, extending as it does from a third-line stone (*c*). White intends to undercut the fourth-line Black stone above it, but White's left side position is too low. As you will learn, Black 19 dare not extend to the fourth line, lest it be undermined by a move extending from White's nearby third line stone (*d*).

After Six Days...

War broke out. Despite all the unclaimed land remaining, the inhabitants of paradise became covetous of the others' areas and tried to steal them.

"The battle is joined" in the midgame. Both players have to strengthen or expand their positions, create new territories in the center, attack their opponent's positions, and defend against attacks on their own positions — all at the same time!

The midgame normally begins when all opening moves are exhausted (all corner and edge areas are claimed). However, if you conclude you are falling behind during the opening, you must declare war. You must invade your opponent's areas before they become secure. That means parachuting a few stones into danger behind enemy lines. Thus the midgame can start even before the opening is complete.

Maybe you will launch a full-scale invasion, putting all your might into it. Or maybe those brave few will become sacrifices to distract the enemy from your real intentions.

In Diagram 9, Black must decide between continuing the opening sketching phase by playing at *a* or launching the midgame by invading White's area at *b*. Is Black falling behind? No. If you compare the size of the shaded areas for Black and White, it should be obvious that Black has a lot more claimed territory than White. Black should continue the opening phase.

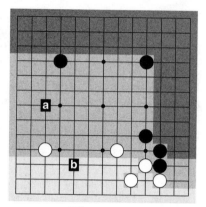

Diagram 9

In Diagram 10, Black did continue to sketch, but played a conservative choice (the marked stone). Now White must decide to continue the opening with *a* or launch the midgame by invading with *b*. Is White falling behind? Yes. White is far behind in claimed areas and will still be so even after playing *a*. White will want to invade Black's area with something like *b* and hope for the best.

If White did play at *a*, the opening game would be over. The midgame would start anyway. Black could choose to secure Black's claims, perhaps playing at *b*. *b* is a good move whether or not White has played *a*. Or Black could invade White's claims. Since Black's claims are bigger than White's, Black would prefer to defend, rather than attack. The game is all about the size of things. Stake out the biggest

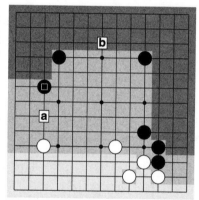

Diagram 10

areas first. Attack or defend the biggest areas first. Being first somewhere is huge advantage. There is even a Go technical word for it, *sente*. To have sente is to be able to play first elsewhere. A move is sente if it forces a reply, leaving you with total freedom.

Stones can be captured and removed from the board (described in detail in the next chapter) and the midgame is filled with the threat of capture. Capture is not the purpose of the game, however, making the most territory is. Capture can lead to making or losing territory, so both players must constantly bear in mind the safety of the stone about to be played, as well as stones previously played.

By the end of the midgame, all areas of the board have been surrounded by one of the players or the players have jointly ruined areas with their mutual presence. All major collections of stones have either been made immune to capture or have suffered death. The game, however, is far from over.

GO

Ending Not with a Bang …

Lots of quibbling and last minute recriminations over missed opportunities characterize the endgame. Of course the game might end with a bang, if someone is forced to resign in the midgame due to the death of a large group of stones. But that isn't the rule. Usually the game continues past the midgame into the endgame. The endgame is your last chance to eke out a win in a close contest.

In Diagram 11, Black and White have clearly divided the board into Black, White, and neutral (unowned) areas, but there are still a few gaps in each player's territorial boundaries. As it stands, Black has twenty-seven points and so does White. The game is tied; it is Black's turn.

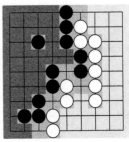

Diagram 11

A good endgame magician can work miracles of sleight of hand, moving territory boundaries slightly this way and that. Since you only have to win by a single point, each dent you can create in an enemy boundary and each bulge in your own boundary provides the potential for victory.

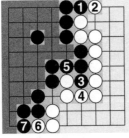

Diagram 12

In Diagram 12, Black puts stones on White's boundary gaps. Each time Black does so, White loses the possibility of territory next to Black's stone. Since each Black move threatens to steal more, White blocks each thrust. When Black runs out of places to thrust into, Black 5 prevents a White thrust, and Black 7 stops another.

After the moves of Diagram 12, all boundaries are sealed. Black has twenty six points; White has twenty five. Black has converted the tie into a win by quibbling over boundaries. The game is not over yet. There is still one place left to play between both sides' positions, though neither player can create new territory by playing there. When you learn about capture, you will learn that such moves can also make a difference (White may have to fill inside White's territory to protect stones from capture). But even if White needs no defense, White cannot win. It is too late.

At last the game approaches its finale. In Western culture it is the dramatic scene, the falling villain or the checkmate. In Oriental culture it is a moment of meditation and peace, the completion of a joint work of art. When every move you can make would cost you points (e.g., filling in your own territory), you say *I pass* (you make no move), disturbing the board no more. If your opponent does likewise, you have both agreed the game is over — and it is. If your opponent doesn't pass, then clearly somebody is out of touch with reality. You can play again if you wish, or pass again. Eventually both of you will pass in succession, ending the game. All that remains then is to count the points and see who won. If you have at least one point more, you won.

Philosophy and Go

Go evolved out of a method of divination used in China. Black and White stones were cast on a board covered with astrological and geomantic symbols. We talk a lot in this book about violence, killing, and capture — the aggressive, competitive side of Go. This is a part of the picture and the easiest way to memorably explain what the game is about and how to play it. But there is more to Go than fighting — Go has a spiritual side, a reflection of Oriental philosophy. To concentrate only on the concepts easily understood in the Western tradition would not make a good Go player. To become a strong player, you need qualities that seem unexpected at first, but which can have repercussions in everyday life.

Duality: In Oriental philosophy, everything in the world can be seen as the dynamic interplay of opposite qualities: Yin and Yang, female and male, receiving and giving, rest and activity, faith and rationality. Within every individual are *both* opposing qualities. The West tends to think of opposites as opposing, whereas the East thinks of opposites as cooperating parts of the same whole.

The dynamic tension between opposites is called *balance*. While in specific situations expressing only one side of oneself can be valuable, overall one should strive for balanced expressions of both parts. Awareness that both qualities coexist allows you to look in any specific situation to see which quality is most appropriate. You need not be locked in to only one side.

For example, the Western mindset is heavily biased in favor of action and often neglects the value of its polar opposite, inactivity or resting. Allowing situations to "ripen" and delegating action to others come less easily to us. In Go, a weaker player is tempted to make overplays, feeling that the only way to get the opponent to make a mistake is to take action to force the opponent to pick badly. Stronger players are content to be passive and play a non-threatening peaceful move. They know full well that if you give a weaker player the initiative, the weaker player will usually pick a bad move without any help.

Radical Change: If opposites coexist in all things, then the ability to change radically also exists. While locked in deadly combat you feel aggressive Yang energy. Once the group is alive or dead, you can repose in Yin and admire the beauty of it. Yang becomes Yin. A group is alive in one moment and dead in the next— transformation from one extreme to its opposite.

Oriental philosophy and mysticism are steeped in the concept of the coexistence of opposites. Hard/Soft, Cooperation/ Competition, Love/Hate, Life/Death, Success/Failure. This simultaneous is/not- is quality is often baffling to the Western mind, but it is a key to action in the Orient. It is not that the two qualities lie at either end of a straight line. It is more like the two qualities are next to each other on a circle. You can either take the long way around from one to the other, or you can simply move from one to the adjacent other directly. Assume both qualities exist in a situation or a person and look for the most efficient lever to move something or someone across the thin boundary. A small action can result in what seems like an impossibly large transformation. Enemies become friends, the weak defeat the strong, the dead become alive.

For example, success may be the opposite of failure, but they are not far apart. Being successful does not place a company at a great distance from failure. Behind each failure lurks an unseen opportunity for success and behind each success lurks an unseen risk of failure. Businesses can fail rapidly *because* they are successful. Fast growth, however much desired, is dangerous. Whenever your company doubles its size in short order, all of your established systems will be stressed beyond endurance and you need new systems. If you don't watch out for this — poof! Or consider this: if you accomplish what you set out to do, you are successful. Then what? You are in danger of drifting ever after until you find a new vision.

Cyclical Change: Once you admit change occurs from one extreme to the other, then you must also admit that it can change back again. Not just *can* change back again, but *will* change back again. A quality builds toward its zenith and then collapses back into its opposite. Over time this change may occur in predictable cycles. The bleak cold of winter will give way to the rebirth of spring, which becomes the sweltering heat of summer, which becomes the dying of fall, which becomes the bleak cold of winter again. The economy grows and then enters recession. Success leads to failure which leads to success. It is not surprising; it is

inevitable. If you are aware of this cyclic nature, you can prepare for the next turn of the wheel. This cycle can take only a few seconds, like the cycle controlling your heartbeat, or it can last for centuries.

Centralization has been a trend for centuries. In earliest times people organized themselves into small groups, each of which was self-sufficient. Over time this gave way to tribes. As agriculture overtook hunting, interdependence led to forming larger aggregations of organization— the city-states. Industrialization created broader dependencies for raw materials and markets to sell in, and nations replaced city-states. Continuing this trend is the European Common Market, a sort of mega-nation. And yet, this trend may not be a linear growth resulting in the eventual unification of all of Earth. It may instead be merely a vast cycle.

There are signs that centralization has peaked and decentralization is the next wave. Businesses are breaking into smaller pieces, returning to their core strengths. Nations like the Soviet Union and Yugoslavia are fragmenting into pieces. Quebec threatens to secede from Canada. Hawaii wants to leave the United States. Libertarianism, the politics of individual responsibility, is becoming popular. As technology makes global interconnection probable, it also reduces the need for local connectivity. The pendulum is either swinging away from centralization on a slow march back to small units, or is about to cross the narrow threshold and radically change our political universe. What took thousands of years to evolve may suddenly transform within a century. People unaware of the cyclical nature of development will find themselves surprised at the changes and their rapidity.

Preparation: Preparing is a matter of expecting things to change, but it is not *just* a matter of expecting things to change. The current phase of the cycle has embedded in it the seeds of the next phase. When a phase transition comes upon you suddenly, consider what advantages can be salvaged from the preceding phase.

In winter buds are dormant but preparing to bloom. In the failure of one business can come the inspiration for a successful new business. For example, 3M's famous PostIt Notes product stems from a failed glue that wouldn't stick enough. Instead of viewing it as a failure for what they wanted, it was considered in a new light and led to a successful product. Another example might be that if you gain lots of experience in bankruptcy court due to your failed business, you could form a new business based on advising others in similar situations. In Go, if you suddenly realize your stones will be captured, instead of despairing, look to see how that might be a blessing in disguise, how you might sacrifice them gladly while your opponent is thoroughly distracted with success.

Surrender: If you feel that only actions (control) can save you, you neglect the value of external support. Surrender, the opposite of control, is an often overlooked technique. In Go, surrender can enable you to let go of a group that is in trouble and look for other ways to use your moves. Outside of Go, if the world is not submitting to your will, if you just cannot bludgeon it into going your way, then consider doing something else. Have faith that there is a direction you should be moving in and prepare for the moment when that direction becomes clear. This is a good policy on the Go board and in life.

Surrender is not the same as resignation. This becomes abundantly clear when you consider your choice of resigning the game versus reconsidering your position and options. It is better to treat the setback of losing a group as an opportunity to change your approach to the game instead of an all-time damning event.

It is an act of faith to see the universe as supportive. I like to operate on the belief that the universe is on my side. The positive attitude can enhance more than just your game. If you stop developing defeatist paranoia, you gain flexibility to try again in a different way rather than keep banging your head against a wall. This will aid your ability to learn as it removes the negative feedback and makes all experiences positive in some sense. It also makes it easier to take risks: there is less to lose and more to gain. This can lead to more than making a radical move or just speaking out honestly on a topic, it can help you develop integrity.

There is also an element of self-forgiveness in the quality of going beyond one's mistakes and trying again. By removing the urge to fear-driven effort, you give yourself permission to receive insights from information that is all around you. This can lead to creative solutions not available to those obsessed with macho, controlling behavior. You may find your game takes longer as you abandon the pressing fight to allow your intuition to work on other solutions, or you may play faster as you get out of your own way. You may find less pressure in your day-to-day life as you let solutions offer themselves.

The Dinosaur's Hind Brain

They say two heads are better than one. In the case of the big dinosaurs, two brains were essential to survival. It took too long for messages from the far end of the tail to reach the brain in the head, so nature evolved the hind brain. It didn't think, it just reacted. Today this design carries through into humans. When you stick your hand on a hot object, you don't spend time thinking about whether you should release it. A message travels to your spine which sends an action response back without thought — a reflex action. The amazing thing is that humans can consciously override this reflex. You are able to keep your hand there and let it burn. This is not usually a good choice.

Reaction follows perception. To react to something you must be aware of it. If you are a raw beginner at Go, you see only a mass of stones scattered on top of the board. To improve, you must detect things above mere stones. You must see strings, links, territories, and groups, and be able to recognize when they are in danger. Then you can train your hindbrain to reflexively save stones threatened with capture, solidify endangered links, and keep your groups alive. Then you can train your forebrain to dispassionately analyze the whole board and determine your best course of play.

Strings

Stones of one color that touch each other horizontally and/or vertically along the grid are *strings*. Diagonally placed stones are separate strings. In Diagram 1, all *a*'s are one string. *b*, *c* and the *d*'s are separate strings.

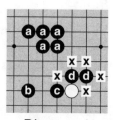

Diagram 1

The rules say you can put a stone on *any* empty intersection (subject to suicide restrictions which are unimportant, so I will ignore them). After all your work to surround a territory, the enemy can just plonk a stone in the middle of it to dispute your claim. Fortunately, the rules also provide for capturing stones to defend territories you create from just such invasions. Strings, not stones, are the fundamental units of capture.

Empty intersections touching stones horizontally and/or vertically (but not diagonally) are *liberties*. In Diagram 1, the *a* string has nine liberties, *b* has four liberties; *c* and *d* have three and five liberties respectively. All liberties of *d* are marked with *x*; *d* and *c* share a common liberty.

Give Me Liberties or Give Me Death: By the rules of Go, when a string has no liberties, it is removed from the board.

Diagram 2a

In Diagram 2a, White's string has just one liberty. Black can capture it with one more move. White's string is in *atari* (threatened with immediate capture).

In Diagram 2b, Black played on White's other liberty and removed White's two stones from the board. Black gets to keep them as prisoners. They add two points to Black's score. Black also has two points of territory now.

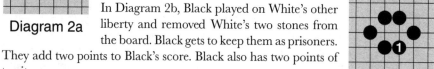

Diagram 2b

Last One on Wins: In Diagram 3, White has just played 1. Both Black's marked one-stone string and White's three-stone string including 1 have no liberties. What happens? The rule is whoever played last wins. It's like an underwater fight. Whoever takes the last deep breath before submerging will win. The correct sequence of events is: put a stone down; remove all enemy stones with no liberties; remove all friendly stones with no liberties.

Diagram 3

In Diagram 3, the removal of the single marked Black stone leaves White's three stones with one liberty, so they remain on the board. Because they are now in atari, Black could replay where the marked Black stone used to be to capture three White stones; Black would then be the last one on and end up with two liberties. The situation wherein multiple stones capture a stone and get immediately recaptured is called a *snapback*. In reality White's two marked stones were doomed to snapback, and White shouldn't have played White 1 to save them.

The Eyes Have It: In Diagram 4, Black has two liberties. How will White capture it? If White plays on either of the two liberties, White's move will have no liberties while Black's stones will still have one liberty. White's move would be removed as a suicider. (Suicide is illegal in some rules, just stupid in others.) It is not possible for White to capture Black. Black has two eyes.

Diagram 4

An *eye* is a liberty surrounded on all sides by stones from a *single* string (or stones that could connect elsewhere to become a single string). If a string has only one eye, then to capture that string you must fill the eye last. The string is then removed per the rule of **Last One on Wins**. If you fill the eye before filling all other liberties, your own move dies and the opponent's string remains.

If a string has two eyes, it is immune from capture. You can never fill the eye last, because there are two of them. Strings with two eyes can never be killed. They are alive.

False Eyes: If more than one of your strings bounds the eye, then the opponent may be able to capture just one of them to occupy the eye. In Diagram 5a, White has something that looks like an eye but it is bounded by two White strings. To join them into one string, White would have to fill in the eye itself. Since Black can capture into the eye without killing all bounding strings at once, such an eye is called a *false eye*.

Ko: It is possible to create a situation where, after capturing the opponent, your stone is capturable, and, after you are captured, you can recapture your opponent, and so on. Such a repeating situation is a *ko*, meaning eternity. The recapture recreates the previous position. This is illegal in Go. You may not recreate previous board images.

Before recapturing in a ko, you must play elsewhere for one move, making a *ko threat*. This breaks the repetition by changing the board elsewhere. Your opponent either wins the ko (e.g., connects the stone in the ko) or responds to the threat. If your opponent responds, then you recapture the ko stone and await your opponent's threat.

Diagrams 5a-c illustrate a ko. In Diagram 5a, White's marked stone is in atari. In Diagram 5b, Black 1 captures White. In Diagram 5c, White 2 captures Black 1; the situation now looks exactly like Diagram 5a. This is illegal. White must first play a move elsewhere. (If that had happened, White 2 would have been labeled White 4).

Diagram 5a

Diagram 5b

Diagram 5c

The rule of ko gives Go an extra strategic dimension. It teaches indirection. The threat of ko requires constant consideration of the creation and neutralization of ko threats, even without a ko happening.

Saving Strings: There are two ways to save strings threatened with capture:

> 1. **Play the last liberty yourself.**
> 2. **Capture an adjacent enemy string.**

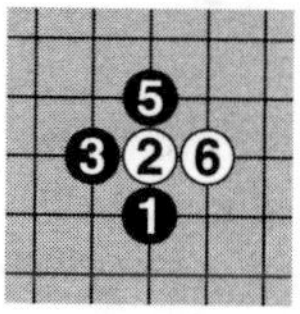

In Diagram 6, Black 5 threatens to capture White 2. (White chose to play move 4 elsewhere.) White saves White 2 by extending with 6, creating a bigger string with new liberties. Black now has to fill three more liberties to capture White.

Diagram 6

In Diagram 7, Black's two marked stones are in atari. If Black extends to *a*, they will still be in atari and White will capture all three by playing right of *a*. Black can save the marked stones in Diagram 7 by playing at *b* and capturing two White stones. The removal of White's two stones will leave Black's marked stones with three liberties.

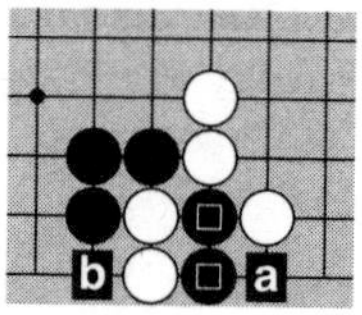

Diagram 7

Dead as a Doornail: Sometimes you should override the hindbrain's saving reflex. In Diagram 3, capture didn't help White. In Diagram 7, extending didn't help Black.

Diagram 8

Here, in Diagram 8, there is no salvation whatsoever for White after Black plays 5. (White chose to play elsewhere for the 4th move.) White can neither capture nor extend to safety. If White extends with White 6, Black persists with Black 7. When White now plays at 8, Black can kill the White string with 9. Three White stones would then be removed from the board. White should not play at 6 and 8, since escape is impossible. White 2 is dead and White should play elsewhere.

Go is a bit confusing in its terminology. Stones that are removed from the board are called captured, and stones that cannot avoid being removed from the board are called dead. Yet captured stones can never be rescued (unlike prisoners of war), and dead stones can be rescued (as though resurrection of the dead were possible). They should have reversed the use of these words.

Automatic Capture: If stones cannot find safety by the end of the game, they will be removed as captured, *without having to fill in their liberties*. Both sides just agree there is no escape and that the stones are dead. If both players fail to agree on the life and death of stones, they continue playing to prove their beliefs. Anyone who passes during this resolution phase must hand a stone to the opponent as an automatic prisoner. This keeps the score balanced as one side fills in to kill and the other side passes.

Links

Strings are easy to see. Links, the foundations of more complex relationships, are slightly harder. A *link* is an invisible association between close friendly stones (a stone link) or a stone and an edge (an edge link). The stones forming the link are *endpoints*. Edge links have only one stone endpoint; the edge of the board acts as the other.

Links tie friendly strings together to form barriers and these barriers fence off areas of the board from enemy access. Stones lying on the same line or only one line apart horizontally or vertically create this barrier effect. If stones are more than one line apart in both directions, they leave a gap that is easy for the enemy to penetrate.

So, to be a link, the endpoints must be within one line of each other in one direction and relatively close together in the other direction. As the endpoints move farther apart, they change character abruptly, as described in *Call of the Wild*. If two stones (or a stone and the edge) are not related via one of the patterns shown in Diagram 9, they do not form a link. They are too widely separated; their barrier is easily breached.

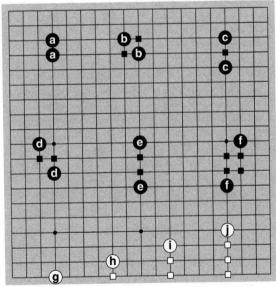

Diagram 9

Stone links (in black):
a in-line extension
b diagonal
c single-skip
d small knight
e double-skip
f large knight

Edge links (in white):
g in-line extension
h single-skip
i double-skip
j triple-skip

The marked points in between the two endpoints are *path points* that you can occupy to join the ends into a single string or that your opponent can occupy to prevent you from forming a single string. As a rule, shorter links are stronger than longer ones. Straight line links are stronger than bent ones of equivalent length. In-line links are stones solidly connected into a single string and I mention them only for completeness.

Links are threatened or attacked by enemy stones placed near them. Answer threats and attacks promptly, as a hindbrain reflex.

Threatened Links: An enemy stone touching adjacent or diagonal to a path point threatens a link. Immediately secure a threatened link from further attack by playing on the path point closest to the enemy stone. The exception is: never react on the first line if there is an open second line path. Play on the second line path point instead to avoid having your move captured. In-line and diagonal links cannot be threatened.

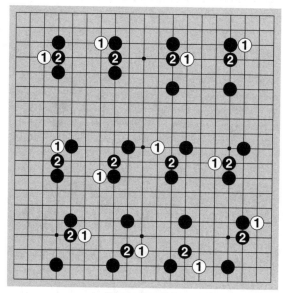

Diagram 10

Diagram 10 shows some (not all) threats against stone links (White 1) and correct defenses (Black 2). In response to White's threats, which are always adjacent or diagonal to a link path point, Black responds on the threatened path point.

Attacked Links: An enemy stone placed directly on a path point attacks a link. Always defend the link even if you cannot reconnect the endpoints. This will help you attack your opponent's stones later by keeping them separated or denying them easy access to a region. The act of preventing two stones from joining is called *cutting*, and the enemy stones doing that are *cutting stones*. Capturing cutting stones is valuable because it allows two strings to join into one.

The move defending an attacked link attempts to go around the opponent's stone to rejoin the endpoints. This move creates two shorter links, one from each endpoint to the defending stone. These will become the focus of further attacks if your opponent is insistent about separating your stones.

Diagram 11 shows White attacks (White 1) against Black links and correct Black responses (Black 2). Each response forms two shorter links, which become the focus of continued attack and defense. Sometimes White must take time out to save stones from capture, giving Black extra time to reinforce links. White's attacks are always on the link path point while Black attempts to rejoin endpoints by linking around the attacking stone.

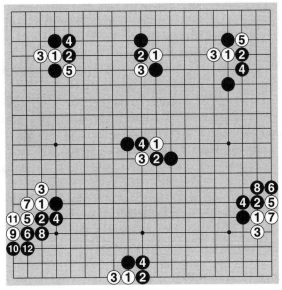

Diagram 11

Your opponent's attack may prevent you from connecting your two endpoints. Most of the attacks shown in Diagram 11 keep Black separated. Even so, the defended link remains as a barrier preventing the enemy stones from connecting.

Territory

A territory is a cluster of empty intersections enclosed by only one player's stones and links. (It may also contain embedded enemy stones considered dead — remember **Dead as a Doornail** earlier?) *Territory*, the collection of all territories, is the game's treasure, its *raison d'être*. Whoever has more territory at the end of the game wins.

Guard the Doors to the Treasure Room: Imagine that a territory is like a room with walls of stones and open link doorways. All the valuable treasure lies inside the walls. Nearby are thieves who would like to steal your treasure. If a thief approaches a door from outside, what would you do? You would close the door immediately (put a stone on the threatened link to secure it) to keep the thief out.

Suppose the thief somehow appeared inside the room, grabbed some treasure, and ran toward the door. Again you would close the door immediately. But this time you would immobilize the thief as well. You don't want a thief running around in the room trying to find another way out.

What would you do if the thief appeared standing in the doorway? You would try to slam the door. But the door wouldn't completely close. You should then build a new smaller door *between* the thief and your treasure. This is illustrated in Diagram 12a.

Diagram 12a

You could try to build up a door on the outside, entombing the thief in your room, but this is riskier; the thief might fight back. In Diagram 12b, Black seals White in, but the sequence White *a* through Black *d* might result in White living within Black's room.

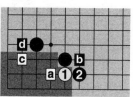

Diagram 12b

In short, when the enemy plays near or on a link doorway, defend the link immediately. Your hindbrain should already have mastered this as the link reflex, but it is also a territory reflex. If you have two links to defend simultaneously and only one is a territory doorway, make sure your hindbrain defends the doorway link first.

Tit-for-tat, Score Remains Pat: When you trap enemy stones in your territory, usually you do not need to execute them. They can't escape and at the end of the game they will be automatically removed. In fact, filling in all their liberties costs you points — you are filling in your territory. You only want to respond as needed to immobilize them. If your opponent invades and you defend move for move, preventing your opponent from living (making two eyes), there is no change in score. For each move you play inside your territory (losing one point), your opponent has placed a stone that you get to remove at the end of the game (gaining one point).

In Diagram 13a, Black has eight points of territory. In Diagram 13b, White invades with White 1 and Black 2 immobilizes the thief. White persists with 3, and Black

again keeps White solidly contained. White will not play any further. All White's moves put White in atari. At the end of the game Black removes the two White stones and counts six points of territory and two White prisoner stones for an unchanged eight points.

Diagram 13a

Diagram 13b

Once you have mastered the reflex of shutting the door on a thief, your territory is usually secure when it is sketched. That is why you sketch in the opening game instead of building solid walls immediately; you will have time to defend the doorways. But there are situations where your territory is not stable as it stands and you may want to defend it before the thief arrives.

Open 3-3 Instability: The first case involves a territory built in the corner. If the territory contains an unoccupied 3-3 point (third line from the edge in each direction) and you have no stone immediately adjacent to the 3-3 point, then your opponent will invade there as in Diagram 14. In doing so your opponent immediately creates a tiny room of four points. Suddenly you may have lost your territory.

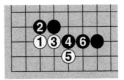

Diagram 14

Diagram 14 shows a typical 3-3 invasion. White invades with 1, Black seals the nearby door link with 2, but White marches onto the other interior link with 3. After Black 6, White has built a room of eight points out of Black's former territory. With a few more moves, White will be safely alive.

3-3 invasions can be prevented by playing on or adjacent to the 3-3 point first. In Diagram 14, Black could play at Black 2 to seal the corner before White invades. The extra defensive move touching the 3-3 point makes it easier to kill any White invasion.

Fourth Line Instability: The second case involves a territory with those wide doors so popular in hotel conference rooms. If the territory doorway is a fourth-line stone, it is hard to close the door on a thief.

In Diagram 15, Black has a territory with a fourth-line door. White can slide to *a* on the door, and Black cannot easily create a new door. The preemptive defense for the big door is to erect one or more smaller doors. Black could play at *a* or one above it to better secure the opening into Black's territory before White slides on in.

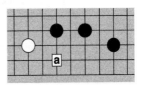

Diagram 15

Double Big Link Instability: The last case involves a territory using two large doors hung off the same small hinge. This hinge can barely stand the weight of the doors. When a thief arrives at one of the doors and you try to close it, a partner rushes the other door, which snaps off.

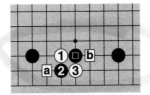

Diagram 16

In Diagram 16, Black has two double-skip links from the same central stone. White 1 and 3 are a sacrifice combination (White abandons one of these stones), after which White can play at *a* or *b* to break apart one of the two double-skip links. Each move threatens to capture a stone, so Black will have to save that stone and allow one of the links to be broken.

If Black wants to secure a double-door in advance of White, Black should add another stone above the center pivot or shrink one of the two doorways.

Groups

A group is a collection of strings connected by links. The strings of a group could become one string by playing on all the path points. Therefore a group acts as a virtual string. That is, a group bounds territory and has eyes by virtue of its links.

In Diagram 17, there is one Black group and one White group. The link paths are shown with marks of the appropriate color.

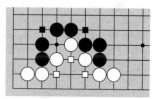

The group is the primary unit of analysis in the midgame. If the group as a whole cannot get two eyes, then each and every string in the group also can't get two eyes. Eventually all strings of a dead group can be

Diagram 17

captured. The ability to recognize whether a group is alive or dead is essential.

Two Point Extension for Safety: As strings need liberties, groups need territory. So much so, that extending along the edge to gain territory is a group hindbrain reflex, overriding the general opening rule of extending into the widest areas first.

In Diagram 18, Black's stone initially has room to extend in two directions. But when White plays 1, Black must rush to play *a* to gain some territory. Otherwise White will play near there, and Black will never get an easy base for life.

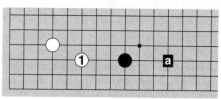

Diagram 18

What is a Weak Group? As you will learn, Go is driven by issues revolving around weak groups. Whether a group is weak or strong depends upon your Go strength and the configuration of stones. In terms relative to your strength, if you think *you* could attack the group, then it is weak. If you are nervous your opponent could attack it, then also treat it as weak. In absolute terms, a group is strong if it has enough territory and time to form life or if it has a lot of maneuvering room around it to grow into. Having five or more different single skips that could be played indicates you have enough room to maneuver. The moves must not be adjacent or diagonal to any enemy or friendly stones nor should they be on the first or second lines.

In Diagram 19, White's marked single stone group has one stone capable of supporting single skips (marked with *x*'s). Of the four possible skips, only two can be counted as maneuvering room because one touches Black's stone and another skips into the edge. The group is weak.

White's big group has five stones supporting six safe skips (marked with *y*'s). It is strong.

Black's middle group has four stones and three safe skips (marked with *z*'s). It is weak.

Black's corner group has territory enough for two eyes. It is strong.

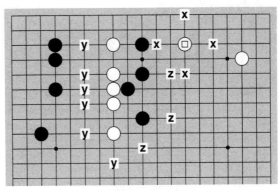

Diagram 19

Review: Diagram 20 shows examples of the basic structures. See if you can identify all the examples of each type:

- •**String:** adjacent stones that are captured as a unit (7 Black, 8 White)
- •**Links:** short range connectors and barriers (don't miss the large knight's move link of White's on the left-middle side) (12 Black, 13 White)
- •**Groups:** linked strings (4 Black, 5 White)
- •**Territories:** vacant points bounded by a single group (3 Black, 2 White)

All link path points are shown in boxes. The neutral region is the center of the board and space between opposing stones along the edge of the board.

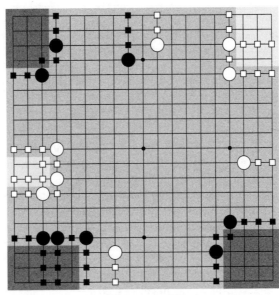

Diagram 20

If you have mastered these fundamentals of perception, you are off to a great start.

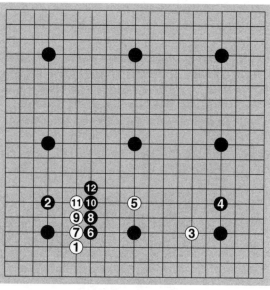

One of the great virtues of Go is its handicapping system. Two players of widely different strengths can play an even contest where both have an even chance of winning. Black, who always plays first, is assumed to be the weaker player. To compensate for this weakness, Black is given extra initial moves. Instead of placing one move, Black places as many moves as necessary to start off on the right foot. Usually no more than nine handicap stones are given, but more are not impossible.

Diagram 1 shows the start of a nine-stone handicap game. Black starts with control over the entire board. Among professional players, the unmarked nine stones would result in a victory of about 140 points for Black. If Black can just keep stones connected out to safety, White will be in for a losing battle. Of course if this were easy for Black to do, Black would no longer get a nine-stone handicap.

Ranks are defined based on handicapping. If you have to put down three moves on your first turn to have an even chance of winning, then you

Diagram 1

are three ranks weaker than your opponent. As a raw beginner you start at a rank of 35th *kyu* and improve toward 1st kyu. As you improve past 1st kyu, you become 1st *dan* (black belt rank). From there it is up the dan ranks until you are as strong as anyone in the world (about 10th dan). A 5 kyu player gives a five stone handicap to a 10 kyu. A 5 dan player gives a five stone handicap to a 1 kyu player. (There is a one stone difference in strength between 1 kyu and 1 dan.) How many ranks are there in Go? If the weakest player is 35th kyu and the top pros are 10 dan, there are 45 ranks in Go.

People have asked how much stronger than a professional player is God? While the match has yet to be played, most estimates place God three ranks above top professionals. One pro is reported to have said he wouldn't bet his life against God without a four-stone handicap.

The Wolf Pack

There is violence in nature — predator stalks prey, to eat and to live. But this violence exists to preserve balance. If every herbivore lived, there would be immense herds of starving animals wandering over barren plains nibbled down to the dust. There is balance in nature and, though the individual scenes of death horrify us, this balance ensures that the complex ecology continues.

The rhythm of depredation followed by population recovery continues onto the Go board. Groups are attacked and die while new ones are created and thrive. A predator that goes for too much can be turned on and killed. No group is totally helpless and, just as in nature, sacrificing the weak helps others to live.

Hunting with the Pack

There are savage creatures on the Go board. Wild and untamed, they will do anything to survive. Packs of wolves hunt these creatures. They corner one of them, surrounding it with a baying pack then closing in for the kill. Think of your stones as the wolves. Wolves work together to surround and enclose their victim. Maybe the hunt starts with a daring raid by an opponent's creature on your territory. Maybe you make a deliberate attempt to surround and trap one in the wild. Or maybe you try to cut one off from a herd of its friends. When you do attack it, sometimes it will turn and attack you, fighting desperately for its life or at least trying to take you down with it. These creatures are strings and can be as tiny as one stone or as big as you can imagine until they become the full fledged monster — a group. There are two steps to capturing the wild and wiggly strings: enclose the target and then go in for the kill.

Enclose the Target

To enclose strings you must encircle them with your pack of wolves. Otherwise they can run around (add stones to gain liberties) and become harder to kill. Enclosure is automatic when the enemy string invades your territory. The walls of your den surround it immediately. Trying to catch a string out in the open is much harder. You need to coordinate several wolves to keep your prey from running away.

An encirclement is composed of wolves with small spaces between them, i.e., links. Shoulder to shoulder wolves (in-line links) like Diagram 1 are inefficient. The prey won't wait for you to complete the wall of bodies and will easily escape. You can encircle more quickly and with the same effect using the longer links of Diagram 2a.

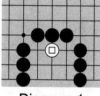
Diagram 1

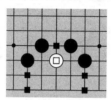
Diagram 2a

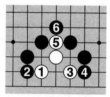
Diagram 2b

Once White's stones are encircled they are trapped. If they try to escape by slipping through the links, reflexively defend them (see Diagram 2b).

In order to set up an encirclement, locate where the enemy stones have open access to the rest of the board, then make a move that creates two links closing off the open access. An enclosing move always results in the target becoming surrounded by a continuous ring of stones, link path points, and possibly the edge.

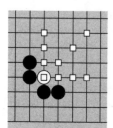

In Diagram 3a, White's stone can expand in the directions indicated by the white boxes.

If Black plays at 1 in Diagram 3b, Black creates two single-skip links to contain White's stone. White is now enclosed. There is no more open access.

Diagram 3a

Diagram 3b

There are typically many moves that enclose a target in links. To select among the possible choices, apply the following rules in order:

1. **Don't create links already under attack.** The enemy will just finish destroying the link. Threatened links are OK. You will still have time to defend them after the enemy responds. In Diagram 4a, Black 1 creates a large-knight's link to the marked Black stone, but the link is already attacked by White. White 2 completes the destruction of the link and Black has made no progress in enclosing White.

Diagram 4a

2. **Select the shortest and closest links to the target.** The tighter the noose is around a victim's neck, the faster the victim will die (the fewer liberties it can acquire by wriggling around). In Diagram 4b, Black contemplated playing *a*, but Black 1 creates a shorter pair of links to the marked endpoints.

Diagram 4b

3. **Pick the move with the most liberties**, if you still have multiple moves to choose among. This improves your stamina in a fight.

Diagram 5

Diagram 5 shows all possible enclosing moves. Symmetrically equivalent moves have the same letter. *a* and *b* form links already under attack (i.e., links that have an enemy stone on one of their path points) and must be rejected. *c*, *d*, and *e* are acceptable. *d* creates the shortest link pair and is therefore best.

In Diagram 6, White 1 has just invaded Black's position. If Black wants to kill White 1, Black must first enclose it with *a*, *b*, *c*, or *d*. Applying the rules:

1. Discard *d*; it forms a link already under attack.

2. Discard *c*; *a* and *b* produce shorter links.

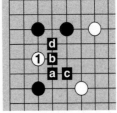

Diagram 6

3. *a* and *b* are similar (though *a* has one shorter diagonal link it also has one longer large-knight link; *b* has two small-knight links). *a* is preferred because *a* gets more liberties than *b*.

Go in for the Kill

Once your pack has encircled the victim it's time to finish it off. It's important to do this right or you may lose members of your pack. The victim may even get away, leaving you and your family to starve. You can only go after and fill one liberty per turn, so it's important to pick the right one.

To select among the possible choices, apply the following rules in order:

1. **Attack from a safe base**, playing liberty-filling moves that are adjacent to or diagonal from your existing stones. This will help protect them from counterattack.

2. **Fill your opponent's best liberty**, the one that would provide the most liberties if your opponent played there.

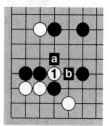

Diagram 7a

In Diagram 7a, White 1 is already enclosed, with liberties at *a* and *b*. If Black played at either *a* or *b* that would be attacking from a safe base. The best liberty is *a*. If White played there, White's stones would have four liberties. If White played at *b*, White would have only three liberties. Black should play at *a*.

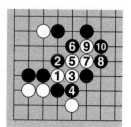

Diagram 7b

If Black applies the liberty-filling rules at each move White will be captured as shown in Diagram 7b. At the end of Diagram 7b, five White stones will be removed by Black.

Can the Prey Climb a Ladder?

There is a potential exception to avoiding attacked links when enclosing strings. This exception is the ladder.

In Diagram 8a, Black would normally pick none of *a*, *b*, *c*, and *d* to enclose White, since all form attacked links. White has only two liberties, however, so Black *may* be able to pick *a*, putting the White stone in atari and loosely enclosing it.

Diagram 8a

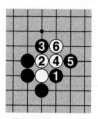

Diagram 8b

In Diagram 8b, Black tries to capture White by playing 1. White 2 breaks Black's enclosing link. To re-enclose White, Black must play 3. This sequence is repeated through White 6. How will it end? If nothing else is in the way, the moves will zigzag all the way across the board, and White will run out of liberties at the edge. This is a *ladder* capture. Each move must keep White in atari or White will turn around and attack Black's weak line of stones.

If a White stone appears in the way of the ladder, as in Diagram 8c, the ladder fails and Black will be in trouble. *Never play out a ladder whose result you can't figure out.* You will lose the game quickly.

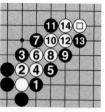

Diagram 8c

Leader of the Pack

When prey stumbles into your den, killing it is easy. It is trapped. But sometimes the intruder is not just a food creature but another wolf, and both of you are trapped. You surround each other. In such cases a fight to the death develops. Whoever fills in the other's liberties first wins and becomes leader of the pack. This is a *capturing race*.

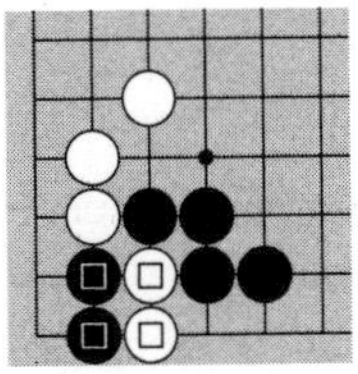

In Diagram 9, Black and White have marked stones caught in a deadly struggle. Black has two liberties and White has one. White will lose this capturing race, no matter what.

Diagram 9

In Diagram 10, Black has two liberties and so does White. Whoever plays first will win, so it is urgent to play here.

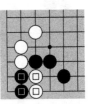

Diagram 10

Generally speaking, whoever has more liberties wins without playing further. In case of a tie, whoever plays first wins. If you do play further, you need to be careful. It's a tight space with no room to maneuver. Turn your back for a moment and you will lose.

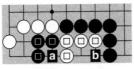

Diagram 11

In Diagram 11, Black has three liberties and so does White. Time is of the essence If Black plays on the shared liberty (*a*), suddenly the race is two-two, and White proceeds to kill Black. To win, Black must play at *b*, making the race three liberties to two liberties.

The rule in the capturing race is to fill in liberties from the "outside" first, away from the other stones involved in the race. Fill in shared liberties last. To remove White in Diagram 11, Black must play at *b* first, not *a*.

Is Cutting Feasible? Knowing about capturing races, you can decide if it's safe to cut somewhere. Imagine you have just cut. Will your cutting stone be surrounded? If not, it is safe. If it is surrounded, will any opponent's stones be surrounded? If not, your cut is dead. If both of you are surrounded, what will be your liberty counts? If your counts are at best even and you are enclosed, you will die. You must have more liberties than your opponent to win.

In Diagram 12, Black has a diagonal connection in the territory wall at *a*. If White cuts there, Black and White will both be enclosed. White will have two liberties. Black will have three liberties on one adjacent string and two liberties on the other. Since White is not stronger in liberty count than Black and it will be Black's turn after White cuts, White will die. Therefore White won't cut, and the territory boundary is safe enough for now.

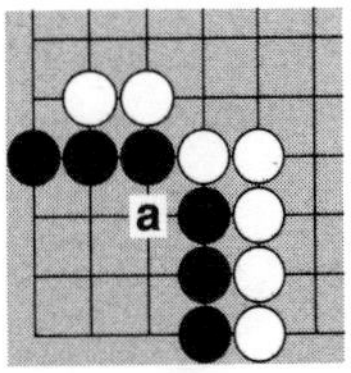

Diagram 12

In Diagram 13, Black has a diagonal connection at *a*. If White cuts there White will have two liberties and Black will only have one. Since both sides will be surrounded and White will be ahead in liberties, White can cut and Black will lose two stones.

Diagram 13

Play Dead: When you have lost stones in a capturing race, don't play it out just to see if the opponent will match you move for move. Play dead. Later you can use these moves as ko threats to reverse the race. Or maybe your opponent won't notice the moves that threaten to revive your stones later, but would be paying attention now.

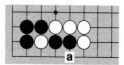

Diagram 14a

In Diagram 14a, White has clearly lost the race, one liberty to two. White should not play *a* now but should save it for a ko threat.

In Diagram 14b, Black gets careless and plays endgame moves against White's stones. After Black 3, Black has the same number of liberties as White's unmarked single stone, so White can capture the four Black stones. This may seem unlikely, but only slightly more complex variants of this happen all the time.

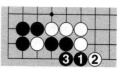

Diagram 14b

Capture or Territory? Holding or extending your territory is more important than killing for fun. Only kill if you need the food. It is not efficient to kill unnecessarily. This admonition usually falls on deaf ears. You can gain points by capturing strings or by enclosing territory. Beginners are often overcome by blood lust, and most players enjoy the thrill of the hunt. However, capture is not the objective of the game — surrounding the most territory is. Capture's purpose is to defend your claims.

In Diagram 15, Black takes six moves to make nine points of territory. White takes six moves to make four points by capture (two points of territory and two prisoners). Black made more points going for territory than White did going for killing a string.

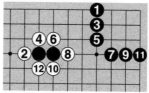

Diagram 15

Kill strings to save your stones, to make eyes for your groups, to join a weak group to a stronger group, and to protect territory. If you kill for fun, don't expect a large profit.

Go on the Information Superhighway

The easiest place to find out almost all you could want to know about Go is on the World Wide Web. Provided you have the computing resources, a modem, and access to the Internet, there is lots of Go information out there. Ideally, or even presumably, you will have a net browser such as Netscape Navigator and a choice of search engines to find things for you. You need an Internet account with telnet capability in order to play Go easily on the Internet. Your public access provider must have a local phone number or you will be in debt forever if you find you enjoy playing Go on the Internet. Outside the US this is presumably going to be a problem as you'll often have to pay for connect time. Best idea is to go back to university and get a free account there or move to the US.

The general clearing house for the latest Go information is the newsgroup: **rec.games.go**. Read the latest news, scandals, tournament postings, news of new products, questions and answers, then add your own comments on Go issues. From here you can obtain the Go FAQ (Frequently Asked Questions) — a list of Go information. Useful items in the FAQ are: an explanation of what Go is and how to play, some help with terminology, where to get Go books and equipment, understanding Go rankings, how to find a club to play at, what programs are available to display game records or play you at Go, and how to find out more about computer Go.

If the FAQ isn't currently posted in rec.games.go, go to Fred Hansen's Home Page:
http://www.cs.cmu.edu/afs/cs/user/wjh/public/Home.html

The FAQ is just a part of the Go goodies on offer at the Go archive site: **ftp://bsdserver.ucsf.edu/Go**. This site also features amplified information mentioned in the FAQ and compressed files of clients, programs, translators and a huge assortment of game records and other useful Go stuff. Another route into the archive site is: **http://bsdserver.ucsf.edu/go/ftpindex/top.html**
You can also access the FAQ via: **http://www.smartpages.com/faqs/**

There are a number of World Wide Web Home pages which deal largely with Go matters, from gossip, photos of well known players, discussions on Go programming theory, tournament arrangements, and Go songs, but as these are available as personal whims and likely to change we will not list them all here. Any one will lead you to the others. we recommend Ken's Go page as the best link interchange. It's the Grand Central Station of Go. Here's the address:
http://Ltiwww.epfl.ch/~warkent/go/golinks.html

It has everything we can think of: facts, services, people, history, articles, a Go dictionary, study advice, links to many clubs and Go Associations, plus information on Go authors on the Web and ftp sites to get take-away goodies.

Official Go information in Great Britain is available on the British Go Association page: **http://www.eng.ox.ac.uk/people/Harry.Fearnley/go/BGA.html**.

The American Go Association has its page: **http://www.usgo.org**. Its snail address is: PO Box 397 Old Chelsea Station, New York, NY 10011.

Computer Go has an official mailing list for those interested in this special field. Contact: **listproc@listproc.anu.edu.au**.

But for the fun news see Michael Reiss's Computer Go page at:

    http://www.mth.kcl.ac.uk/~mreiss/compgo.html.

It features what's new on the Computer Go scene, where to get Go software, software in development, a Hall of Fame with photos, details of the massive Ing prize, gossip, and a lengthy bibliography.

The most useful Go pages for beginners are written by Mindy McAdams. Sample: "How to Play Go on the Internet" at

    http://www.well.com/user/mmcadams/igs.howto.html.

This is a wonderful, detailed, clear account of all you need to know to get started playing Go with people from all over the world. It covers getting your own Internet account and obtaining a client as well as how to use the IGS and its etiquette. It also links to the No Name Go Server page. Also try her page on "What is Go?"—
http://www.well.com/user/mmcadams/gointro.html. It describes the game, the players and other sites to visit and is less massive an encounter than some other pages.

There are currently three resources for playing Go on the Internet. One is in Korea, the Internet Go Server at: **igs.nuri.net** (port 6969). Another is in America, the No Name Go Server at: **imageek.york.cuny.edu//nngs** (port 9696). The third is in Germany, at: **grizu.uni-regensburg.de** (port 9696) All require you to register as a user to play regularly. The telnet connection only gives an ASCII view of the game. There are a number of clients available at the Go archive site to present a 'user friendly' interface.

You can play Go by modem link without involving the Internet. This is more sensible than postal Go. There is the specification and sample code of a Go modem protocol for developers obtainable from the archive site. The modem protocol was written by Bruce and is the world standard for computers to exchange Go information. Almost all top programs implement this protocol since it is required for the Fost Computer Go Competition.

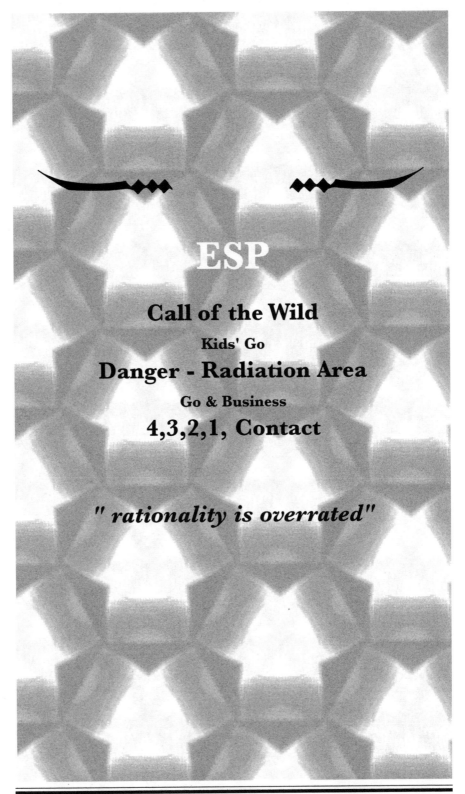

ESP

Call of the Wild

Kids' Go

Danger - Radiation Area

Go & Business

4,3,2,1, Contact

" rationality is overrated"

Call of the Wild

A t the beginning of a game, the Go board is a great open space. As development progresses, structures arise to limit that space. But a group that wants to live needs space to avoid capture and make eyes. Hence the call of the great open spaces and your opponent's predatory urge to close you in, enclose your groups, and domesticate them into small tame creatures or kill them to fatten his own growing groups.

Stay Free — Avoid Enclosure

To stay free, you need to develop the ability to sense when your enemy is closing in on you. If you notice you are surrounded, it is too late. The first scents on the breeze are the warnings you must detect in order to run in time. Like an antelope being stalked by a lion, your groups must learn to flee before the attack, not after.

Weak players fear being enclosed by stronger players, and well they should. White's tactical abilities are like magic to Black, who is virtually defenseless. Maybe you feel strong and unworried by the threat of enclosure. Be worried. As players get stronger, they also get foolish. They lose their fear of enclosure because they know they can live.

Stay fearful. Although sometimes unavoidable, becoming surrounded is costly. It is always a strategic cost to become enclosed. This is what might happen to you:

1. **Your Group Might Die.** Sometimes death happens because of a tactical error. How often have you heard "I would have won if ...''? Expect to make errors. Such errors will be tragic if your group is enclosed.

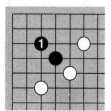

Diagram 1a is a joseki in which Black lets White surround Black's corner in exchange for other outside moves. Black 1 is the joseki move to gain life.

If you don't know the joseki, Diagram 1b shows a quick and easy way for the corner to die. It may not look dead yet, but trust me that it is.

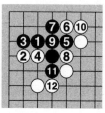

Diagram 1a

Diagram 1b

2. **You Lose Targets Because Your Opponent Unites While Engulfing You.** Diagram 1c, where Black improves on Black 5 of Diagram 1b, shows Black gaining life. White, however, gets a strong, unattackable wall.

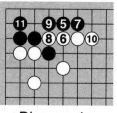

3. **Your Group Becomes Isolated.** Black's surrounded group can provide no assistance to other weak groups, nor can it act as a base from which to extend toward enemy potentials.

Diagram 1c

4. **You Will Lose Points in the Endgame.** Making life means playing additional stones within your territory to form eyes, lessening your profits. Small enemy endgame plays you might have ignored now require response because they threaten your eye space. What began as a large profit gets whittled away into a mere handful of points.

Diagram 1d, which fixes Black 7 of Diagram 1c, is the correct joseki. If Black carelessly captures White 14 with Black 15 instead of playing as shown, Black dies. Otherwise, Black barely lives; with a profit of only 3 points after White plays forcing moves. Aiming to attack White's stones justifies becoming so enclosed. Few Black players ever carry out the attack.

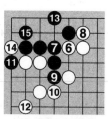

5. **Your Opponent Gets a Source of Large Ko Threats.** While your group is hostage, you must be more careful fighting everywhere else, lest a ko fight demolish you.

Diagram 1d

Enclosure Alert

The first early warning you should master is the one-move-before-enclosure alert. You should be able to spot immediately all moves which can be used to enclose your stones (create links all the way around them). As learned in *The Dinosaur's Hind Brain,* do not consider enclosures that create links already attacked.

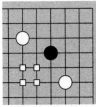

In Diagram 2, for example, Black should quickly see all four marked points as places White could play to enclose Black. There are no other places.

Diagram 2

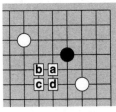

Diagram 3

In Diagram 3, of the four lettered intersections, only two actually enclose by creating links. Do you see them? The two are *b* and *c*.

Do you see danger in Diagram 4? White can enclose in one move, and there is exactly one place to do so. See if you can find it. Hint: creating a large-knight's link is NOT the move, since it contains Black with a link already under attack.

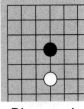

Diagram 4

Sector-lines: Invisible Fences

Perceiving immediate enclosure (via links) is easily mastered. Anyone can see a fence. Well, maybe. I know someone who works for the Invisible Fence Company. Their product? Dense impenetrable shrubs that act like fences but don't look like fences. Go has invisible fences too. Spotting them requires understanding sector-lines.

Anywhere on the board, two stones of the same color or a stone and an edge point can be thought of as the ends of an imaginary line. If there are no intervening obstructions such as stones or links, then it is possible to play to join the two ends into a continuous line of stones. Many such lines exist during the opening and midgame. At short range, these lines are called links. At long range, if the lines divide the board into useful strategic regions, they are called *sector-lines*.

While links are actual barriers, sector-lines are potential ones. Both divide the board into *sectors* (regions containing groups or collections of potential territory). The sector becomes a basic unit of analysis. If multiple groups of the same color reside in the same sector, there will be no significant attack to be made on them. They can join too easily. Sectors containing a single group, however, become a prime focus of analysis for attack and defense.

Diagram 5 shows some imaginary lines radiating from Black 1. Line *a* is a sector-line, containing a single-stone White group to its right. Line *b* passes through an enemy link and is thus broken. Line *c* divides the board into regions containing multiple White groups. Neither line *b* nor line *c* is a sector-line.

The *d* sector-line to the upper edge contains another White single-stone group. When considering sector lines to the edge, only do straight lines along a grid line. Ignore diagonal lines (four shown).

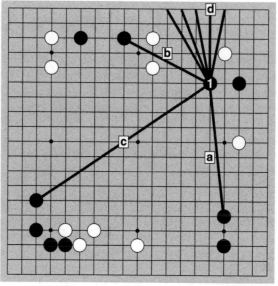

Diagram 5

When deciding upon sector-lines containing a group, use the one providing the tightest containment. This gives least maneuverability and provides the group with the most danger.

Sector-lines may be of any length. However, don't concern yourself with ones more than ten intersections long. This allows a line to run from a side handicap stone to the next one, containing a corner. Lines longer than this are usually too weak to be important. Thus, even if line *c* were otherwise good, it would be too long to notice.

The Carnivore and the Herbivore

The midgame revolves around the attack and defense of weak groups. Perceiving the board strategically requires seeing it from the point of view of both the attacker and the defender. When you think about moves, consider their impact with respect to each viewpoint. To be a good hunter you must understand the prey, and to survive as the prey you must understand the hunter. Although a weak player taking a handicap from a stronger player may feel like an antelope being stalked by a lion, it is important not to give White too much psychological advantage. Even the herbivore can turn and attack when cornered. Each species has its weapons or shields.

The attacker sees the board divided into regions of potential enemy victims and hunts for the sector-lines bounding each enemy group. If a weak group is isolated within its own sector, the attacker licks his lips in anticipation. If the group is not in its own sector, if it is part of a herd, then the attacker tries to split it off from the herd.

Diagram 6 shows the board from Black's attacking viewpoint. Black has lines containing all but one of White's groups. Only two of those lines (on the right) are short enough to count as sector-lines.

The defender sees the board the same way, divided into sectors of potential victims, but in this case the victims are the defender's own groups!

Diagram 7 shows Black's defensive viewpoint (White's attacking viewpoint). All of Black's groups are in separate sectors. Black's upper right group requires two sector-lines

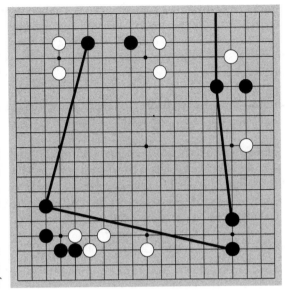

Diagram 6

to contain it. All lines are short enough to be dangerous to Black, whose freedom is threatened everywhere. Fortunately, not all of Black's groups are weak.

When considering the implications of a sector-line for a group, look at the line most closely containing the group. If the group is not bounded by enemy sector-lines or the lines are too long, any attack will fizzle quickly and can be rejected. The group can expand freely. Groups within sector-lines less than ten points long, however, are in serious danger if they don't already have two eyes or have secure territory worth two eyes.

A group lying exactly on a sector-line *may* be in danger. If your opponent is stronger that you, the group *is* in danger. If you find yourself with a weak group contained by a short enough sector-line, what should you do? Run.

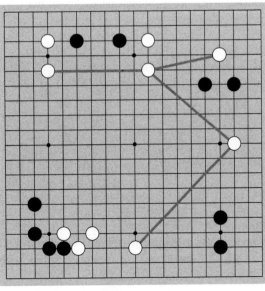

Diagram 7

Run Across the Line: This is just a continuation of **Avoid Enclosure** on a broader scale. Don't stay within a sector-line if your group is weak. Running consists of adding stones to the group (see *Flight and Fight*). Place your next stone to form a link with any of the group's stones, so as to make the group spill across the containing sector-line and into another sector.

Should You Always Run? Don't be silly. You don't *always* do anything; 80% or more of the time you run, which is why it's the rule.

In Diagram 8, Black has a corner group within White's sector-line, but Black shouldn't run for two reasons. First, Black is not in danger. Black has enough secure territory already to make life if need be. Second, expanding to *a* or *b*, Black can acquire lots more territory. Making a two-point extension was a basic group reflex in *The Dinosaur's Hind Brain*. Do that instead of running.

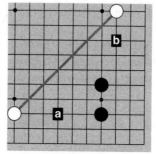

Diagram 8

Running assumes you don't have enough secure territory and can't easily get enough in one move.

Running is Not for Ultimate Safety: You do get safety, but only temporarily. When you escape the sector-line, your opponent can play more moves and create new lines so that you are back inside again. Sometimes you seek only temporary security in order to have time to play some really big move. Mostly, however, waiting to be attacked later is a bad idea. Instead, the purpose of running is to secure the high ground from which to turn around and attack those who seek to contain you. They are forced to stop attacking you and defend themselves. You either get the initiative to play elsewhere or the fun of an attack.

White plays 1 in Diagram 9, placing Black's group within White's line. Black has territory, but it is undercut from both sides, so while Black could live, it wouldn't be worth much. Black runs to 2, crossing the sector-line.

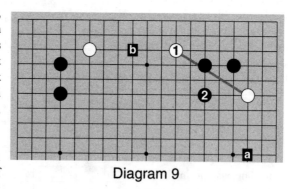

Diagram 9

From here Black will turn around and attack at *a* or *b*. If White defends one side, Black rushes to attack the other. Black must rush to attack. Otherwise, if White defends both sides, Black's running move is meaningless and White will continue to attack Black later.

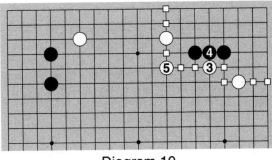

Diagram 10

If Black fails to react to White's sector-line, White will follow up with White 3 and 5 as in Diagram 10. Now Black is enclosed. This is an instant strategic loss. White's potential territory is much more secure, and Black is risking the three-stone group to a serious mistake. With perfect play, Black can still break out of containment; but most players aren't perfect. I use this enclosure all the time on black-belt rated one- or two-dans, and they stay enclosed and sometimes die.

Don't Run: Most of the time running makes you temporarily safe and promises attack. If running promises no attack, don't run. Make life or sacrifice.

In Diagram 11, Black will not be able to attack White after crossing the sector-line, so Black should play 1 to live instead. Later Black has a good continuation to *a*. Playing one point higher (at the 3-3 point) is a pure defensive move with little threat against White's lower stones.

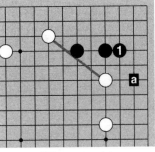

Diagram 11

Quiz: In Diagram 12, if you were Black, where would you play next?

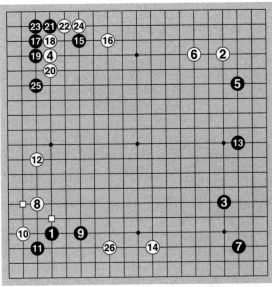

Diagram 12 (moves 1-26)

Black's lower left corner is within White's line from 26 to 8. Look closely. Make sure you agree. Here is how to see it. Notice that from 26 to 9 is a small knight's move. Make two more similar knight's moves from 9 (shown as marked intersections), ending up just to the left of White 8. If White 8 had been on the mark to its left, Black 9 would be exactly on that sector-line. But White 8 is where it is, to the right, so the line is slightly right of Black 9, meaning Black 9 is within it. It's a subtle distinction, being in or not in. Many will miss seeing it, but it makes a world of difference. I hope you didn't miss the easy lines from 14 to 8 or from 26 to 12. Black is clearly within them also.

Running will not help Black counterattack White, so Black should play left of Black 11 to secure corner life. Black's territory is insecure in two places. Black 11 solves one of them, and threatens to capture White 10.

Did you realize that this Black group needed defense? If so, you were better than the real Black, who chose to play elsewhere and was left with an insecure group.

When the chance arose, White attacked as in Diagram 13. Black defended as shown, and White turned elsewhere. Black is not yet alive. White can turn the corner into just one eye, but that is premature now, since Black can easily make an eye outside. The outside is more valuable. Since Black can only defend the corner, at no profit, Black will be in no hurry to do so. Therefore Black must be careful in any center fighting from here on. Having an insecure group is a major strategic liability with ramifications throughout the board and the rest of the game.

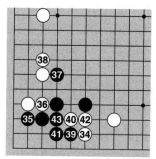

Diagram 13 (34-43)

Valley of the Jolly Chartreuse Giant

The midgame is not just about the attack and defense of groups. It is also filled with the attack and defense of large potential territories. *Potential territory* is the vast acres of open space along the edge, between stones of the same player that are members of different groups. If the stones were of the same group, they would be connected by links and those links would be doorways of real territory. Since the stones are in different groups, the territory is only potential. The doorways, in this case, are sector-lines.

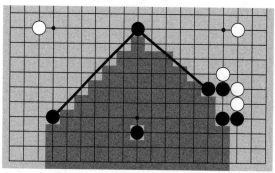

Diagram 14

In Diagram 14, Black has an impressive potential territory of almost eighty points within two sector-lines. (The real territory Black already encloses is not shaded.) This potential territory is not necessarily all going to become real territory, but a lot of it will. White will have to be extremely careful in playing here.

Plays within the sector-lines (on shaded intersections) are *invasions*. An invasion voluntarily creates a weak group within enemy sector-lines, allowing that group to be severely attacked next turn. **Invasions are dangerous**.

The alternative is to play on or just outside of the line. This is a *light reduction*. It creates a group in no immediate danger, but it encourages the opponent to secure much of the potential territory by sealing the line in the vicinity of the light reduction move.

Beware. For with a mere shift of a single intersection, a move can cross the sector-line, switching from being a light reduction to an invasion, with consequent major strategic ramifications. For further details on these two kinds of moves, see *Fools Rush In*.

With groups, we were interested in the closest sector-line to the group. With potential territories we want the line making the biggest claim, containing the most points.

In Diagram 15, of all the lines shown, *a* is the true boundary of the region.

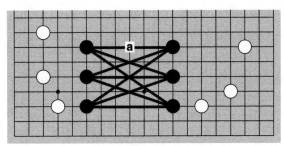

Diagram 15

Perceiving and acting with respect to sector-lines is something easily taught to weaker players. Amazingly, most strong players are not truly conscious of these lines and the distinctions they engender. They learned Go before the concept of sector-lines was fully articulated. They base their play on having been in similar situations, but not on seeing the actual lines. This means that strong players can sometimes be blind to dangers that weaker players, trained with sector-lines, can easily see. It's funny to watch when that happens.

The sector-line is a simple concept. So simple, it has been overlooked for thousands of years of Go play. It provides an important early warning system for players, even if they don't understand the theory underlying it.

Teaching Go to children is primarily a concern of Go-playing parents. However, it is beginning to be a concern of national Go organizations, which realize a supply of new players is vital to the game's continued growth and popularity. In England there are some schools lucky enough to have Go-playing teachers willing to pass on their enthusiasm for the game to others. Increasingly at Go tournaments there are special events arranged for children. And so the cry goes up — how do you teach children to play Go?

The Instant Go lectures by Bruce were a beginning. Some teenagers attended them, learned devastating ways to beat their friends, and spread the word. But even the drama of these lectures was not enough to completely captivate children. Recently we have been working on special, short, Kids' Go lectures involving more audience participation and fantasy than a regular Go lecture. We encourage children's natural competitive spirit to help them understand game concepts. Human beings enjoy being stimulated and excited. Stimulation also makes description of things in a book more enjoyable and interesting. Stimulating events are more memorable than plain happenings. So we use stories to illuminate our meaning and help you remember what could be a very dry set of injunctions.

Currently there is a guilt in the use of violence to entertain. Many people are complaining about the rising violence in society, especially among the young. We feel it is important to be aware of how easy it is to misuse violent metaphors just to make a dramatic point. The more violence there is in the environment the more we all become inured to it. Children are subjected to a huge amount of violence on TV and in the computer games that are produced for them. Accepting violent solutions as normal is producing a violent society. We have tried to reduce the violence in this book. It is difficult and patently ridiculous to remove all allusions to life and death and killing from a game which has used such terminology for many, many centuries. But we found ourselves tending to exaggerate the violence in order to make a point more vivid. So we have rewritten parts of the book using metaphors that we hope are equally vivid but do not involve human-human or human-animal violence. (We have discussed related issues under *New Age Go* and *Philosophy and Go*.)

There are plenty of other ways to make Go understandable by kids. Relating events on the board to physical actions makes the game less abstract. Slam a door in someone's face is more vivid than defend a link. Cut up a pan of brownies explains territory. Measure which child in a group is the tallest and ask "would you pick a fight with this person?" Children, too, can then experience the thrill of adrenaline at confrontational moments in the game, because they now understand it *is* a confrontation. Bruce illustrates the rules of capture by having one child stand up, and then surrounding him or her on three sides with other kids. Then Bruce asks if the target can escape, upon which he or she promptly wriggles out. Then Bruce adds the fourth child in front of the target, and asks the children to huddle together to "crush" the center child.

Bruce then repeats this by adding a "friend" to stand with the target child, and show how much more work is involved in surrounding both children and crushing them. Children love physical behavior and you should exploit this in teaching them.

You can then move on to issues of territory in 9x9 games. The thief metaphor taught in *The Dinosaur's Hind Brain* is quite popular, and immediately teaches them the basics of blocking access into space.

Children are incredibly impatient. 9x9 games end rapidly and are the ideal starting point. These games are all tactics and no strategy and can be played very simply for territory and prisoners. Competition with other children brings on Go talent better than anything else and children love to compete. Schools or clubs

Kian and Christie Wilcox playing Go in Hawaii.

Children love capturing stones, engaging in contact fights and building impressive fortress walls. Initial games, particularly with children age 5, should focus on allowing them to capture stones and avoid issues of territory. They will delight in tricking you into letting them capture you. After a few games, you can start saving your stones for a moment, only to let them capture bigger clusters of stones. From this they will firmly master the principles of capture and saving stones. Avoid life, death, and eyes at this point.

are the ideal place to learn and play in junior tournaments.

If you are playing a game against a beginning child, it is critical to lose if you can. Give the child a big enough handicap to win. If you must win, make sure you make it tantalizingly close, so the child has incentive to try again. Your goal is to have them like the game.

NOTHING IS WORSE than using your skills to destroy the beginner's stones. Come to think of it, this is equally applicable to the adult beginner. You want them to enjoy their experience. You don't want them to realize how far they have to go to become as competent as you.

Kids' Go is not the scene of silent absorption found in most adult Go clubs. Kids' Go is noisy, full of discussion and cries of triumph, disbelief, or defeat. The excitement and noise go together. Until children are of an age to appreciate strategy and silent concentration, encourage them to play Go among their peers.

Other ways of encouraging children to play Go include:

Pennyante Go — both players get a penny for each point of territory or prisoner they capture in a game.

Sudden Death Go — first player to lose a stone loses. Great for teaching capture and getting games to end quickly.

Pair Go — they have to learn to cooperate, at least in teams of two.

Three Color Go — add an extra dimension and player to the game.

The Big Five — each side leaps ahead five stones every move .

We discuss these and other novelties in *Variations on a Theme*. The significance of the variations is that children are not put off by changes in the rules. They delight in tricking and discomfiting each other — being able to change the adults' rules.

For the solitary child with no fellow Go players there is computer Go. We hope that our invention of a program with a selection of different personalities will provide enough variety and interest to gain a child's attention. Our shareware program EZ-GO (see *How to Form a Go Club*) has two personalities. **Psycho** plays the Great Wall opening in even games and is generally wacky in his strategy. **Leaper** leaps from situation to situation across the board, rarely responding as you expect.

Good luck with your efforts to involve children in Go. Once they learn how exciting it is, they are hooked. In the Orient, children younger than 10 become black-belt rated (*dan*) players. As with so many areas of learning, one can be a child prodigy at Go.

Remember, however, that you should not push them to play. Playing is something they should want to do. Maybe they will want to play because they see you doing it and want to do it themselves or see it as a way to get some of your precious time. Maybe they will want to play because they have incentives (as in Pennyante Go). Or maybe they will want to platy because they intrinsically find it fun.

Computer Go is particularly useful because no one sees them losing, and a program doesn't mind how often they cheat and take back moves or use the computer to help visualize territory or safety.

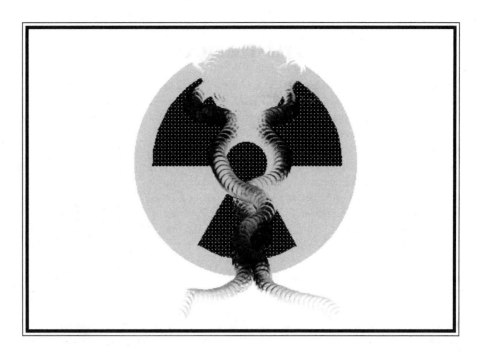

Danger—
Radiation Area

H*e pinned on the green badge, thinking what a nuisance it was to have to wear the oversize ID pin. This'll wear holes in all my shirts he thought grumpily as he mooched along to his new office. Hardly had he settled into his chair than his morning mood was shattered by the whooping of alarm klaxons. Boy, this place is really uptight about safety drills he mused as he strolled back into the corridor. One of the hurrying workers glanced his way and suddenly paled. Pointing at his badge, she hurried past him as if he had the plague. He glanced down. At first he didn't notice anything, then he thought,* Didn't the badge used to be green? *Now it was red. Bright red. What had they said at the induction session?* Your pin will record how much radiation you have been exposed to, it goes from green through yellow to red. It's easy to remember, just like the traffic lights. Red means stop. Stop; you've received a dangerous dose of radiation. You need treatment fast and even then it could be fatal. *He never knew how it happened. He saw and felt nothing.*

In Go, you can't see it, hear it, touch it, taste it, or smell it either. But a Go player **knows** it's there. It builds up over many moves and can be cumulatively fatal. What is it? Influence.

Influence

Imagine each living stone is a chunk of uranium. It radiates over nearby intersections, its power diminishing rapidly with distance. Black stones radiate positively charged energy; white stones radiate negative. Where positive and negative meet, they neutralize each other. This metaphor is part of almost every computer Go program written. It's been used to "see" territory, groups, walls, and potential territory. Each living stone adds fixed amounts of influence to nearby points (see Diagram 1). Black stones add positive numbers, White stones add negative. The total influence of a point is the sum of all stone influences upon it. Writing code to update the "influence map" of the board using this model is easy. Each time a stone is placed you add its influence to the nearby intersections, and each time a stone is removed you deduct its influence from nearby intersections.

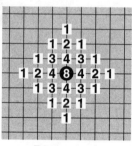

Diagram 1

Each intersection of the board is thus influenced positively by Black, negatively by White, or has zero influence. Then the board is segmented into regions of same-signed influence. Empty regions of points with same-signed influence become potential territory. Regions of contiguous influence above a specified magnitude become "groups" and/ or "territory".

Diagram 2 is a normal board position early in the game. Notice how you view it.

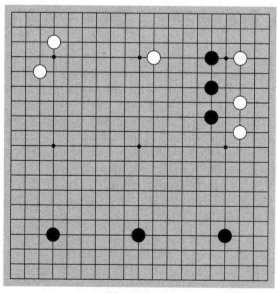

Diagram 2

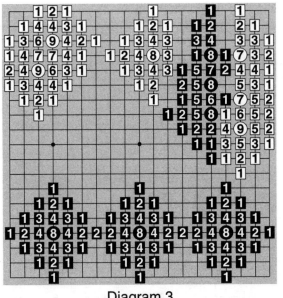

Diagram 3

In Diagram 3, influence values for each stone were generated and the resulting numbers printed out. On the left- middle side of the board there is a large region of neutral points, suggesting opening play there. On the middle- upper side, a play by White could merge two separate influence fields, helping to defend a potential territory.

The influence model creates tantalizing images of how we might view the board. At least this model has some appropriate properties. Power diminishes with distance. Power is stronger in straight lines along the board grid than it is diagonally. Power is canceled by opposing power. Power is amplified by clusters of like stones.

There are flaws in the model, however. Power ceases only four units away from a stone. In Diagram 3, Black runs out of power in holes along the bottom, yet in real Go that isn't true. That flaw can be patched by radiating farther, but other problems remain. Distinguishing territory is not easy. White has a blob of radiation in the upper right and Black has a blob immediately to its left. White's blob is mostly territory and Black's is not. How do you tell the difference?

There are questions about radiation. Can you radiate through solid stones? Through links? Does it matter, since presumably the sign of the influence is still valid? Where is the boundary of an area? With influence it's vague. You need to stop dead stones from radiating, so somehow you must keep track of which stones changed status each turn. Go players find links and sector-lines, which are precise and suggest specific moves. This all means lots of design and code for Go programmers to work out.

As a human, you are not adding little numbers up. Instead you immediately have a vague visual sensation that point x is nearer to Black than White, or is nearer to lots of Black's stones at once. The exact numbers don't really matter.

Every time you place a stone, you make a statement about what area of the board you are trying to affect. That's because each stone exerts influence over intersections. A small amount of influence from a single stone isn't interesting. However, the accumulation of influence from a line of stones facing some direction, a wall, is interesting.

Walls

A *wall* is a line of stones of the same color, which breaks the board into separate regions and exerts coordinated influence on nearby points perpendicular to the wall. Diagram 4 shows some shaded walls and the direction of their influence.

Whereas single stones radiate diffuse power in all direction, walls radiate concentrated power in two opposite directions.

In Diagram 4, Black's walls show only one direction of power radiation. With one exception, the other direction of each Black wall is neutralized because it faces an opposing enemy wall. The exception is in the lower left corner, where the opposite direction actually contains territory. The primary direction is neutralized by White's stones. Wall power facing enclosed territory is generally not mentioned by Go players. A wall and its power always refer to "outward facing" power and the ability to affect the future on the rest of the board.

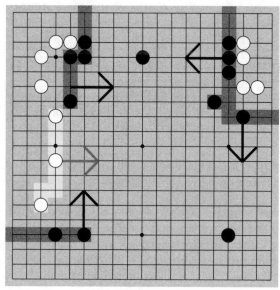

Diagram 4

A wall has two uses. The boundary properties of its stones and links can be used to make territory or its stones can be used to make sector-lines to attack a weak group.

Life Ruins Walls: A living group ruins almost all enemy wall radiation *moving toward it*, no matter how far away the source of that radiation. By being in front of the wall, the group prevents significant territory from being formed. By being alive, the group cannot be attacked.

In Diagram 5, the radiation from Black's marked stones is moving toward White's safe marked group, so Black's power is almost worthless (a mere gote six points).

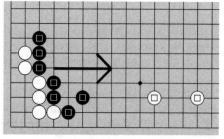

Diagram 5

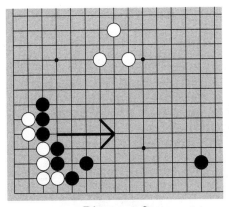

Diagram 6

In Diagram 6, however, Black's radiation is not moving toward White's group, but is moving perpendicular to radiation from White's group. Black's wall is not neutralized by White.

Black has a potential territory on the bottom. If White invades, what happens to Black's influence? As long as White is weak, Black's influence has value and can be used somehow. The instant White gains a completely living group, however, Black's influence is negated by White.

Walls are Convertible: In physics, energy can be converted to matter or into other energy. In Go, a wall can be used to make territory, or it can be used to make another wall in a different area.

In Diagram 7, Black has a lot of influence facing White's stone on the top. If White were strong, Black's wall would be worthless. Since White is weak, Black's influence washes over White's stone and into the potential territory beyond it. Black has two choices for

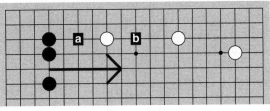

Diagram 7

using this wall. Black can merely extend in front of the wall to *a*, making territory (a small move), or Black can invade at *b* behind White's stone, and attack (a large move). Were Black to kill White, the territory gained would be huge, but presumably Black cannot kill White. What will happen instead is that Black will use the invading stone as a basis for further play, trying to push White's weak group toward Black's corner wall.

Diagram 8 carries out Black's invasion. White 2, White 4, and White 8 cross Black's newly created sector-lines, while White 6 defends a link. After White 8, Black's wall in the upper left corner has no more outward influence value, but Black has new influence created where the invasion was. The new wall's influence washes past another White stone. That is how Black "moves" a wall from one area

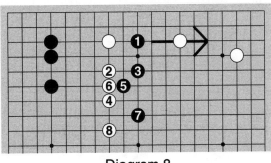

Diagram 8

to another. To move a wall, attack a weak group and build a new wall while making sector-line threats against the weak group.

Walls with Leaks Collapse: Enemy stones that undercut you farther up the edge form an edge leak and ruin your wall. You can never afford to take the time to plug the leak.

Diagram 9 shows a professional strategy by White. The marked White stone on the left side is strong, and makes Black's left edge leaky. By initiating a contact fight with White 1, White makes both sides build walls (contact fights build walls). White's wall enhances the potential of the bottom. Black's wall faces the leak and will be hard to use efficiently.

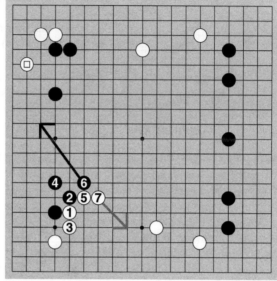

Diagram 9

Walls Die of Age: At the beginning of the game, walls have great value, and at the end of the game walls are useless unless they enclose territory.

Walls Built in Gote Never Last: *Gote* means playing last in a situation. It's the opposite of *sente*, having the right to play first in a new situation. Building a wall in gote is often suspect. If you build a wall in gote, your opponent has the right to play anywhere. Maybe your opponent can just stick a strong stone near your wall and ruin it.

In Diagram 10, Black picks a joseki that builds a wall in gote. (White fills 13 at 6.) In this diagram all White has to do is use White's sente to place a stone near *a* and Black's wall is useless. To play Black 2, Black must already have a stone near *a* to make the wall part of a useful framework.

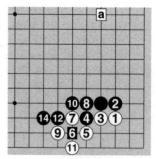

Diagram 10

Evaluation: In Diagram 11, it is Black's turn to play. Let's analyze the board from the point of view of walls.

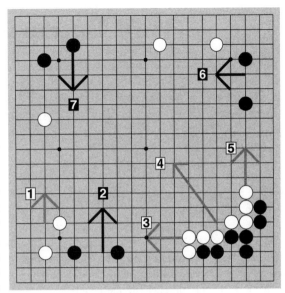

Diagram 11

White's wall #1 helps claim the left side. Black's wall #2 faces a strong White stone to its left, so it is useless at present. White's wall #3 faces strong enough Black stones and is useless. White's wall #4 faces a distant strong upper left corner, so the wall is useless for now. White's wall #5 faces a strong enough upper right corner and is useless. Black's wall #6 faces a weak White position; Black can invade. Black's wall #7 faces a weak White stone; Black can invade.

Just because a wall is useless right now, doesn't mean it will necessarily always be useless, and just because a wall is useless doesn't mean your opponent played any better. Black didn't make all that much territory in the lower right corner in exchange for White's walls in the lower right (#3, #4, #5), so White is not unhappy with the trade. White still has prospects for this wall.

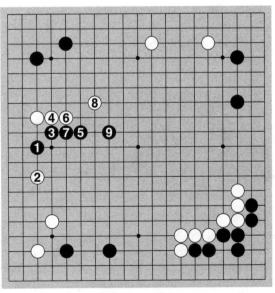

Diagram 12

Black should invade to use the corner wall, as in Diagram 12. White 2 stops easy life for Black. Then both must run through 9. White builds a wall having no effect on Black's upper-left corner. Black builds a wall ruining White's left side potential. This result is bad for White. Also, White 8 is just on Black's sector-line (9 to upper left corner), so White remains nervous.

Wall Extensions

Considerations of safety and influence control how far you extend from or to a wall.

A wall is *thick* if it has no weaknesses. The enemy must be extremely cautious approaching your thick walls, because you can spend all of your time attacking with no concern for defense. Avoid thickness, whether it is yours or your opponent's. Stay away from your opponent's thickness because it is dangerous to you. Stay away from your own thickness because it is inefficient. You won't get enough territory.

Walls using links that can be cut are *thin*. If the enemy plays next to the link, you need to defend the wall by securing the link.

When you want to claim an area, you put walls on both sides of it. If the walls are too close together, then you have spent too many moves for too little territory. This is called *overconcentration*. In geometry, the square is a "perfect" shape. It encloses the most area with the least circumference (smallest walls) of all the four-sided shapes. This principle applies in Go, as we shall see.

When you extend, pick one of three extensions: the safe extension, the safe follow-up extension, or the squeeze extension.

Safe Extension: Make a safe extension when you are concerned about making a base for the group you are extending from. You do not want to extend too far, lest the enemy invade and cause you grief. The rule is count how far your highest stone of the wall is from the edge, count over that amount along the edge, and place your stone on the third line. Choose the third line because that is the line of territory. Any higher and you do not control the edge well.

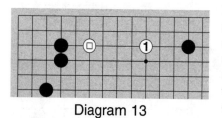

Diagram 13

In Diagram 13, White wants to defend the marked stone and so plays White 1. Black can invade between the two White stones, so White is going to be in deep trouble. You must be careful never to overextend from a weak group. If your opponent invades, you end up with two weak groups.

In Diagram 14, White counts up three from the edge (it's a short wall), and so can extend only three over, to the marked intersection. This forms a double-skip link, so there is no possibility of an invasion separating White's two stones.

Diagram 14

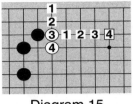

Diagram 15

In Diagram 15, White's wall is one line higher, so White can extend one line farther.

In Diagram 16, White has an even higher wall, allowing an even longer extension. This continues to apply to walls even higher.

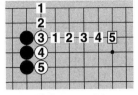

Diagram 16

If you make an extension smaller than the safe extension, it is overconcentrated. If you make it greater than the safe extension, it can be invaded and you will have one or two weak groups (a liability). The safe extension is optimal.

Distant safe extensions like Diagram 16 look invadeable, but they actually aren't. The geometry of the sector-lines involved allows you to catch and kill an intruder.

In Diagram 17, Black 1 invaded behind White's safe extension. In the sequence to White 6, White has links containing Black's stones, and Black's stones have no territory for eyes. If Black stays contained, Black will die. Black's only play from here is to use the sequence *a-d*. However, Black's original invading stones get cut off when White plays *d* and White captures the invasion. (Black, in turn, gets center strength.)

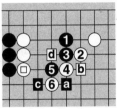

Diagram 17

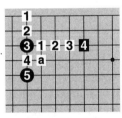

Diagram 18

When walls are thin, you have to deduct one unit of extension distance for each breakable link. In Diagram 18, Black's wall is five off the edge, but White could cut the link or peep at *a*. Therefore Black deducts one from the planned extension and can play only four away.

When walls are bent, you still count height, but always from the top of the wall. In Diagram 19, Black's wall is seven high, and Black can extend seven units away from its top. Black does not deduct one line for thinness because no links can be cut (only threatened and the threat doesn't access the open space).

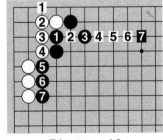

Diagram 19

Safe Follow-up Extension: Though you may not be concerned about the group you are extending from, you do have to worry about the stone you are extending with. If it is approaching a strong enemy position, you still want some kind of safety. Either your move must be a safe extension, or it must leave room for a follow-up safe extension. By definition this follow-up extension will be three lines farther over, since your stone will be a single stone wall three off the edge.

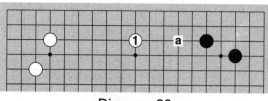

Diagram 20

In Diagram 20, White 1 is too far to be a safe extension from the upper left corner, but White has left room for a follow-up safe extension to *a*. If Black invades behind White 1, White will play at *a* immediately. If Black extends toward White 1 from the upper right corner, White will defend to prevent a subsequent invasion. White defends by making a single-skip toward the center, or a double-skip along the third line back toward the White corner.

Squeeze Extension: When the enemy is weak, you can play close. Your opponent dare not invade, lest the invasion and the existing weak group come under dual attack from your extending stone. This means you can play close, either two or three lines away (avoiding contact).

In Diagram 21, White is not concerned about the safety of the upper left corner and so can extend as far as *a* or White 1, close to Black's weak stone.

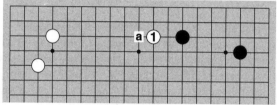

Diagram 21

Wall Attacks

When you build walls using contact pushing and crawling, you have little choice about where the wall will be built. You must follow the flow already inherent in the touching stones. When you build walls by attacking a weak group, you have complete control over where the wall is built. By threatening to enclose enemy stones and forcing them to run, you build up a wall of stones in one of many directions. One side of this wall faces your opponent's group. The other side is the side of interest. This is why you build the wall.

Before building a wall you should have a plan that will use that wall profitably. You must see that a particular wall could be useful and know how you will follow up to exploit it. The following pages show some prepared plans for attacking in one area in order to construct walls designed to influence another area. The moves creating a wall all threaten to enclose a weak group and cooperative opponents will do everything they can to avoid becoming hemmed in. This is not always their best strategy. Although one rule of sector-line theory states **Avoid Enclosure**, there are times when it is better to totally abandon stones rather than spend many moves trying to save them. Dead groups are stable — they need no defense.

The wall plan will consist of wall-building and whatever additional moves are needed to utilize the wall profitably. Such a plan may never bear fruit, but working it out organizes your thoughts and moves into a smooth, coherent framework, which leads to playing better Go.

Remember, a wall is built for any of the following useful purposes:
1. to build a large potential territory.
2. to neutralize enemy walls.
3. to neutralize potential enemy territory.
4. to support an attack on an enemy group.
5. to support an invasion.
6. to make territory.

Only Build Useful Walls!

A wall is built by forcing a weak group into running at your command. Your goal is to accomplish something useful while letting it live. Don't get distracted and start trying to kill the enemy group! If you focus on killing the enemy stones, the odds are you won't succeed; you may or may not build a wall, or if you do build a wall it won't be placed usefully. As long as your opponent responds, maintain your focus and complete your wall. If your opponent ignores you, however, you must abandon your wall plan and punish that group, frequently by killing or enclosing it.

In each of the following diagrams, understand the flow of the stones; see how the attacker channels the movement of the defender's running plays so that the attacker can place stones optimally. The intent of each wall-building method is to build a wall where you want one.

Wall Plan #1 — The Squeeze

The Squeeze wall plan presses an enemy group against some of your stones (each move is linked to a prior one) and leaves only one escape route. The opponent has little choice but to take that route and continued squeezing builds a wall.

In The Squeeze Diagram, as Black threatens to enclose along the line through 1 & 3, White runs along the line formed by 2 & 4. Black gets a wall facing the arrows.

The Squeeze is the most common plan. The wall it builds is a simple continuation of an existing position and is attached to safety.

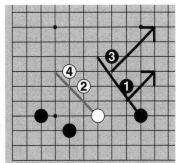

The Squeeze

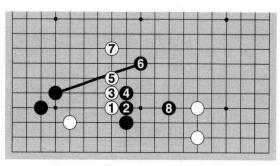

Diagram 22

Diagram 22 shows the result of a pushing and crawling fight into the center; both sides gain temporary stability. Each of White's moves crosses a Black sector-line. But suppose White were greedy and didn't play at White 7 (which crosses Black's shown sector-line). What if White tried to stop Black from gaining eye space?

In Diagram 23, White 7 blocks Black's extension and threatens to cut. Black 8 protects the cut; White 9 protects 7 from being captured. Black has sente and launches a punishing squeeze attack with 10, threatening to surround White. White tries to escape. With the sequence through Black 14, Black builds a long thin wall. Black 16-18 secure life in the corner and White eventually gets precarious life with White 21. Now Black thickens that thin wall into an

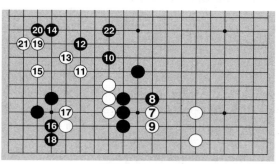

Diagram 23

imposing barrier with Black 22. This wall dominates the rest of the board. This is why White **Runs Across the Line** with White 7 in Diagram 22.

Wall Plan #2 — The Flying V

The Flying V wall plan begins with an isolated capping play, i.e., a play which does not link to other friendly stones, placed in the middle of the obvious single escape route that splits it into two narrow escape routes.

The Flying V Diagram gives the general idea (shaded areas represent Black stones in those areas). If White runs out along line 2, Black continues to attack with line 3, linking from the capping stone. If White runs at line 4, Black blocks with line 5. Notice that the

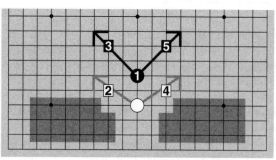

The Flying V

wall created is laid out directly in front of the natural escape route of the weak group. In favorable circumstances, one can use the "V" to completely smother a group. Although killing is not the normal intent of wall-building, if the opportunity presents itself, don't turn it down. It is unlikely, however, that you will ever see the completed V shape. The goal of running is to escape containment. Therefore the defender should only run out one side. Once the defender has escaped, it is bad play to run out the other side.

The Flying V is rarely used as a plan. It requires two strong adjacent positions (shaded areas) to work and creates a broad wall facing the rest of the board. Usually the wall would face strong enemy positions — i.e., is worthless.)

In Diagram 24 Black begins an attack with Black 1. White might as well abandon the marked stone because it can't live locally, and running offers no opportunity for attack. When White 2 is played elsewhere and Black follows up the attack with 3, the classic capping play, it is the height of folly for White to try to flee and live now. White begins

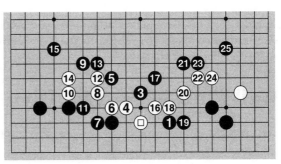

Diagram 24

running out toward the open areas, with Black in hot pursuit. In this example White will crash into the sides of the board and never escape. White may live, but Black's wall will win the game. If White had planned to live, White should have run with 2 instead of playing elsewhere.

Wall Plan #3 — The Sacrifice

The previous wall plans assumed the existence of one or more strong supporting positions for the attacker to use in creating a new wall. **The Sacrifice** assumes you are weak, and strengthens you by offering up a sacrifice.

In The Sacrifice Diagram, you *strengthen* supporting positions by sacrificing the initial attacking stone. Again start with an isolated capping play, only this time abandon it and squeeze from the sides.

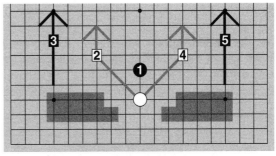

The Sacrifice

Diagram 25 is a common handicap situation. White begins this wall plan by capping at White 1. Inexperienced Black players tend to think that their capped stone is under assault, and panic. White welcomes this belief and Black's accompanying fear. In theory, however, Whites' play is only a sacrifice to strengthen White's own weak groups.

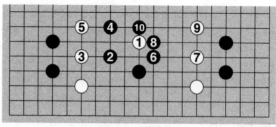

Diagram 25

Diagram 25 shows two separate escape and wall-building operations, one on each side of the cap. Remember, it is a mistake for the defender (Black in this example) to run out both sides. Once is enough.

Wall Plan #4 — The Divide & Conquer

The previous wall plans need only one weak group to work with. **The Divide & Conquer** needs two.

The flow of the attack (1) in The Divide & Conquer Diagram forces the first weak enemy group to run (2) toward the second. Just before they unite, the attacker drives a wall between them (3). This last-minute wedge has tremendous impact on the second group. After the first group escapes (4), the attacker either kills or encloses the second group (5).

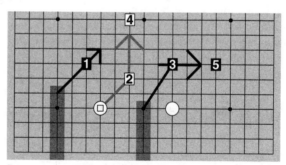

The Divide & Conquer

If you intend to run in the wedge direction anyway, this is a good flow. Force your opponent to create a narrow gap, then run through that gap with the wedge.

The Divide & Conquer is generally a lethal plan; it gives the opponent no time to defend a weak group. This is the primary reason one should never have two weak groups on the board at the same time.

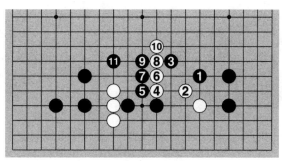

Diagram 26

Diagram 26 is a clear example of **The Divide & Conquer**. Black begins with Black 1, trying to push White's single stone into running toward White's 3-stone unit on the left. After White gets close enough with White 4, Black drives stones Black 5, 7, & 9 between White's two groups. When the first group finally escapes with White 10, Black encloses the second one with Black 11. Enclosing is immediately valuable, whether or not Black can kill the enclosed group. And White's other group is still a weak group to be attacked in the future.

In the Real World

In Go, when you use the Squeeze plan you do two things. You induce enemy motion in a particular direction and you build a wall that "hides" a region from view. In the real world, when someone creates circumstances that seem to force you in a particular direction, it's good to ask yourself not just do you want to go that way. Also ask yourself what is being hidden.

In Go, the isolated capping move is made in preparation for a Flying V or a Sacrifice plan. Capping creates two directions for running. It polarizes the opponent's choices, but the opponent still chooses. In the real world, pressuring someone into making one of two choices does not mean they will make the choice you want. Be certain you will be happy with whatever choice is made. Even if you think there is only one choice, they may find another action is also possible. Give consideration to the consequences of them making either choice.

For example, when Sun Microsystems tried to rally support for standardizing on a particular version of the Unix operating system, many companies using Sun's Sparc processor chips became concerned that this operating system would get embedded in the chip and give Sun an advantage. So they formed an opposing standard and rallied to create a new organization. Sun's action polarized the situation, and their competitors responded in an unanticipated way.

Go & Business

While the purpose of this book is to teach Go, Go is also a strong business metaphor.

John Reed, CEO of Citicorp Bank, wrote in the Harvard Business Review (Nov.-Dec. 1989) *Competition among the top thirty players around the world is about occupying space. It's about positioning yourself wisely over time, not wiping the other guys out on a specific product. I approach competition a little like the Chinese board game Go. You see where the other players have put their chips, figure out why, and decide where to put your chips.*

Territory: The purpose of Go is to secure more territory. Correspondingly, the purpose of business is make more profits, generally by securing a greater market share. The Go board represents the consumer marketplace. Territory is a particular marketplace for a particular product line. The corners are those areas where it is easiest for you to gain marketshare. Maybe they represent the local or domestic market, or maybe a niche where you have the only product.

Developing and keeping a corner (local base) is important because it costs much less to start there. The sides and center are correspondingly harder for you to gain share in. When you do expand, do so in related markets, along the edges adjacent to the corner of your advantage. Perhaps international markets, or areas where you have some products or expertise.
The two eye concept of Go is also important in business. A business dependent upon a single income source

(eye) is highly vulnerable to attack. Businesses need a mix of products (multiple eyes) to insure survival.

The Go model says that throughout the game you and your opponent will both compete and cooperate. Sometimes you will tacitly allow your opponent some area in exchange for another area. Sometimes you will peacefully divide up an area (as in a joseki). Sometimes you will fight to the death in some area. At the end of the game both players will coexist on the board in harmony. Victory is not all or nothing, it is a small percentage difference.

Stones and Links: Stones are people in a company or products that you have to offer. Strings are companies or product lines. Links are business relationships between people, from one company to another, that allow them to work together. Or maybe links are relationships among collections of products, some form of vertical integration. Links act as barriers to entry into some marketplace.

Go player Bill Gates understands links. When Netscape forged a link in which they would supply the Internet browser for AOL's millions of users, Gates reacted that day. He called the head of AOL and within hours AOL announced it would feature Microsoft's Explorer, with Navigator relegated to relative obscurity.

Groups are the collection of businesses needed to supply and control some market. They are joined by links. Links which appear to run from group to group (or business to business) actually run from stone to stone (or person to person). Thus it is often possible to break specific links without having to attack a group or company as a whole.

Principles and Issues: If you follow this metaphor and are a passably good Go player, certain business reflexes and ideas become manifest.

In Go, links are the foundation of almost everything. So it is in business. You need to perceive what actions threaten or attack your relationships (links) with other companies and which links are important boundaries for controlling your marketplace. You must discover the nearby businesses you need to build relationships with to control an industry and how to disrupt the links of your opponents.

In Go, breaking an opponent's boundary link of a territory will result in the opponent losing some or all of that territory. Generally it does not mean you get the territory. Instead, the territory becomes junk space where no one gets an advantage or value because you both share it. Translate this into business and the conclusion would be that while you can harm an opponent's market (profits) and acquire some of it for yourself, you can't take it over completely once it has been developed, unless, as in Go, you can kill his group. Death, in this case means bankruptcy or acquisition.

Our chapter on balance discusses how you can balance moves made by your opponent, and moves made by you. I explicitly warn you in Go that balancing by matching (doing what your opponent does) is a weak style which allows your

opponent to control the agenda and that means you are always behind and catching up. This is equally true in business. Companies that try to copy an opponent's successful ad campaign, discount fare, or whatever may be unaware of other balancing mechanisms. Pay attention to the distinctions of balance described in the *A Question of Balance* chapter and see how you might apply them in your business to gain an advantage.

Efficient play is needed in Go and in business. You have limited resources and can't build new relationships, strengthen old ones, and attack enemy relationships all at once. You need to build a secure base from which to expand and have enough product variety (eyes) to insure you won't be blinded by sudden market shifts.

Lessons: Go teaches a variety of useful business lessons. It teaches productivity, to achieve maximum results with available resources. The optimum return on investment occurs on the third or fourth lines in the beginning. The third line corresponds to conservative making of profits, the direct goal. The fourth line corresponds to innovation, the future potential of profits.

Go teaches balance of the third and fourth line activity. Play entirely on the third line for profit and you may be blown away later by innovation. Play entirely on the fourth line for innovation and you may never find a way to capitalize on your position and convert it into profit. Finding the correct balance and timing of behavior is essential, which means constantly looking for the right moment to take action.

Go inculcates perseverance, to play for the long haul, to be willing to face setbacks and regroup one's thoughts (there's always another corner or part of the board). It teaches you priority, that urgent moves must be made before big ones.

Go makes sacrificing a way of life, be it wringing advantage from misfortune or intentionally trading one thing for another. And Go teaches the concept of enough; knowing when to stop the endless quest for more money, more power, more fame, more anything. Go is not about dominating or crushing others. Go is about sharing and having just enough more. Competition in Go provides incentive to do better and be better, without taking it to the extremes that damage relationships with people.

Contrast with Chess: Chess teaches the value of specialists. America is a nation in love with specialists. Specialization works well in short-term single-focus battles. Go emphasizes generalists. Each piece or person is able to perform all roles. Generalists are needed for the long-term, multi-focus, complex environment, such as that found in today's business world.

The chess model says that when you win, your opponent will know it immediately and give up. Go teaches you that the game continues even after you have won, and that you can lose it again. The chess model teaches the use of concentrated power to smash the opponent's position. Go teaches the use of balance and coordination to achieve almost invisible results.

Search for the Metaphor: As you read through this book, other perceptions, strategies, and tactics can be related to the business context as well. As you learn Go, ask yourself what some Go situation might mean in a different context. Is there an analog of ko in business? How do sente and gote work? What is a light reduction? Go is valuable as a rich source of metaphors. Metaphors suggest new ways of perceiving other areas, and make new suggestions of ways to handle old problems.

Go and Personal Development: In addition to being directly useful as a model for business strategy, Go is an excellent domain in which you can learn about yourself and train yourself. Go is a mirror of you. Your default styles, your preferences for strategy and tactics, your focus or lack thereof are all reflected in how you play.

Go (at least as I teach it in business seminars) affords you an opportunity to view how you react in rapidly changing environments. You learn to constantly reinterpret the board as the game progresses and as the rules change. Learning how you do this and how else you might do this would be hard in the real world because the time frame is slow. Your commitment to perceiving yourself in only one way would blind you to seeing yourself in different ways. Go is a nonthreatening environment in which to see yourself and to have others see you and tell you what they see.

Practice: It is not enough to intellectually understand something. Instead, the learning must become embedded in your being, a reflex created from endless repetition. A big value of Go is that you can play games of Go to completion much more rapidly than you can play games of business to completion. Playing allows you to embed Go philosophy and styles of thinking into your existence and then translate them into the business domain more rapidly than if you tried to acquire them directly from practice in the business.

4.3.2.1.Contact!

If you're locked in a room with a homicidal maniac, what would you wish for, apart from a key or Bruce Lee? A gun? I would. The safest way to handle an attacker is from a distance. You'd only want to use your bare hands as a last resort. Getting in close is dangerous. You could get hurt. So why do it unless you have to? Yet Go players routinely wade in and play in contact with enemy stones, with no thought about danger and no thought about purpose.

Contact occurs when stones of the opposite color are immediately or diagonally adjacent to each other. Diagram 1 shows the two basic contact positions. A contact fight occurs when either or both players' stones in contact are unstable. It is urgent to respond and keep responding in a contact fight until you are stable, and usually until your opponent is also

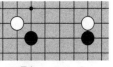

Diagram 1

stable. If you leave a contact fight too soon, you may suffer a large local loss. If you leave too late, you may end up wasting moves and losing sente (control).

If you're going to get into hand-to-hand combat you need to learn something about technique, or it's just going to be a brawl — and you'll be the loser. Take some lessons from the martial arts: Judo, Tai Chi, Kung Fu. Be aware of your balance, advantages, and purpose.

Balance

Balance involves dynamic tension between polar opposites, in this case motion and immobility or motion in one direction versus motion in a different direction. If you are unbalanced or unstable, it means you are stuck moving in the direction of one extreme and will become an easy victim.

Given a choice of standing still or motion in the wrong direction, which do you prefer? You can change direction of motion faster than you can change from non-motion to motion. A boat heading the wrong way can change the rudder and be moving in a new direction quickly. A boat sitting still cannot use the rudder and must first build up momentum. Prefer motion to motionlessness.

All martial arts focus first on your stance, how you place your feet on the floor relative to the rest of your body. Balance is not just standing there. The passenger standing waiting for a train is not balanced in a martial arts sense, cannot switch rapidly to motion, is not ready if attacked. The martial arts balance means being ready to change extremes quickly, to both attack and defend easily. Knees slightly bent, ready to flex, in a sense already in motion. While the stance makes you ready for motion, it is not committed motion. To attack implies committed motion. Attacking implies becoming unstable. It is easier for the defender to remain balanced and stable than for the attacker.

Stability

When, in Go, are your stones stable? Your stones are stable if they can't be cut apart and they have at least five liberties (hence the chapter name *4.3.2.1.Contact!*). This is absolute stability. You can also have relative stability. If you have more liberties and fewer defects than your opponent, you are relatively stable. Your opponent will probably abandon stones rather than fight at a disadvantage.

Mind Dangerous Defects: A *defect* is an imperfect connection between two stones (all points marked *a* and *b* in Diagram 2 are Black defects). Connected stones share liberties and fight as one. Disconnected stones fight separately. Since you get only one move per turn, disconnected stones must wait their turn for rescue, which might come too late. A defect is dangerous if, when the opponent occupies it, you cannot make an alternate connection or capture the

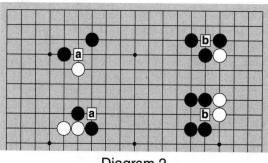

Diagram 2

cutting stone "quickly". Quickly here means your opponent is unable to get more than two or three liberties. You shouldn't have to read out how to capture. If you find yourself doing tactical reading, if you don't just "know" the answer instantly, the defect is dangerous. Even if you read out that the enemy string can't survive the cut, having to read it means the potential of unfavorable interaction with other situations is too great.

Diagram 2 shows dangerous defects marked *a* and safe defects marked *b*. From here on in, only defects that are dangerous matter. So defect implies dangerous defect.

Don't leave defects lying around. You may freely create a defect during fighting, but don't leave the fight until you have resolved it. It is OK to make two defects during a fight if your opponent also makes one. Don't expect to survive a fight where you make three or more defects. Don't expect to survive if you have two defects and your opponent has none.

Survive with Five: With furniture it takes three legs to make something stable. With Go stones it takes five liberties. This is because unlike your floor, the Go board is being manipulated by an actively hostile opponent who is constantly trying to push your furniture around. So you need a broader base. The rule of five works in Go for several reasons.

First, it works because most tactical tricks that can harm you require a shortage of liberties to work. Empirically it turns out that they simply fail to work when the liberty count reaches five. You get enough time to muster your defenses.

Second, five liberties gives enough time for your own tricks to work. In most tactical situations, there is a wide variety of moves to choose from. You want to pick one that does multiple tasks, but that may mean it does not do the primary task optimally. Will you have time to delay the primary task? With five liberties your stones are absolutely strong and you can try the full set of responses in any situation.

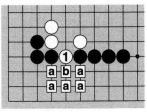

Diagram 3

In Diagram 3, any of the points marked *a* or *b* maintains the connection between Black's stones (although only *b* is common). Liberty shortages diminish your set of usable responses. This is especially serious if your tactics are weak; you might miss the only workable move!

In Diagram 4, Black is unable to connect because of a liberty shortage. Black must spend time defending the three stones to the left of 1, at the cost of losing the link.

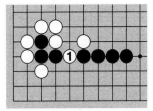

Diagram 4

Whenever you have fewer than five liberties, watch out for unpleasant tactical tricks that can be pulled on you.

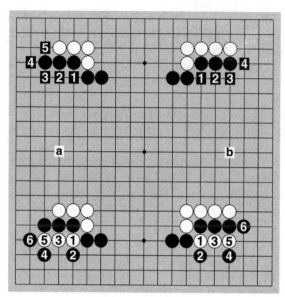

Diagram 5a & b

Third, five liberties protects a cutting point.

In Diagram 5a top, Black has five liberties (marked).

If White cuts in 5a bottom, Black plays 2 and uses a local net capture with 4 to kill White.

If Black has fewer liberties as in 5b top, then Black cannot capture White locally.

Black 4 in 5b bottom fails because Black has to save stones with 6. Yes, Black might succeed by using a ladder capture instead of a net.

However, unless the ladder is quite local, sooner or later White will play a ladder block and Black will lose something.

Contact Fights Yield Joseki: Let's apply the notions of defects and liberties to the joseki shown in Diagram 6. The invasion of White 2 contacts Black 1, causing a fight. Black 3 makes Black stable (5 liberties, no defects), while White is not. White responds with White 4. Black is again unstable and pressures White with Black 5. You could choose *a*, but 5 as played is more severe and only introduces one dangerous defect. White 6 tries to gain more room, and Black 7 indirectly protects the dangerous defect at *a*, while keeping White enclosed. After White 8, Black must again respond (the cut at *a* is dangerous again and Black has only three liberties for Black 5 & 7). Responding with *d* for Black 9 is wrong, creating a second dangerous defect while White has none. Black 13 protects the dangerous cut *c*.

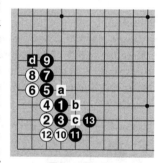

Diagram 6

Count Virtual Liberties: At this point the joseki ends because the position is contact stable. Black's 5 & 7 & 9 string has five liberties, so it is strong. But the remaining Black strings have either three or four liberties, so what about them? Black 13 is stable because it is not in a contact fight. Black 11 and 1 & 3 have only three liberties each and are in contact; considered alone they are unstable. But you can think of 1 & 3 & 11 & 13 as forming a solid unit, a "virtual string", because they cannot be cut apart. In the virtual string they share virtual liberties, but that is not the final count. Since it is the opponent's right to force the virtual string to become a real string (White *b* for Black *c* in this case), you must count liberties after all threats and connections have been played. The correct virtual count is five, so those stones have enough liberties. Similarly, White's two-stone string with only four liberties is safe with seven virtual liberties (if you know Black can't cut on the second line without getting squashed quickly).

That just leaves the cut at *a*. The cut at *a* is interesting. If you know enough, it is not dangerous. If you don't, it is. Dangerous is a relative term, relative to your own strength.

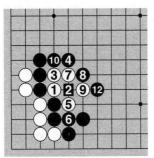

Diagram 7   11@ 2

There is a local sequence to capture the cut (Diagram 7). This means all of Black's stones are a virtual string. But it depends upon knowing about the trick of Black 8. If Black defends Black 2 when White ataris it (with 7) by playing 8 at 9, White escapes and the cut was dangerous. Knowing the trick, the cut is not dangerous. But if Black loses one liberty on the three-stone string (White at *d* of Diagram 6), then the cut at *a* immediately becomes dangerous, no matter how much you know. With only four liberties, the enclosure sequence of Diagram 7 fails.

Now you know about contact balance and when something is stable. The next topic is how to play out contact fights.

Advantages

Whenever you fight, you want to utilize your advantages. Advantages may be innate or environmental. Are you heavier, taller, faster, or smarter than your opponent? Is there a wall behind you? Like a duellist who gets to choose the weapons and locale, you need to know what suits you best. There are often many ways to fight. Your advantages dictate which ways you will prefer. You must also consider your opponent's advantages. What can you expect your opponent to do to utilize them?

Before you can use your advantages, you need to be familiar with the full range of options. Know what is the normal way, and what is your special way. In contact fights the normal way is to gain liberties quickly and/or prevent your opponent from doing so. At the same time you want to avoid getting cut apart.

Play the Best Liberty

Whenever you play to increase your own liberty count, you want to increase it as much as possible in one turn. Given a move that acquires two new liberties, and one that acquires only one new liberty, play the higher liberty-count move.

A well known proverb is "Don't make empty triangles." In Diagram 8, if Black plays at *b*, gaining three new liberties and losing one old one, Black has a net increase of two liberties. If Black moves at *a*, making an empty triangle, the net increase is only one liberty. How inefficient.

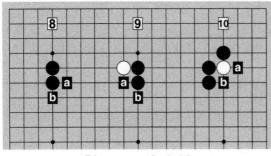

Diagrams 8, 9,10

In Diagram 9, the move at *a* does not make an empty triangle. It gains only one liberty, but it also reduces White by one. Relative liberty count is also important. If you have only two liberties and your opponent has only one, you are winning the fight. If White's stone in Diagram 9 had more than five liberties, then *b* might be better than *a*.

You can only decrease enemy strings by one liberty at a time. If you can cut, you can decrease multiple strings at once. Which liberty to fill is not arbitrary even if you can't cut. Play where the opponent would get the most liberties by playing there.

In Diagram 10, the optimal Black liberty fill at *a* yields a ladder, while the inferior choice *b*, lets White get away. If your opponent has more than one excellent liberty, choose the one that reinforces your weaker stones.

Play Near to Friend and Foe

Reasonable liberty moves are adjacent to or diagonal from your stones **and** from your opponent's stones. They participate maximally in the fight.

In Diagram 11, what should Black do to continue the contact fight with White? To defend a single stone, the "Best Liberty" rule says Black can play any liberty *a* or *b*; they all yield five liberties. But *b* walks away from the fight. Black's other liberties (*a*'s) aim to continue the fight and are better. To attack White's stone, *c* is no good because it is not near a previous friend stone. It will just become a new weak string. Black should play one of the *d* moves, which are near to friends and near to foes.

Diagram 11

Watch out for strong stones

Don't Contact Strong Stones: Playing against stones that have more than five liberties is a partial waste of your move. It is like a child trying to push on a sumo wrestler. Much better to push on things you can actually move.

In Diagram 12, White should not play *a*. If White wants to play around here, White should play *b* or, if fearful of being cut, left of *b*.

Diagram 12

Don't Block Stones Stronger than Yours: If you block stronger stones while creating a dangerous defect, your opponent will cut and the fighting goes against you. Before you play a diagonal block, count your opponent's liberties and count yours. If your opponent has more, don't block.

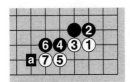

Diagram 13

In Diagram 13, Black wants to block at *a*, but White has four liberties to Black's three. Also blocking would create a second dangerous defect when White has none.

If Black blocks (Diagram 14), White cuts and Black must struggle to keep both sides alive. Black ends up crawling on the second line, and White is happily marching on the third.

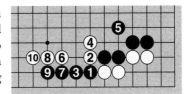

Diagram 14

Skip with Six Liberties

After a contact fight, frequently one or both parties will play non-contact skipping moves in the same area. These moves are sector moves, maintaining access to open board regions.

Consider Diagram 15. White's marked stone was weak and inside Black's sector-line, so White contacted Black with 1. Black 2 at *a* would fail to cross White's line (not shown), while Black 2 as played moves onto the line. White 3 is the obvious contact response to continue escaping. Playing a blocking move at 4 instead of 3 would be blocking stronger stones and should be avoided. Black 4 is not needed for contact stability, since Black already has five liberties. But Black is within White's line and wants to run. Black does not have enough liberties to skip yet and so continues contact with 4. Since White becomes unstable as a result, Black 4 is a good move. Once again White 5 is forced, combining contact and sector.

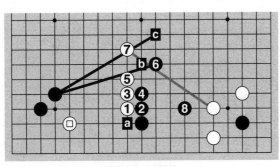

Diagram15

Now Black has enough liberties to run across White's line, so Black skips with 6. Skipping to *b* would be unsafe. If White pushes into the small knight's link that Black actually played, Black still has five liberties, and White's cut is met with a local net capture. White 7 now runs across Black's sector-line. Black is not within White's new line from 7 to the corner and jumping to *c* with Black 8 would not put White within Black's new line from *c* to the Black corner (hence it has no impact on White), so Black makes eyespace with 8.

Tie-breaking Choices

Even though you may know how to choose a move in a specific location, actual fights get complicated.

In Diagram 16, after White 7 Black not only has several move choices in a single contact location (such as *d* and *e*), but also several areas of contact to choose from. Each of the following guidelines can help choose which contact area to play:

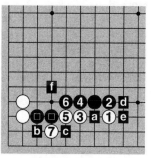

Diagram 16

1. **Attack or defend the weakest stones first.** White 7 is weaker (has fewer liberties) than White 3 & 5.

2. **Play the highest lines first when near the edge** (lines 4 to 1). Try to press your opponent closer to the edge and keep yourself away from it. Thus: *a* is higher than *b*.

3. **Look for moves that shift the movement of stones** 90 degrees. These contact pivots are immensely valuable, especially if they can be occupied in sente. Black at *b* is a pivot point.

4. **Play the severest move you can**, without causing yourself risk. In-line links are solid but passive; diagonal blocks away from other enemy stones (outside diagonal blocks) are aggressive but less severe than inside diagonal blocks . Cutting is the severest move of all, but in this example *c* is just foolish.

Here are some common contact sequences that might be reasonable for both players. Which sequence to choose depends upon global considerations, just like a joseki choice does. See Diagrams 17 and 18. There are two ways to initiate contact, playing diagonal to an enemy stone (shoulder hit), and playing adjacent to an enemy stone (attachment).

a: Simple. White 2 and Black 3 are direct stone extensions. Each player builds a wall with Black sticking out one side and White out the other. Solid, with each side maintaining liberty count.

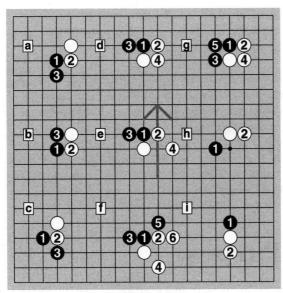

Diagram 17

b: Used when Black wants to move upward or when the enemy liberty count is important.

c: Most aggressive, Black gets large influence while restricting White. It is dangerous if White can safely cut, since Black is blocking stronger stones.

d: Black 1 is an attachment; White 2 applies pressure to Black. After Black 3 relieves the pressure, White defends the cutting point.

e: The hanging connection is an alternate defense that reaches farther. It can be peeped, which is sometimes an irritation. This 3-stone "arrow" should point in the direction in which White wants a wall. In this diagram White has a vertical wall, protecting the region to its right. White can resist Black trying to move to the right from 1 & 3.

f: White 2 is a hanging connection in the wrong direction. Black comes around with 5, and White must back down with 6. If White wants a vertical wall (as in **e**), this isn't it.

g: This could become messy if White cuts with 4, but it ends simply when both sides just connect as shown. White could have cut with White 4 at Black 5, but then White must do tactical reading. White 4 as shown is safe and solid.

h & i: Unorthodox. They violate the principle of aiming toward a stone. Not acceptable!

j: The crosscut pattern. Both sides extend for liberties. A proverb says *When caught in a crosscut, extend.* There is one extension in a third/fourth line crosscut that should always be examined. This is shown in Diagram k.

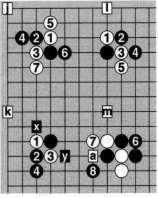

Diagram 18

k: The extension to Black 4 on the third line threatens to crush White 1 against the edge with *x*. The extension also threatens a ladder against White 3 with *y*, and if the ladder works, Black has no worries.

l: Here is the result if you fail to extend as in Diagram j and instead atari with Black 4. After White 5, Black's position is worse than before. One of White's strings is now stronger, while Black's stones are as weak as ever. Black now also has a dangerous cutting point between 2 and 4.

m: Continuing Diagram l, if Black protects the cut with 6, Black may lose a stone by ladder (White at *a*), uniting White. Even if White can't capture and so plays White 7, after Black runs with 8 (a special shape move), there is a big difference between this and Diagram 18j: White has sente.

Purpose

Purpose is your motive for fighting. Why are you doing this? Are you fighting to kill, is this an exhibition, or are you teaching skills? If you forget your purpose you may pick the wrong methods, emphasize the wrong direction, or linger too long in the fight.

By definition contact fights are not fights to kill. If you want to kill, you use the rules for killing strings given in *The Wolf Pack*. Nor should contact fight rules be used when you are drastically outnumbered (instead see *Fools Rush In*). Contact fights are for fights among stones almost equal in strength.

Contact fights, by their nature, cause both sides to add lots of stones locally. They are used to gain strength or influence. Contact fights build walls of influence. Since contact fights build walls, aim the wall in a useful direction.

Diagram 19. In response to White 1 Black chose Black 2 instead of the symmetrical move at *a* because a wall facing Black's marked stone would be cramped. By playing at Black 2, Black is able to use the marked stone as a part of a massive outward-facing wall. Building walls is one of contact's two major uses. The other is defense. When you are weak and outnumbered, you need to gain strength. So you initiate contact with a weak enemy stone.

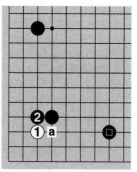

Diagram 19

Initiate contact carefully. Contact can create a fight where the best tactician wins, usually this is the stronger player. If you are Black, wait for White to start a contact fight if you can. Don't start it yourself. Once in a fight, respond and keep responding until your stones are stable.

Contact fights settle a situation. This is good if fluidity and uncertainty are to your disadvantage. That's why as the defender you want a contact fight. You are nervous about the potential interactions of your weakness on the rest of the board. Fluidity and uncertainty are vital, however, if you are already losing the game. You need unusual things to happen. So don't follow contact fight rules when you are losing. Create your own magic.

Abusive Contact

A contact fight strengthens both sides, so it's a great way to defend and a lousy way to attack.

To see the difference between starting contact and avoiding contact, compare the top and bottom openings in Diagram 20.

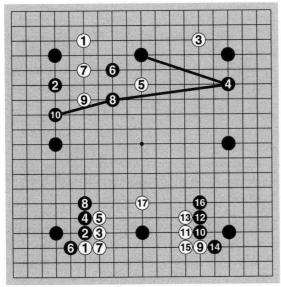

Diagram 20

At the bottom Black has played contact as much as possible. This triggers a flurry of moves as both sides conduct contact fighting. Black's lower side handicap stone is dead, giving White stability and territory. Black has strong outside stones, but Black's corners and sides are still open to invasion. The overall position is simple to keep track of, White has made territory and is stable.

In the top Black avoided contact, causing fewer moves to be played. The situation is more fluid but favors Black heavily because White has no territory and has all weak groups. Black's stones on the left are safe. The top middle handicap stone has been extended to Black 8, which is across the 5-9 sector-line. White's groups have no eyes and are within dangerous sector-lines. Any White invasions will further weaken White's outside stones, so White will not dare invade the corners for now, unlike the bottom where White can safely try to invade Black's corners. Provided Black carefully watches sector-lines and links, there is no reason for Black to get into danger, and White will be pressured for many moves to come.

In the Real World

To many, avoiding contact to attack seems counter-intuitive. Good! Important rules are counter-intuitive. If a rule is obvious, everybody does it and nobody gains significant advantage. Looking for counter-intuitive knowledge pays off bigger. Who would have thought that to prevent someone from getting a disease you would first give it to them. Yet that is exactly the principle behind inoculation.

You only think you attack with contact. But, you wouldn't attack with contact someone who is obviously a better fighter than you. And you don't first-strike someone your own strength. Unless one of you gets lucky, all you will do is exhaust both of you. Since you can't guarantee victory in either of these two cases, you don't attack with contact. You attack from a distance, with a gun. You attack with contact someone weaker than you (you bully). And bullies don't usually attack to kill. They attack to reinforce their own self image, or to get the victim to hand over something. So it is with contact fights; you push your opponent around to gain influence.

There are times to attack an equal. You spar with an equal when in training. Why? It increases your skill. It also increases your opponent's skill. This happens in tennis. If your backhand is weak, your opponent learns to target it. Over time, all that extra practice with your backhand makes it improve, so it can no longer be targeted.

What does all this suggest in business? Suppose you have competitors who are stronger in some area while you are stronger in some other area. Should you attack them in their area of strength? No. If a small airline launches a price war with a big airline, usually the small airline gets killed. Battling money against someone with much more than you is a losing strategy (unless you have a cost advantage). Instead, you find where you have more strength than the competitor — or some new weapon.

Miller Brewing tried exactly that when competing with Anheuser Busch, which had a much bigger share of the beer market and could afford more advertising. Miller invented Lite Beer (a new strength) and put on an advertising blitz. They attacked with segmented marketing, another new strength. Instead of making a single ad and showing it to all audiences, they created multiple ads that targeted different market segments. This was highly effective and increased Miller's market share dramatically. But it didn't get anywhere near killing Anheuser Busch. So Busch learned the same trick, but with a much bigger advertising budget. Net result? Busch got stronger. Miller's initial advantage dissipated.

Contact fights make both sides stronger. If you want to kill your opponent, attack from strength and land a fatal blow. If you can't, consider shoring up your weaknesses. Build strength without strengthening your opponent. How? Fight with some other competitor in some other marketplace using your weakness. You both get stronger, but your original target doesn't. Then attack using your new and old strength combined.

Group Defense

Darwinian Evolution
Flight and Fight
The Great Escape

Go & Politics

*" to be circumspect
and not to forget one's armor
is the right way to safety"*

Darwinian Evolution

Complexity develops from simplicity. It is a basic principle in nature: complex structures are built up by repetition of simpler ones. Our body is composed of repeated cells; our cells are created from instructions carried on the four bases in DNA helices. Crystals are formed by geometric constructions of repeating atoms and molecules. Evolution is the process by which simpler things become more complex over time. Single-celled creatures become multicellular, then add fins and gills, then add brains, and so on.

In Go, there are also underlying simple shapes of stones that get repeated over and over again to build more complex structures. They are all based on the eventual need for eyes. Initially the board is empty, but as some shapes can form eyes, the evolution of more complex shapes from simple, elemental shapes begins. On the static matrix of a Go board the process is like crystallization. But the pressure is evolutionary and the unsuccessful shapes are as dead in the world of Go as the moa and dodo are in the world of flying birds. Some designs just can't compete fast enough.

Each stone you play can contribute toward your overall success or it can lead toward your ruin. Disregard for detail can spoil even the best of global play. Shapes are a crucial part of that detail. As you learn Go, you become familiar with recurring configurations of stones and you learn standard follow-ups. This is the shape aspect of Go. Shapes are important time-savers. When you are planning to play in an area, look first at the shapes there. They frequently suggest an obvious choice. Some shapes, called "bad shapes", should be avoided and warn you not to play a move. Still other shape-suggested moves, called *tesuji*, can point out objectives to try. Suggestions of goals and where and when not to play are critical in limiting the massive number of available moves to a set you can afford to analyze. This chapter will focus on recognizing good and bad shapes and developing a group's shape.

The study and practice of shapes or forms is at the heart of Japanese learning tradition. They teach imitation of form first (kata) and innovation second. Innovation in the absence of skill is seen as useless. The constant practice involving a large number of similar problems builds up student confidence. Innovation is not treated as some giant step forward, as it is in the West. Instead it is the accumulation of small changes and improvements. These result in a big advancement in quality by many tiny steps.

Bad Shapes

The most common bad shape is the empty triangle, shown in the far left in Diagram Bad Shapes. It is bad because it is inefficient. The empty intersection in the triangle is redundantly touched by two stones. Had the shape been a straight line of three

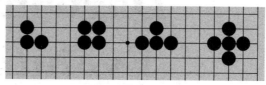

Bad Shapes

stones, they would have touched eight intersections. Instead they touch only seven. A worse shape fills in the empty triangle with another stone of the same color. This clump of four is no more efficient than two stones in a diagonal link form. Similarly, as stones are added to form other clumps (also known as dumplings), they get more inefficient.

You want to avoid bad shapes. The empty triangle is the biggest clue. If you are about to make a move forming an empty triangle — STOP. See if you can find a better move that does the same job.

Diagram 1a

In Diagram 1a, Black wants to play *a* to secure the link to the edge. This would form an empty triangle.

A better choice is *b* of Diagram 1b. It reaches farther, undercuts White, and cannot be cut off by White. If White could cut it off, Black should try *c* instead. It backs off to gain safety.

Diagram 1b

If you cannot find a move to "fix" the empty triangle, consider playing elsewhere. Find something else to do. If you absolutely must play the empty triangle, treat it as a symptom that you did something wrong in the area several moves ago. You have an opportunity to discover an earlier mistake.

Not all empty triangles are wrong. There are two excuses for making empty triangles.

The first excuse is to make a trade in which both you and your opponent make bad shape. In Diagram 2, Black 1 peeps White's connection. White 2 is the standard response, yet it forms the dreaded empty triangle. White should not avoid this move. While White is left with an empty triangle, Black is left with a "bad shape" too. Black has a stone in a bad contact fight. Even if Black spends another turn defending it, Black will still be unstable, and White will still be stable.

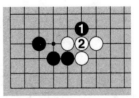

Diagram 2

The second excuse for forming an empty triangle is to make an eye. An eye is made of empty triangles pasted together (consider the eyes at right). It's so bad, it's good. The super concentration of power forms a black hole, and all enemy stones die when placed in it. While an eye is good, it is slow to make. Make eyes only if you have to. If you can find a way to prevent having to make eyes, so much the better.

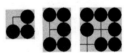

Good Shapes

The good shapes can be remembered by fanciful names: muffin, brownie, baklava (left to right, top), cupcake with cherry, and cream puff (left to right, bottom) in Diagram Good Shapes.

To get to any of these shapes you have to make many moves. The shapes created along the way (subset shapes) also have value and are good shapes.

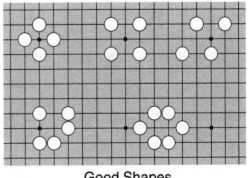

Good Shapes

Good shape provides for connection and prepares for eye formation. But good shape is more than that. A good shape move does future work as well. It wards off dangers you may not even be aware of. By contrast, bad shape moves barely manage to accomplish their current tasks, never mind future ones.

Shape Development

The process of building shape starts with the first stone. It is a shape by itself, albeit not a very powerful one. Additional stones can be added to form more complex shapes, until finally the stones combine to form one of the complete eye shapes shown in the Good Shapes Diagram.

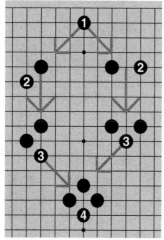

Muffin Development

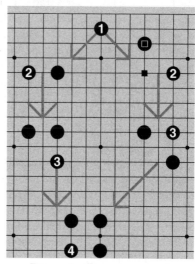

Brownie Development

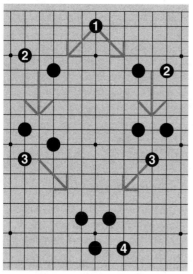

Baklava Development

In the Muffin Development Diagram you see the ways a single stone shape develops to a two-stone shape, then into a three-stone shape, and finally into a muffin. Each move of these transitions is also a good shape move.

Similarly in the Brownie Development Diagram you see transitions from a single stone to a brownie. One of them, however, is risky. Black 2, developing from the marked Black stone, is not a link. This is a poor way to develop, since you may get split apart before getting to Black 3.

The Baklava Development Diagram does not show one of the transitions from a single stone to two stones because it is also not a link. Can you figure out which move that would be? Again it is poor, so don't play it.

The wealth of possible transitions goes beyond the ability to show it in the Cupcake with Cherry Development Diagram. Again one of the second stage developments is omitted because it is not a link.

The Cream Puff Development Diagram explodes outward with many choices just for the second move.

The key understanding to have is that all sub-shapes of the five basic complete shapes are potential good shapes. Learn to see how to take stones and see the inherent complete shapes in them.

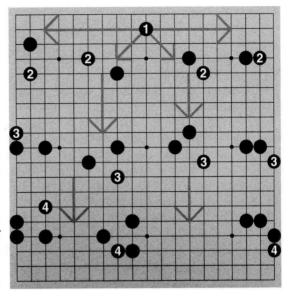

Cupcake with Cherry Development

For example, how many complete shapes can you reach from Diagram 3? The answer is two, the cream puff and the cupcake with cherry.

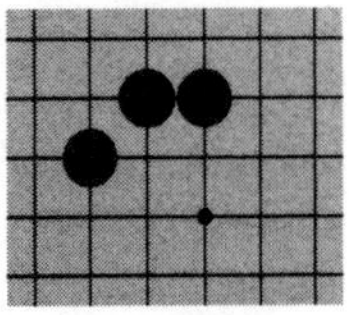

Diagram 3

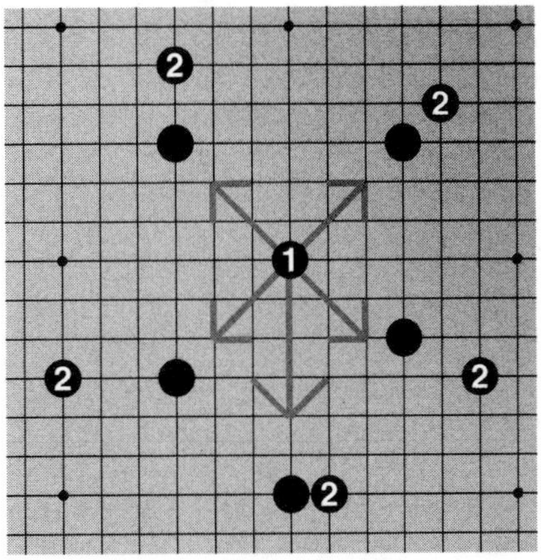

All subset shapes are *potential* good shapes. This is because to be considered useful, they must have the possibility of becoming a complete shape. If enemy stones occupy essential points preventing formation of a complete shape, then that potential will never be fulfilled and the subset shape you create has no meaning.

Cream Puff Development

In Diagram 4, Black 1 is clearly aimed at making a muffin, but White occupies the last vital point. Since the muffin can never be completed, Black 1 is not a "good shape" move. It is just a move.

Flexibility: While all subsets are good shapes, it is not good to create all subsets. The key to developing good shape is flexibility. Make moves that support multiple shapes. That way, if the enemy intervenes in one, you can continue with another.

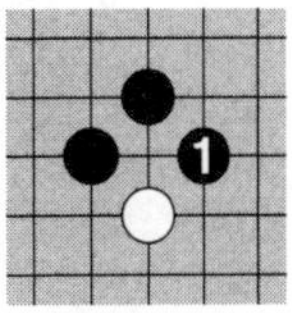

Diagram 4

In Diagram 5, part *a*, Black 1 is a bad shape move because it can never complete a muffin.

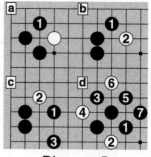

In part *b*, Black 1 invests three moves to form a shape, only to have White 2 take a critical point and lay waste to Black's formation. At least it cost White a move to block Black's moves.

In part *c* we see optimal good shape development at work. Black 1 aims for the same complete configuration as in part *b*. When White 2 destroys the cream puff shape, Black merely switches to building a cupcake with cherry using Black 3, illustrating flexibility.

Diagram 5

The 3-stone subset of the muffin shape created by Black 1 in part *d* can be stopped by White 2 but Black can continue creating muffin shapes close to completion until Black cannot be stopped from reaching a completed muffin.

Notice something about part *d*: White was determined to stop shape formation at all costs and failed. Even if White had succeeded, White would have created many strings much weaker than Black's one connected group. Unless White were backed up by thickness all around, Black could build new shapes by attacking White's stones: White would be unable to resist effectively.

Developing a Group

A secure group is one with two eyes. The completed shapes are eye shapes. Since the group needs two eyes to live, it needs the ability to form two completed shapes. When building eye shape for a group, the best shape to help along is usually the one that is most nearly complete. Remember, you want life as fast as you can get it. While you are trying to make shape, your opponent is likely to try to obstruct this process, so be prepared. There are several rules to follow in developing shape.

    1. **Make a sente move,** if possible. As always, a free move is worth a lot.

    2. **Work on the most complete shapes,** using the maximum number of your stones. You will accomplish your task sooner.

    3. **Create the greatest number of future shape moves.** If your opponent blocks one, you want a maximum of other shape options.

You will spend a lot of time working from a single-stone base. There are six moves that might be considered in developing the shape of a stone. These are the six link relations:

large knight's move
double-skip
small knight's move
single-skip
diagonal
in-line-extension

Of these, the double-skip and large knight's move should be rejected as too weak on connectivity. This leaves us with four stone-developing moves:

in-line-extension
diagonal move
single-skip
small knight's move

Are there any reasons to prefer one move over another? Yes. Prefer the single skip.

Prefer Single Skips

Significant differences between the four moves lead to preferring the single skip. If you look back at the Good Shapes diagram, you will notice that the single skip is the only link that figures in all good shapes. Since you want eye shape as fast as possible, examine only the shapes using four stones. One is composed entirely of single skips. None includes the in-line-extension. Of the shapes of four shown, the muffin consisting of diagonals or single skips is the most secure, the brownie the next most secure, and the baklava the least secure. Thus there is a clear ordering of moves based on speed and security of eye formation. Single-skips are best, followed by diagonals, small knight's moves, and then in-line-extensions.

Speed and security aren't the only reasons for preferring that ordering of moves. Assuming your opponent is ungracious enough to try to thwart your shape formation, flexibility is needed. You need to be able to switch shapes readily.

For each two-stone shape, Diagram 6 shows the possible development follow-ups. Once again the single skip is a clear winner with 16, followed by the diagonal with 14, the small knight's move with 12, and the in-line-extension with 12. The single skip is the most flexible and is the default choice. The diagonal is used for greater safety if the enemy is close.

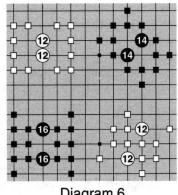

Another reason for the popularity of single skips is that they sacrifice well (see *Sacrificial Lamb* - Trade Links for Influence).

Single skips are so popular, there is even the proverb "Single skips are never wrong." This might be overstating it a bit, but not much.

Diagram 6

Life at Any Cost

When you attack a group, you must choose moves carefully. You cannot sacrifice stones so easily because they might give the defender eyes. The defender has it much easier. The defender can work on shapes without specifically protecting each stone, as each will either be thrown away or become part of the soon-to-be-living group. Keeping groups alive should not be difficult, but I've seen many kyu players go down in flames in situations where there was no reason for it. Either they weren't focussing on the essential matter of staying alive or they didn't know how to best live.

Whenever a group of yours becomes surrounded, you should immediately consider how you are going to get life for it. Now! Don't play that next move. Think! Try *The Great Escape* first. If that doesn't work you should immediately secure two eyes. Speed is critical. The longer it takes you to get life, the more likely you are to die, and the more damage you will suffer on the outside as a result of trying to live.

There are two general principles for survival:
  1. **Widen your eyespace** (grow more territory).
  2. **Split your eyespace** (form two eyes).

These principles can be refined into three steps for easy living. The steps given below are not optimal; they may strengthen the attacker more than is necessary. If applied in time, however, they should get life, which is the basic objective. Later you may learn to optimize, but for now the guide is **Life at Any Cost**. Even if part of the group must be sacrificed. The following steps should generate effective moves for the defender.

Threaten First: By making threats to escape, connect to safety, capture, etc., you force your opponent to respond, giving you a free move. These moves should help you solidify your eye space without allowing your opponent time to interfere. To find forcing moves when a group is surrounded, you should locate the complete loop of enemy strings and links being used to contain you. All links are places to threaten to connect to the outside; all enemy strings are possible targets to menace. First-line threats offer no threat to grow or run. They must threaten to immediately join to some outside group, or they are worthless.

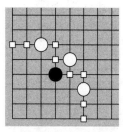

Diagram 7a

In Diagram 7a, Black has allowed himself to be closed into the corner (Don't ask why. Black shouldn't have.) The enclosure consists of three White stones and four links, two to the edge and two between stones.

Whenever you play a link threat, play it on or just inside the link, linking back to your group. Do not play either unconnected to your group or on the outside of a link. The attacker will respond between your move and your dying group, making it worse.

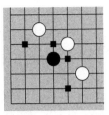

Diagram 7b

Diagram 7b shows Black's useful inside threats. Inside moves are simple and safe, but sometimes it is also possible to play on the link points as well. By playing more ambitiously, you may gain more space if the attacker backs down and plays on the outside. If, on the other hand, the attacker plays inside, you had better be prepared to utilize your move as a sacrifice because saving it is likely to get you into trouble.

In Diagram 8a, Black plays 1 on a link point itself. It does not link back to Black's handicap stone and doesn't sacrifice well. All White did was reply with White 2 and things are now worse for Black.

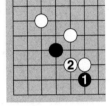

Diagram 8a

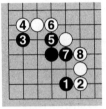

Diagram 8b

Links such as the knight's move have only inside and outside points, both a part of the link. **Threaten First** says Black should play out Diagram 8b (in any order) with the expected White responses shown. Each exchange helps strengthen White and some may not be necessary. But if you can't read out the life-giving sequence, it's better to use too many threats than not enough.

Secure Unstable Boundaries Second: If a string bounding your territory can be captured or if the enemy threatens to penetrate a bounding link, you must defend to preserve your eyespace. Pay particular attention to links to the edge which are undercut, because you can lose a lot of territory quickly. Before an attacker's move on the link, the boundary is stable. When the attacker plays on the link, the move threatens access to much of the territory and a defense is urgently needed. Of course, if the link only leads to one point of territory (which can become a new link), there is no urgency.

In Diagram 8b, Black has several links, but if White plays on them, Black can plug the leak simply. None of Black's edge links is undercut, so there is nothing critical there. Since Black can minimize any White attempt at intrusion, Black has time to employ the next principle.

Develop Eye Shapes Third: You want to make one of the completed good shapes in as few moves as possible. This means looking at the shapes currently in your group, and adding a stone to develop the one closest to completion. Given more than one good move, develop as may shapes simultaneously as possible and set up future shape moves.

Black's most complete shape in Diagram 8b involves Black 1, 7 and the handicap stone or Black 3, 5 and the handicap stone. Black should use as many stones as possible to build a shape. These sets of three stones cannot build the muffin, brownie, baklava or cream puff (since White occupies a critical point). They can only build the cupcake with cherry.

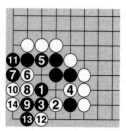

Diagram 9a

The best move is at Black 1 of Diagram 9a. It cooks both cupcakes simultaneously. White 2 jumps safely into Black's eye space. Black now has an unstable boundary link to the left and can threaten White with capture, so **Threats First** and **Secure Unstable Boundaries** apply simultaneously with Black 3. White 4 defends a stone from being captured and Black is left with no vital threats and no unstable boundaries. Black resumes making the most developed shape, securing the boundary of a simple muffin with Black 5. White cannot kill Black from here. An attempt is shown, but fails.

Trying another variation in Diagram 9b after Black 1, White dives deep into Black's eyespace with 2. Black dare not let White escape so Black defends with 3, preventing White from penetrating a boundary. White 4 crawls toward the other bound, but Black 5 stops White and creates an almost eye. White stops the eye with 6. Black 7 builds shape while protecting Black's two stones from capture. White 8 prevents Black from making two eyes simply, so Black has to go back and defend his two stones properly with 9. White pushes into Black's eyespace with 10, but Black 11 is simple and makes another eye inevitable.

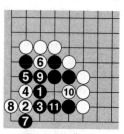

Diagram 9b

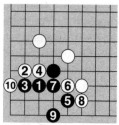

Diagram 10a

If Black knows some joseki, Black might begin with Black 1 of Diagram 10a, ignoring the three steps. This 3-3 move does not aim to build the most complete shape possible, so it becomes easier for White to attack. Life is not quick and easy; Black gets confused along the way. After White 10 Black is dead. Black 1 violated **Threaten First**. It did not threaten White but only made shape and secured boundaries. Given enough maneuverability this move works, but Black made a fatal error at 9. Black 9 was a reasonable response to White 8, but it was not a forcing move while there were several such moves available. It violated **Threaten First**.

Diagram 10b shows one continuation to death. After White 16, Black cannot connect the stone in atari without losing it in a bigger way. Yet if Black captures White 16, White will collapse the eye with a play left of White 14, atariing Black.

So much for life. Keep **Life at Any Cost** in mind. Deviate from its steps at your own risk.

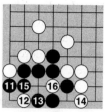

Diagram 10b

Flight and Fight

I*t's late at night. As you walk past a dark alley, you hear a rustling behind you. Your heart starts pumping; adrenaline floods your body. You can feel your natural defense mechanism at work, gearing you up for danger. Your body is now ready for fight or flight ("put up or shut up") as you turn to see if it is a mugger or just a cat.*

In Go, you don't hear a rustling — you imagine a sector-line. That's your cue to gear up for danger. But it's not fight or flight you get ready for. It's flight *and* fight. Mere running, unless it joins you to a safe group, only delays your danger. Sooner or later you will have to run again, and again, and again. So, the purpose of running is to gain the high ground to attack a weak enemy group. That is, run and then attack. Otherwise you probably shouldn't run.

Flight is first, because if you fight first and mess up, you leave yourself in danger of being enclosed and killed. Your instinct may be to fight first, but wait until you have room to swing your arms and room to change your mind. Running is a form of attack. In running you build a wall facing your opponent so that you can then turn around and counterattack. This is like is an old-style aerial dogfight. When a plane is being attacked from the rear (the best place to attack), the defender has to run (climb) in order to get out of the way and then get behind the opponent to counterattack.

Why Run? If you don't do something to protect a weak group, it is likely to be tortured or killed. Running is one of the defenses of a weak group. It is a means to gain space for eyes. But there is no profit in running *per se* and it ends in gote. So unless you have to, you don't run for eyes. You run to attack. If your group is outside of enemy sector-lines, then often enemy groups will be within your sector-lines. It's the nature of a confined board space.

When to Run? If a group hasn't enough space for two eyes and can't get it easily, and if it is contained by an enemy sector-line, it's time to head for the wide open spaces. Without knowing sector-lines, it's easy to miss the moment. This is a common failing of weaker players, who don't realize their danger and fail to run soon enough. If you know sector-lines, it's easy.

But not so fast. First you'd better ask yourself if there's any reason not to run. If a group is heavily outnumbered or not close to safety, you are likely to be better off letting it die. Any time you try to run through an opening towards safety, your opponent may get to reinforce either or both sides of the opening while threatening to close it. Your opponent's moves not only strengthen his stones, but they weaken stones of yours farther out. This is the price you pay for running. Such damage is often worse than just letting the running group die. Affection for your stones makes sacrificing anything a hard choice to accept, but you must learn. The critical question is, if you did run the group to safety, could you then turn around and use it to attack enemy groups? If not, running is too uni-purpose.

Where to Run? *One way is out.* When there is only one way out to safety, it would seem obvious what to do. And it is — if you think of running.

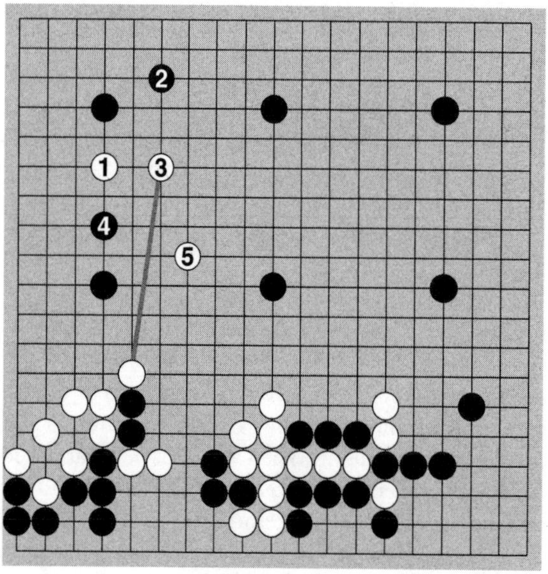

Diagram 1

In Diagram 1, I was playing a teaching game against a 15 kyu. After a fight on the lower side, I had built thickness and had sente. White 1 began an attack on Black's left-side stone. Black 2 was a common variation to defend the corner, but the corner was not yet outflanked (not within a sector-line) and the side stone was. He should have run the side stone out immediately. White 3 increased the White containment, creating the White sector-line shown. Black 4 went the wrong way.

The escape hatch is toward the center stone, across the sector-line. When faced with only one way out, run toward the sector-line, trying to get as far beyond it as possible. In geometry the shortest distance between a point and a line is the perpendicular to that line passing through the point. That is the correct way to run.

In Diagram 1, toward where White 5 was played was the fastest route for escape, How far Black could safely move that way is another question entirely, but knowing the correct direction of motion comes first. White 5 hit Black hard. Black could not get to the remainder of the sector-line before I sealed him in and, eventually, Black died.

Which way out to choose? When a group gets capped there are often two ways to run. Since running causes damage in the direction you run, you don't want to run out every opening, so the problem is to choose the best one. There are three considerations.

First, you must consider *safety*. You must be able to get out or think you can get out. That's your primary objective.

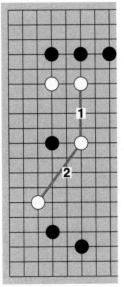

Diagram 2

In Diagram 2, Black sees two sector-lines. Black is farther from Line #1, so Line #2 is easier. Black should run toward Line #2.

Second, you want to run *towards your strength and away from your weakness*. Don't get confused with the proverb "Stay away from thickness." That refers to something else. You run towards your strength because your opponent will be attempting to keep your stones apart (if your opponent doesn't, then the attack ends and your opponent might become the enclosee). Your opponent's separating moves will damage the position you run towards; the stronger it is, the better it will survive weakening. Another way to view it is to think of the other thickness-using proverb: "Push your opponent toward your strong stones."

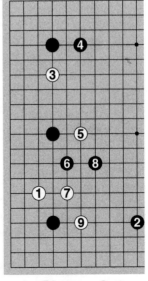

Diagram 3

After White caps with White 5 in Diagram 3, it makes little sense for Black to run with 6 & 8 only to have the lower corner encircled. Black should have run toward the upper corner instead. Black's upper corner is far better able to defend itself from White's follow-up assault.

Third, consider the possibility of attacking your opponent after you escape. You strengthen opponent groups along the side of your escape route; you must expect to attack in the area you didn't run toward. Ask yourself where you'd like to attack, and run the other way.

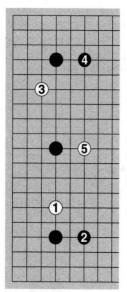

Diagram 4a

This point is illustrated by Diagram 4a. After White 5, which group does Black want to attack and, therefore, which way should Black run? At first glance there seems no reason to run up rather than down, but if you reflect further, you will notice that White 3 on the third line undercuts Black's stones. It can maneuver for life much more easily than can White 1.

Black should run up, between White 3 & 5 of Diagram 4a, as shown in Diagram 4b, and aim to attack White as shown or in some similar manner. Be aware that Black 6 is a running move requiring great skill to handle, since it is not a secure connection. It is a sacrifice running move (discussed later).

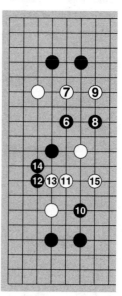

Diagram 4b

Diagram 4c shows Black running using secure running moves. Black 10 stops running for a moment to force White 11 (which stops Black from enclosing White with *a*). Black 12 then escapes and continues to attack White (i.e., White is still inside Black's sector-line). Playing Black 12 without playing Black 10 first is OK (it crosses White's sector-line), it's just that White would then run to 10, and Black's attack on White is less severe.

Sometimes defense and attack considerations conflict. If you run one way, you set up a more promising attack elsewhere but weaken your already weak stones. If circumstances are ambiguous — too bad. That's life. Choose a way somehow. The key thing is to know you can get out the way you are running. If your position is weak or you are taking a handicap, then defense should be the second key issue. Otherwise you are free to consider attack in choosing which sector-line to cross.

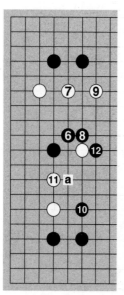

Diagram 4c

How to Run? *Running securely.* Assuming you can find the correct direction to run, you will want to get as far as possible with each move without getting cut off. How do you juggle these opposing constraints? First, I will cover the common safe running moves and then show you why some other secure moves are too slow.

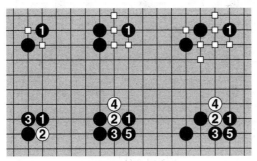

Diagram 5a

Diagram 5a shows three types of secure running moves on the top row. Each Black 1 is a secure connection as long as White has no stones on the marked intersections. On the bottom row White's attempts to cut Black's running moves apart are rebuffed.

Running moves using a small knight's move are also possible, but they are only semi-secure.

Diagram 5b shows knight's-based running moves on the top line (again assuming no White stones on the marked intersections). The middle line shows the usual attack sequences that fail. The bottom line, however, shows attack sequences that may succeed, depending upon what enemy stones are nearby. Even if the attacker does cut, the local fighting usually favors the runner and the runner can usually choose to sacrifice a stone if need be.

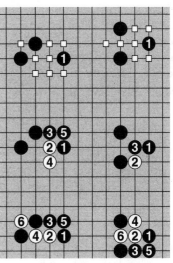

Diagram 5b

If you are going to combine speed and absolute safety, you will do best to "limp out". Alternate weak and strong, fast and slow. First, play an in-line or diagonal move, then play a single-skip or small knight's move. If you play two slow moves in a row, you move much too slowly. If you play two fast moves in a row, your opponent may be able to break one of them.

Diagram 5c shows typical limping running. Notice the attacker need not be as secure in making moves as the defender. White cannot counterattack while escaping.

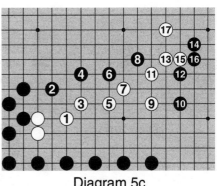

Diagram 5c

Running slowly Since I only showed the single-skip, diagonal and small knight's moves, you should be wondering about the other links. The in-line-extension was omitted because it's too slow.

Diagram 6 illustrates the problem. In a game against a 6-kyu, I began a typical nine stone opening. Black 6 was fine, although, as I determined later, Black really didn't understand that using it depends upon a sacrifice. Black 8 shows that Black felt the need for a more secure move. It struck me instantly as a mistake. The in-line-

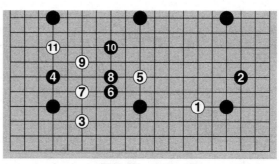

Diagram 6

extension used as a simple running move is far too slow. It is not immediately much slower than a diagonal play, but the follow-ups are poor. In particular, Black then had to play Black 10 to cross the 5-9 sector-line, even though 8-10 was not a secure connection. White then engulfed the corner with 11.

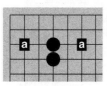

Diagram 7

If it is not obvious that the in-line-extension lacks the follow-up potentials of the diagonal move, consider this. Diagram 7 shows that the direct extension paves the way for a guaranteed faster skip to points marked *a*. But they're going in opposite directions, so one of them is usually aiming in a worthless direction, back into trouble. If White blocks the useful skip direction, you're stuck making another slow move or an unsafe skipping play.

Diagram 8 shows that the diagonal move prepares for skips (to *a*) heading in related directions. White cannot stop both of them. There are however, two cases when the direct extension is OK.

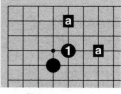

Diagram 8

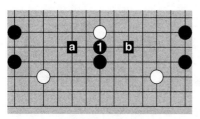

Diagram 9

The first is if running in opposite directions makes sense. In Diagram 9 after Black 1, Black can jump on whichever side White doesn't block.

The other use is in a contact fight, preparing for a safe jump or for advantageous combat. Back in Diagram 5c, White 15 prepared for White 17.

Running fast. The double skip and the large knight's move are ways to run swiftly. Although they are fast, they have horrible safety properties. They are useful primarily when there aren't any enemy stones nearby, and even then they need some skill.

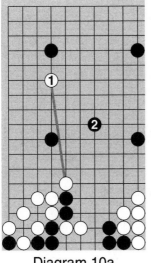

Diagram 10a

Diagram 10a reprises the situation of Diagram 1. Black was advised to cross White's sector-line, and in this open area the temptation is to use a big link and hook up to the center stone with Black 2.

Diagram 10b shows White attacking this link, and, while Black could do much with this fight, Black needs more skill than would exist in this handicap game.

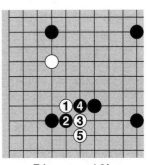

Diagram 10b

Sacrifice running. When trying to escape containment, you don't have to keep every stone connected to safety. Just try to keep a continuous line from stones that must be saved to the outside. You may abandon stones played as running moves if you can make alternate escape arrangements. (See also *Sacrificial Lamb*, under **Trade Links**).

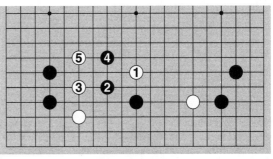

Diagram 11a

Diagram 11a returns to the problems of the 6 kyu. After White caps with White 1, we see the expected Black running sequence. Since neither Black 2 nor Black 4 conforms to the patterns of safe running moves, a sacrifice must be expected. When Black plays the skip to Black 4, White will not cut it immediately, even though White would be "successful".

The disaster of Diagram 11b would make White's joy short lived. White cuts off the "tail", but Black's main force unites with the corner group and swallows two White stones.

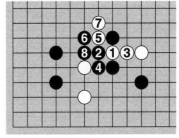

Diagram 11b

The case of a White attack on the knight's move to Black 2 in Diagram 11a is a tougher problem. If White tries to cut it, Black can resist. But while the environment for fighting favors Black, a tactical fight with a weaker opponent favors White. There are too many things for Black to keep track of.

Rather than enter a complex battle, it is simpler (although less obvious) to sacrifice as shown in Diagram 11c. Black thought about this sacrifice, but abandoned the sacrifice lookahead after White 11

because Black felt the position was bad. Black's walls may be close together, but is White doing any better? Keep looking. The right-hand White area is not enclosed territory. Black could run out immediately with another knight's move. (White certainly wouldn't try to

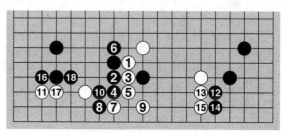

Diagram 11c

disconnect it. That would be ridiculous.) But since Black's side handicap stone is so outnumbered, Black should give it away. Don't resist White's territory, force White to take it! White cannot ignore Black 12 & 14 or White gets absolutely nothing here for all White's trouble. Black secures 18 points of territory in the right corner, granting White a claim of the same amount, and Black retains sente. White still does not completely enclose a claim. Black gives White some small profit in exchange for a slightly larger profit and sente. This is why White doesn't chop off Black's sacrifice running moves.

With sente Black returns to the lower-left corner with 16 and 18. White will have to work hard for life here and Black should get a solid position and sente again.

Sacrifice running is obviously more efficient than secure running. It takes fewer moves to go farther. It does, however, have its costs. You've got to check the tactics carefully and keep up-to-date on strategic changes affecting your stones. The risks of mistakes are higher and there is the possibility of unforeseen interactions making it impossible to solidify in time. Often a running move is made under the sacrifice option and then immediately or sometime soon converted into a secure, simple shape. A player will hunt for excuses to play the simplifying move. If you use sacrificial links for running, be clear what your intent and plans are. Too often players try to save both ends of the link and end up saving a "tail" stone and losing the main group. Don't let that happen to you.

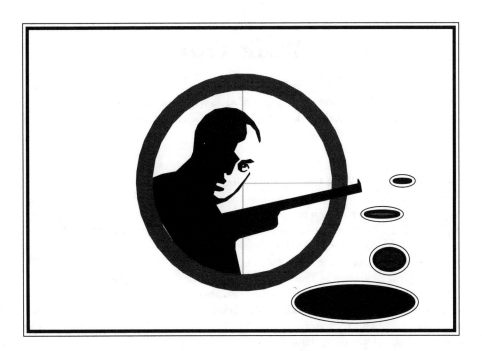

The Great Escape

You are trapped in a prisoner-of-war camp surrounded by barbed wire, round the clock armed guards and land mines. At night the floodlights sweep through the camp, illuminating the barracks and fences in turn. What do you do? Tunnel your way out? Cut through the wire? Climb it? Hide in something moving through the gates? Will you go it alone or work as part of a team? Will an outside force capture the camp and rescue you?

You are in a similar situation if your stones are trapped in one part of the Go board. Living is difficult under conditions where space is tight. Your best bet is to escape confinement before its walls solidify. There are several different escape plans. Try each of them in turn. You never know which plan the commandant will manage to foil and which plan will succeed.

Escape attempts are sente. They cannot be ignored (unless your captor is willing to release you). So you lose nothing by trying every technique that may work. Try in sente or make life if you fail.

The goal of *The Great Escape* is to either pierce your opponent's containment of your stones to regain access to the open board or to capture some of the surrounding wall if your opponent resists letting you out. Capture either gets you out or gives you eyes.

Walk Out

The simplest escape technique is **Walk Out**. You may be lucky and happen across a sleeping guard. If your stones are adjacent to an edge link and undercut it, you might play past your opponent's link, knowing you can't be cut off. Once you do, you're out and that's it.

In Diagram 1, Black is enclosed by the marked White links and should just **Walk Out** to *a*. Black has actually been enclosed for several moves but was too weak to skip earlier, so Black has been responding with contact-fight technique. Stronger players may protest that Black 6 is not the joseki and that Black 6 should be a skip move one intersection to the right. EZ-GO is after easy playability, not perfection. Unless you are stronger than 3 Dan, you probably don't understand the joseki anyway.

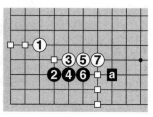

Diagram 1

Contact fight theory says skip with six liberties. Five along the edge sometimes works, but I would probably fry you if you tried skipping without six liberties against me. The ultimate choice depends on the skill levels of the players involved.

Walking out when next to the fence (as in Diagram 1) is easy if you have enough liberties. Sometimes you can also walk out when your stones are farther away.

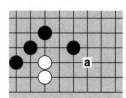

Diagram 2a

Diagram 2a shows a White string two units away from the fence. White wants to walk out to *a*. With the help of White's second-line stone, this is possible.

Diagram 2b shows White doing this and Black resisting. After White 7, White has *a* or *b* to capture or connect, so Black cannot stop White.

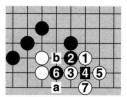

Diagram 2b

If you are three away from the fence, you can't long jump your way past it, even with a running start. Your only hope in that case will be to have friends nearby on the outside who can assist you in your escape by forming a bridge with you.

Form a Living Bridge

Imagine you are with a group of people, half of whom can't swim. As you walk along, you come to a deep stream. You look up and down the stream but see no place to cross it without getting wet. *Let's swim*, you think. That's fine for those of you who can swim, but what about the others? You've got nothing else with you. What can you do?

Do what the ants do. They send a series of ants out to link up and form a living bridge for the others to cross. Since ants can live underwater for a long time without drowning, it's not that big a deal. In your case, you can send out your capable swimmers to act as the bridge. Then you let the nonswimmers pull themselves along in the water, using the human chain as a rope.

In Go you may be able to bridge underneath enemy links to the edge, but only if you have friendly stones on both sides of the boundary.

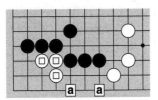

Diagram 3

In Diagram 3, White's marked stones have to cross a stream of Black links three units wide, but help is waiting on the other side. A play on either *a* point will create a living bridge of links, one diagonal and one large knight's move. White can live. Playing exactly in the middle, creating two equal small knight's moves doesn't work; Black can cut White apart with clever play.

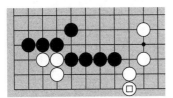

Diagram 4a

That was easy. How about crossing a stream four units wide? Can White connect in Diagram 4a? Given the presence of White's marked stone, it is possible.

White can play 1 of Diagram 4b. If Black tries to interfere as shown, White can still succeed. Notice the role of White's marked stone. Without it, Black could now play to the right of White 1, calling atari and then connecting back to Black's stones above. This would have Black sacrifice a stone to break the connection, but White would only get a false eye out of capturing it, so White would be no stronger.

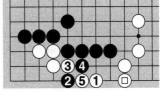

Diagram 4b

Is it possible to cross a stream five units wide? No. You will have to find another way out.

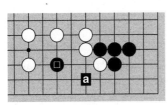

Diagram 5

Bridging can also be done on the second line. In Diagram 5, Black can save the marked stone by sliding from the third line to the second. Black barely creates a link underneath; but White needs to connect the threatened stone and Black will have time to secure the small knight's link underneath.

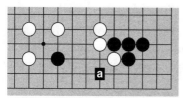

Diagram 6a

It is even possible to slide with the large knight's move of *a* in Diagram 6a. However the tactics get much more confusing. With maximal resistance from White, there could be a ko fight here. Still, ko for life would be good for Black, who is dead otherwise.

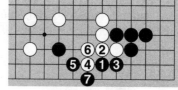

Diagram 6b

Diagram 6b shows less drastic White moves. Black connects safely. These slides work only when the enemy has a weakness that needs defending.

Destroy the Fence

When you can't walk out and you can't bridge out, you will have to escape through the fence. The plan is to weaken the fence. If it gives way immediately, you just escape. If the fence is built of tough material, then cut the wire, dividing it into pieces. Finally, overwhelm the fence by destroying part of it completely, pushing it to the ground, and incapacitating any guards that appear. If you have to destroy part of the fence to escape, you will have ruined the prison. There will be no need to rush after that. You have won and the prison camp is no more.

How Badly Are You Trapped? Before you attack the fence, you should decide how difficult it will be. *As soon as* you become enclosed, locate the links containing your stones. If at least one of the links is a large stone-stone link (double skip or large knight's move), then you should try to destroy the fence. If none of the links is long, destroying the fence probably won't succeed. You can try it anyway, though, because it costs you little. Attempts to escape that fail will strengthen your opponent on the outside, but dying costs you much more.

Assuming you will try to destroy the fence, what do you do? First, **Weaken**. Then **Cut**. Finally, **Overwhelm**.

Weaken

If you see a closed door in front of you, the first thing to do is simply push on it. Maybe it will open. In Go, that means playing stones on the enclosing links. Each time, the opponent must defend the link or let you escape.

Weakening occurs if the opponent's defense creates defects which can be the focus of continued fighting. E.g., White pushing on the bamboo joint at right is worthless because it creates no defects when Black defends.

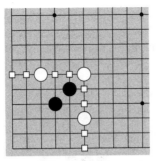

Diagram 7a

Diagram 7a shows a Black group in a White prison camp. The links are marked to show where the fences are. They are where Black should consider playing.

In Diagram 7b, Black has played on White's links. Black can only play on links where the moves will link back to previous stones of Black's, and Black prefers to play in order of most secure play first. Black 1 & 3 were both in-line links from Black's original stones. After they are played, Black can play 5 and 7 as in-line links. But ... playing them makes bad shape. They make empty triangles! This needs to be fixed.

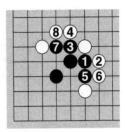

Diagram 7b

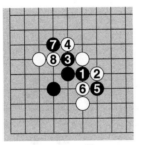

Diagram 7c

Normally you play on enemy links, from inside to outside. If, however, your move would make an empty triangle, fix it somehow. When playing on an enemy's small knight's moves, which have an inside and an outside, play the outside and let your opponent take the inside. Diagram 7c shows Black replacing the empty triangle moves with better ones. The effect is dramatic. Black has two obvious places to cut and yield double-atari. That is, Black cuts and White has two strings in atari at once. One of them must die. Black can capture and escape containment. Diagram 7c illustrates several **Weaken**ing rules. These are:

1. **Only push on stone-stone links.** With edge links your opponent can just drop back and reform a new one, so you can't succeed. In the above example, **Walk Out** doesn't work since Black is not next to an edge link. Therefore Black makes no move against the surrounding edge links.

2. **Play the most connected moves first** to keep things simple as long as possible. Normal order is: in-line, full-diagonal, half-diagonal, and then unpeeped single-skips. Other moves have insufficient connectivity and should be avoided.

3. **Avoid empty triangles.** (Filled triangles are acceptable.) Fix them.

4. **Be aware that all escape moves are potential sacrifice moves.** Don't save them. They weren't there before and were played ONLY to help your preexisting enclosed stones. Saving **Weaken**ing stones is not important.

5. **Attack only links that you can cross if your opponent fails to respond, or that you can cut if your opponent does respond.**

Note: Each **Weaken**ing move threatens to escape if not resisted, so you will be able to play all of them. Playing all of them is not optimal, but EZ-GO is not about optimal play. EZ-GO seeks an easy 80% move that requires minimal tactical lookahead. At higher levels of play, EZ-GO provides an analytic framework for finding the 100% move using lookahead and understanding the risks.

In Diagram 8, Black must consider pushing on each link as part of an escape attempt, but some of the pushes will be obviously foolish and should be omitted. Black's moves *a* & *c* attack links that do not lead anywhere. Moves *b* and *d* attack absolute connections and when the opponent defends, nothing useful is accomplished. *e* may or may not be possible depending on the results of a ladder occurring after White defends and Black cuts. *f* is a cuttable link. Mind you, you can't expect to succeed at destroying the fence in this example since there are no large links.

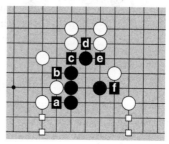

Diagram 8

Cut

Our original example of Weakening left us in an easy situation, with no need to choose the order of cutting. But normally there is a correct order of play. You want to cut so as to create the weakest enemy strings possible as soon as possible. So cut-atari moves have the highest priority, followed by other cuts leading to low-liberty strings.

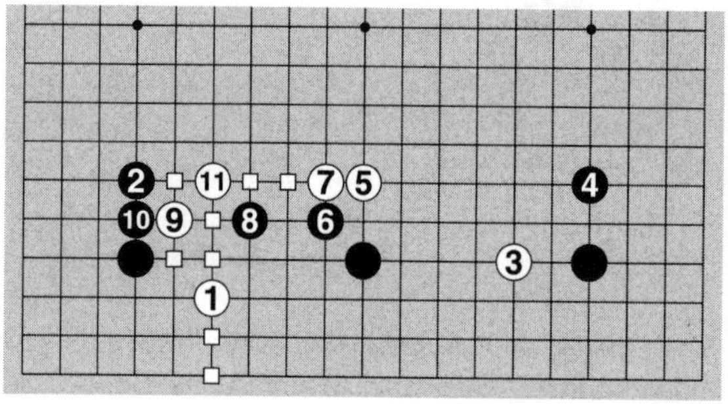

![Diagram 9a]

Diagram 9a

The situation in Diagram 9a arose when Black tried to run (with 6 and 8) but White refused to give up the quest (enclosing anything that moves is a very common White technique in handicap games). Black is not enclosed. Black could run out the right side. But White could just dump a wall around Black again, and ***Running*** tells us to run out only one side. Black should destroy the fence.

Applying the **Weaken**ing phase results in Diagram 9b. Black pushes into the double-skip link, then the double-diagonal, then the single-diagonal.

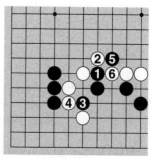

Diagram 9b

Now, during the **Cut** phase, the cut-atari of Black 1 in Diagram 9c takes first priority, followed by the only other cut, at Black 3. WARNING: Don't tactically read ahead. Otherwise you will be tempted to violate the sequence because you think you see a win. Black might be tempted to switch Black 3 to *a*, seeing the capture of White's single stone as inevitable. In the process, Black misses the capture of White's *two* stones, which is inevitable after Black 3 because of the snapback.

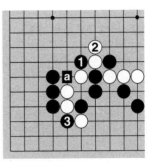

Diagram 9c

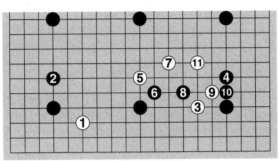

Diagram 10a

Diagram 10a shows another obnoxious attempt by White to bamboozle Black by throwing up a bluff containment. White makes a usual corner approach at White 1 and another at White 3, to each of which Black makes standard responses at Black 2 and 4. White plays a cap with White 5, creating sector-lines around Black, and Black struggles against the impending containment with Black 6 and 8. White threatens to isolate the corner with White 9 so Black connects, leaving White to complete the barrier with White 11.

Weakening this barrier is shown in Diagram 10b. After moves 1-6, there are four cutting points (marked *a, b, c, d*). Of these, only two cuts are acceptable. *b* and *c* fail when White just captures Black 5. Count the enemy's liberties on the strings on either side of the cut before the cut is made to determine which is the best cut to make. Cut point *d* touches two strings with liberties two and three. Cut point *a* touches two strings with liberties three and three. So *d* would be the best cut because it will yield the two strings with the fewest liberties.

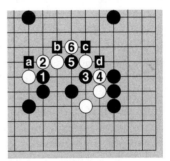

Diagram 10b

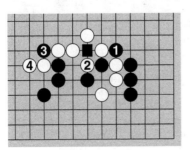

Diagram 10c

The **Cut** phase is shown in Diagram 10c. After cutting with Black 1 & 3, this phase is over. The next phase is **Overwhelm**. Black must kill something.

Overwhelm

If the guards discover your attempt to escape and try to stop you, you must overwhelm them. If your opponent continues to resist, you must now find a currently enclosed target and try to kill it. This is the toughest phase, but the most costly one for your opponent to lose. During **Weaken**, your opponent could have backed down at minimal cost. During **Overwhelm**, however, your opponent risks major damage.

There is a good chance you won't get to the **Overwhelm** phase. When your opponent first enclosed you, it was probably a bluff and your opponent assumed you would misplay early on. Even if you can't read ahead what will happen, your opponent probably can. Your opponent may well fear you will stumble into a kill if pushed hard enough. Thus if you play well in the initial phases following escape rules, your opponent may well back down from such unreasonable play. If not, you get to here.

Locate the Target: Of all the strings enclosing you, one or more of them must be enclosed at present. These are the only possible targets. If you have to spend time enclosing a target, your opponent has too much time and too many options and you will lose the fight.

Restrict the Target: Prevent it gaining liberties and territory quickly. Slides are an important move to block. (A *slide* is a small or large knight's move played parallel to the edge, moving from a higher line to a lower one.)

Reinforce your Weakness: When things are equal, attack from the side of the stones you are defending. Even if you don't kill enemy stones, your moves will reinforce your group and make it easier for you to live.

Stop Quickly: If your opponent has made some territory and you aren't sure you can kill if your opponent fails to respond, stop trying to **Overwhelm**. Switch to making life while you still have the initiative.

Reminder: EZ -GO techniques are conscious ones. You should consciously think "I am starting an escape", and continue each turn with the thought "I am still in an escape during the xx phase" until you have succeeded or failed. Using the label "escape" reminds you of your goal and the steps of the technique so you don't get distracted. If escape fails then try to make life.

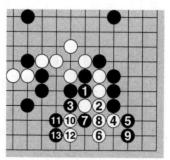

Diagram 10d

Continuing from Diagram 10c, Black has only one target, the three White stones cut off by Black. To kill them, Black must first save a stone with Black 1 in Diagram 10d and then with Black 3 keep White from sliding. When White tries to grow into the corner, Black blocks with 5. After White 6 builds shape and protects the connection, Black 7 ruins White's immediate shape. Black would now like to save Black 7, but it is not necessary. If you didn't know better, you could save it. It would help Black's group life, and both Black and White could get life. If you do know better, you can kill White by blocking White's shape with Black 9. White captures Black 7 and dies with only one eye. (There are two cuts in Black's corner position, but they are manageable.) White's group has so few liberties it would lose a race to capture against the corner.

Mission Impossible: Diagram 11a shows yet another outrageous White attack! Can escape do the job here? Since no large links are involved, I offer no guarantee, but let's take a look. White approaches with White 1 and White 3 to receive a standard response, then caps from a distance with White 5. Black starts to run with 6 but is still inside the sector-line, and by White 9 Black is surrounded by White links on the right hand side.

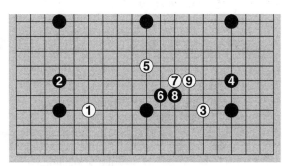

Diagram 11a

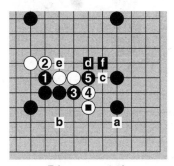

Diagram 11b

After **Weaken**ing with Black 1 and 3 in Diagram 11b, Black cuts with Black 5. The other cut at *e* involves the same liberty counts, but Black 5 encloses White and *e* doesn't. Now White is pickled. To defend White's marked string, White can attach at *a*, slide to *b* or atari at *c* to try to get out. *c* doesn't work because after Black at *d*, White must defend at *e* and Black reseals with *f*.

In Diagram 11c, White struggles with White 1 and 3 but Black keeps White tightly contained and out of the corner. After White 11, Black can play *a* in the center of the dead shape of five and White cannot survive. Even if White could survive, Black would have a secure corner and could now attend to making easy life for Black's other group.

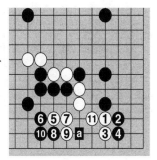

Diagram 11c

The benefits of the **Overwhelm** phase are that the opponent might die, but even if you capture nothing, your own group gets stronger from your opponent's attempts to wriggle into life. This makes life for you all that much easier.

Double Jeopardy: Diagram 12a reprises an earlier attempt to escape. When Black finished the last cut, White tried to trick Black with White 1, aiming to cut at *a*, or save White's marked trapped stones. Black's marked stone is doomed, but it was just a **Weaken**ing stone, so who cares? Black can play at *a* or *b*, but only *a* leads to an escape.

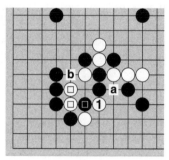

Diagram 12a

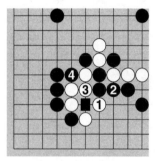

Diagram 12b

If Black keeps cool and connects with Black 2 in Diagram 12b, White gets into the fight shown.

Black 6 of Diagram 12c is played to stop White from sliding to the right of 6. If Black is played one point higher, it would form an empty triangle. Fixing the triangle leads to playing Black 6. When White tries to capture Black 7, Black abandons it with 8 and 10. White 11 makes an eye, but Black 12 prevents the other. White is in trouble now. A simple play at *b* will be met by Black at *a* and visa-versa. White cannot live here without Black's

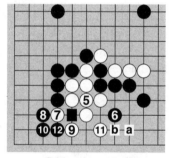

Diagram 12c

misplay. White will play *a* and pray. Black can force White to crawl along the second line and it will be many moves before any eyes can be acquired.

Deadly Games: Here's another escape but with a price attached.

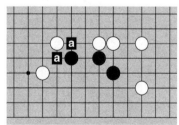

Diagram 13a

In Diagram 13a, Black could be in for a hard time. Black is surrounded, encloses no territory, and is undercut from both sides. There are four enclosing links to choose from (with the two edge links excluded). Moves at *a* are in-line from Black's stones and should therefore be first.

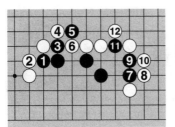

Diagram 13b

If Black pushes in the prescribed order (the numbered Black stones), the situation in Diagram 13b would result (the order of Black 1 & Black 3 may be reversed).

The **Weaken**ing moves have created a number of cutting weaknesses in White's position (marked with lettered boxes in Diagram 13c), which will be exploited during **Cut**. Consider the liberty counts on the enemy strings before each cut is played. The values are as follows: *a*: 5/2 *b*: 2/2 *c*: 4/3 *d*: 3/2 *e*: 4/2 *f*: 4/3. Try to minimize the values to attack the weakest targets: *b* is clearly first and *a* is last, *c* & *d* are pointless since White captures the ataried Black stone to regain connection, *f* is also worthless since White can atari and capture two stones. Obviously Black will need to save stones before trying these cuts. But saving stones is not part of **Weaken** or **Cut** and so is prohibited.

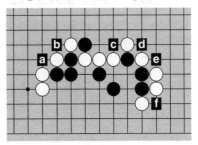

Diagram 13c

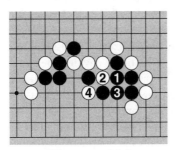

Diagram 13d

Players tempted from the true path of escape will face Diagram 13d where things get worse for Black.

In Diagram 13e, Black escapes with some but not all of the stones. Black 1 is a double-atari, so Black is out immediately. White 2 tries to cut off some stones and Black does not resist. (Black 3 is an empty triangle, but patching it to 5 doesn't work.) After White 4, Black 5 is to be expected to keep a connection. White 6 completes cutting off the marked stones (half of which were just **Weaken**ing moves anyway).

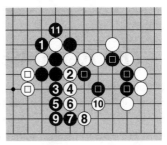

Diagram 13e

Black 7 & 9 are Black's right to make in sente, but needn't be played right now. The main focus will shift to White's stones on the left of Black's group. They are cut off and weak now.

Always remember to keep your focus during escape. Your job is to survive with your group. Don't get fixated on saving cutting moves you make. Abandon them quickly if they don't help you escape with your group and spend your turns making life instead.

Go & Politics

Politics has styles that guide one's actions. Here are some political Go styles.

The Democrat

A Democrat believes in doing what is right. But how can one man decide what is right? The player sitting at the board cannot decide on a move without the help of a committee. He will be advised on the best move, after the implications of the move upon all groups have been weighed. A Democrat worries about the effects of his actions and tries to be fair to all parties. This makes competition difficult. If one person wins, another must lose, so the winner must be penalized to compensate the loser. Why bother to win if it leaves you morally in the wrong and subject to penalties?

The Republican

A Republican believes in being rewarded for his efforts. He will get his friends to advise on the best move or hire expert advice. He aims to profit from the game so he will either bet on the result or rely on winning to enhance his reputation. If he can't actually play, he may take to brokering the advice of others, selling you the best moves. Once the game is underway the Republican is ruthless and goes all out for total victory with the maximum-size win over his opponent.

The Communist

The board belongs to the state, so no efforts made by the players will make any difference to who owns what territory. The player may not get advice as to the best move to make, but there will be many rules to follow in order to play in an approved manner. The game will be observed and non-communist moves will be reported to those in power. The player may be made an example of, to show that divergence from the official line will not be permitted.

The Libertarian

The Libertarian believes in preparing himself as an individual for the challenges of the game. He plays fast, as he has no hierarchy of advisors to consult and no extra rules to hold him back. The Libertarian believes people should pay the true cost of things. The simple cardboard Go board he plays on may have cost hundreds of dollars to account for the effects of deforestation on the planetary ecosystem. The relationship with his opponent matters to him, hence winning by one point is enough, as long as he does win.

The Apolitical

If you've ever played the guy who likes to take his move back when he sees it was a mistake, you know the apolitical Go player. The rules are there for someone else, not him. He'll beef about the rules if he loses and support them if he wins but will never join in a discussion about how they should evolve. He doesn't vote but still wants to rule the roost.

Group Attack

Buy Wholesale, Sell Retail
Rampant Machiavelliism
The Dark Side

A Go Song

*" Only those who will risk going too far
can possibly find out
how far one can go"*

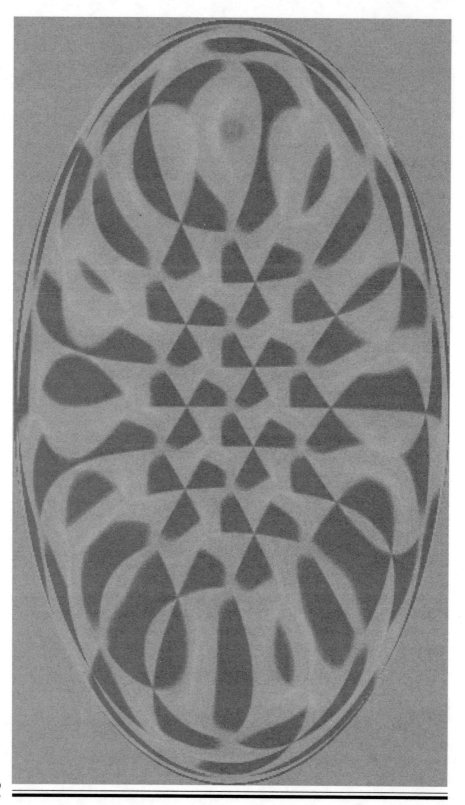

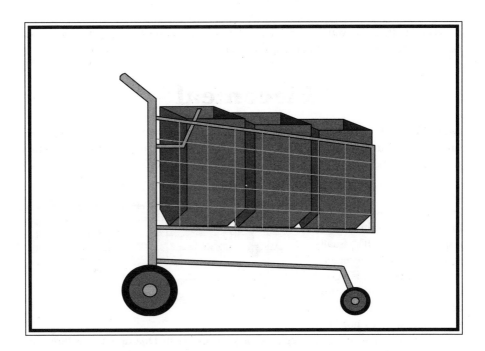

Buy Wholesale, Sell Retail

If you had a choice, would you prefer to buy at retail prices or wholesale prices? Silly question, isn't it? The only reason you buy something retail is because you can't buy it wholesale. Either you don't want as many units as it takes to get the wholesale price, or you don't know where to go to buy wholesale. Buying wholesale usually requires planning. If it's an impulse buy, expect to pay full retail prices.

String = Retail

In Go, trying to separate or capture a single string (*piecemealing*) is buying retail. You will pay maximum cost for minimum acquisition. Your moves will often be single-purpose, having no effect on the rest of the board. Because you are trying to buy only a few stones, your opponent can choose whether or not to sell them to you. Your opponent can resist your taking them or offer them to you in a trade for something of yours. If you succeed in capturing, you will have gotten some stones. A smart opponent will have gotten something else in exchange. So, did you really need those stones? If you didn't, then it's like shopping in a tourist trap. The prices you pay are outrageous compared to the value you receive. Many players go after stones on impulse. *Sacrificial Lamb* and this chapter should cure them of that.

Piecemeal

Avoid Yours: It's easy to detect and reject piecemeal moves you are about to make. Any time you attempt to cut your opponent's links, you are playing piecemeal. Stop and consider whether you can really justify making a piecemeal move.

Diagram 1 shows a couple of piecemeal examples. When Black plays 2, White might respond at *a* or *b*. It's visually obvious that *a* is piecemeal, and *b* is wholesale. *b* is a good move in almost any context because it faces the outside. But *a* may or may not be a

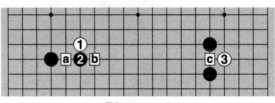

Diagram 1

good idea. It requires extra thought to play. White 3 in Diagram 1 is a threat to piecemeal. If Black ignores it, White must then follow up with a piecemeal move at *c*. Locally, Black will lose a lot of safety and territory if Black allows this, but is it the most important move on the board? Who knows? Unless you are a pro, you can't know. So as White, you can't be certain the threat to cut is not just bad piecemealing.

Confound Your Opponent's: Detecting piecemeal is a good way to criticize opponent moves. If your opponent's move is piecemeal, decide if you can give away the piece. It will surprise your opponent greatly if you give it away, sort of like in Judo when the attacker rushes the victim and gets thrown to the ground.

A 6-dan played White 1 in Diagram 2a against me in a tournament. He must have thought of this move as a profitably big slide that threatened to cut apart my marked

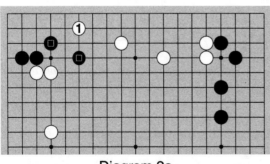

Diagram 2a

Black stones. I thought about defending, but I knew my response would be passive and shapeless. His move was a piecemeal threat to cut, so I thought about it some more. We're in the early game. His move didn't face the outside, and it came from an already secure group. In other words, as a move it was worthless, except for its threat. Could I use his move against him?

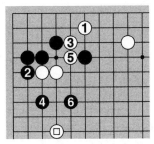

Diagram 2b

I responded with Black 2 in Diagram 2b, making my corner independently alive and threatening to come into White's area. White rushed to play 3, overjoyed at being able to actually cut me apart. I continued with Black 4, offering White a choice. White could connect his stones together with White 5, as shown, allowing me to jump with Black 6. This is the ultimate "success" of White's piecemeal move. White gets to sever Black and join up White in sente. Unfortunately, Black's corner has escaped to the center and Black can invade below White's marked stone. White moves in the upper left corner build redundant strength but aren't useful. White didn't like this.

This is what really happened: White played 5 in Diagram 2c to keep Black out of the center. Black 6 threatens piecemeal, but White has clearly declared an intention to keep his wall intact, so White 7 is assured. White is guaranteed to answer all of Black's moves 8-14 in only one way, as White wants to keep the cut that White originally threatened with White 3. Black 16 was not 100% sente, but it wasn't piecemeal, and White pretty much had to answer it (contact fight stability). The result is Black has converted a White sketch into Black territory, Black can invade the lower side and Black has sente.

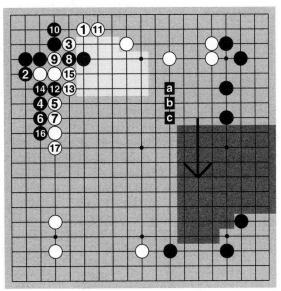

Diagram 2c

White has a defective left-side wall facing the center, but this wall faces Black's living stones on the right and was built in gote. Black can now play one of *a*, *b* or *c* to ruin the wall while laying the groundwork for a wall to face Black's shaded area. White succeeded in piecemealing Black, to White's regret.

Group = Wholesale

Threatening the life of an entire group is a *wholesale* action. Capturing a group is usually so strategically big that you expect your opponent to resist and you don't expect to capture it. You expect, instead, to make advantage elsewhere. That is, your attacking move performs two tasks, and your opponent's defense neutralizes only one. For that to be true, usually your attacking move must face somewhere else on the board while it also faces your opponent's group.

Wholesale

Wholesale is an attitude. Your aim is an entire group, not a piece of it. There are several kinds of moves that can be considered wholesale attacking moves.

Threaten to Enclose: One way to attack wholesale is threaten to enclose a group. By definition, this will face other regions of the board. Since threatening to enclose builds a wall, you must make sure the wall faces either a potential territory of yours or another weak group of your opponent's.

Invade: Another way to attack wholesale is to invade to isolate a group from friends and prevent it from securing life along the edge. This way is risky, because you create a weak group. You could cause yourself much grief. On the other hand the value is high if you succeed, since a large area is neutralized. Invasion is best if it creates two attackable opponent groups, not just one.

Secure Nearby Fourth-Line Territory Boundaries: Securing your territory boundary is immediately valuable, but it doesn't face the outside. It works best if your securing move has a follow-up threat against your opponent, for example a slide into opponent territory or a direct invasion. It is even better if your group is weak, so the move helps you.

Diagram 3 illustrates the three kinds of wholesale moves. White's marked stone is a weak group and Black has three wholesale moves to consider: *a*, *b*, and *c*.

a is an invasion. Features in favor of it in this position are that it isolates another weak group immediately above it. Also, Black has no other seriously weak groups on the board. If Black did, invasion would be too dangerous.

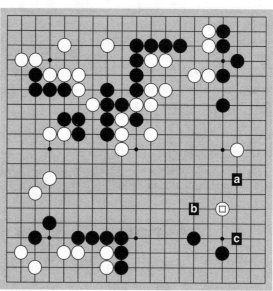

Diagram 3

b is an outside enclosing-type threat. It does not threaten to enclose next turn, which is a negative, but it does make a Black invasion next a strong positive. *b* also expands Black's potential territory to its left, which is good.

c secures the fourth-line corner boundary. It threatens to invade or slide into White's position, which is good. It does not create new sector-lines, which is a minus.

When is Piecemeal OK?

When can you attack a group piecemeal? Either when you really need to capture a piece for your own safety or when the group is too strong to attack wholesale. If you are piecemealing because the group is too strong, find another wholesale attack first.

Separating Groups Is Not Piecemeal: Piecemeal means trying to attack a string, a piece of a group. Separating groups is a good idea because you create no new liabilities, and your group gets access to a new area at the same time as your opponent's stones are being made weak.

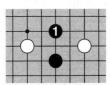

Diagram 4

In Diagram 4, Black 1 separates two White groups and accesses new space. This is great.

In Diagram 5, White 1 aims to separate (piecemeal) Black's stones. White expects Black to connect. But Black chooses to attack White's new weak string instead with 2. White cuts, but must defend for several more moves. Black is building up outward-facing strength, and White is picking off a useless stone. Black's trick will be particularly effective if White has a weak group to the right. White's initial peep at 1 was probably made to strengthen that group, but instead that group is much weaker with all those Black stones near it.

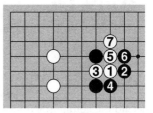

Diagram 5

Piecemeal If It Creates No New Units: If you can cut without creating a new liability, do it.

Piecemeal If You Cannot Wholesale: During the endgame, piecemeal and quibbling about boundaries are all there is to do. That's because the wholes are already safe.

Piecemeal If You Need the Piece: In Diagram 6, Black's group will die unless Black captures some White pieces. Black at *a* is clearly a piecemeal move, but that's reasonable here.

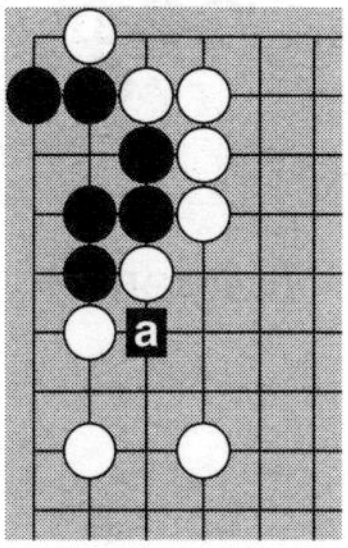

Diagram 6

Threaten Piecemeal If Your Opponent Will Defend: The reason to avoid piecemeal is that your opponent might not defend and will thereby find a better move than yours. If you know your opponent will defend, then piecemeal is fine. How can you know? If your understanding of value is good, then you know when things are too big for your opponent to let go. But that's an easy place to make a mistake, even for strong players. It'•
s easier to know if your opponent has just played a committing move, one that you know your opponent intends to follow up. Then you can threaten to piecemeal as a way to attack your opponent's shape in sente or patch a weakness of yours in sente.

If your opponent has just cut you, your opponent will save the stones involved in the cut. Otherwise, why bother to cut?' If your opponent has just made a hanging connection, expect your opponent to react to any peep.

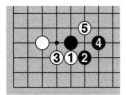

Diagram 7

Diagram 7 is a joseki. When White plays 5, White is reasonably certain Black will connect below 5, otherwise why did Black bother to play Black 4?

Another time you can predict your opponent's move is when your opponent has played a move to kill you. You can expect your opponent to protect stones from capture because your opponent intends to keep trying to kill you (at least until your opponent realizes you can't be killed).

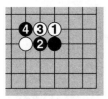

Diagram 8a

Diagram 8a is from a handicap game. Black 4 has just attacked piecemeal. Many are the ways Black can go wrong.

A wholesale way to play would be Diagram 8b. Black 4 is played to defend the cutting point in sente, not to try to cut White apart. Black has solid territory and White must then fret about White's group.

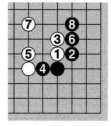

Diagram 8b

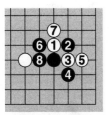

Diagram 8c

If White cuts with 3 in Diagram 8c, this is piecemeal. Black gives White the piece and instead forces out into the open with Black's handicap stone. Because White has cut Black with 3, Black can be certain that Black 4 and 6 are sente. Additionally, Black would be happy with a piece in this situation. Although White didn't give Black a piece, Black is safe. White can capture Black's isolated stone at Black 2 in gote and Black can continue attacking everything White has.

Such a simple thing, wholesale vs. piecemeal, yet so powerful. It is rules like this that make it possible to play fast Go. Piecemeal situations involve lots of tactical reading. But if the overall goal is flawed, lots of tactical reading is just not productive.

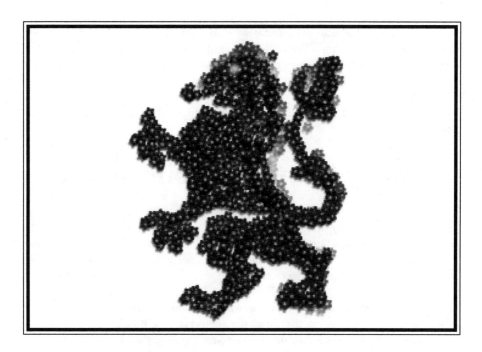

Rampant Machiavelliism

Do politicians from opposing parties want to kill each other? Sometimes you might think so the way that they go on about each other. But politicians are experts at coming out of a fight ahead of their opponents without committing murder. In fact, both sides will try to convince you they have come out ahead at each encounter. A politician's first desire is to survive every fight. A politician also realizes that sometimes you win more by appearing to give something away.

How good are you at plotting and scheming? Can you appear to do one thing while intending another? Perhaps you would make a good politician. *The Wolf Pack* described the thrill of the hunt, the joy of capturing strings enjoyed by the beginner. This is a primitive form of entertainment. The more sophisticated sport is leading groups astray. Watching them writhe and struggle as they try to elude your schemes for them is an especially fiendish pleasure. This is the Machiavellian way — manipulate and control them. Machiavelli would have fully subscribed to the Random House dictionary definition of politics as *the use of intrigue or strategy in obtaining any position of power or control.*

Your average Go cretin will only be content if an enemy group dies, but the real artist will take pleasure in letting it live while conquering the remainder of the board. The opponent is so grateful to survive, he barely notices the game is over. Both sides feel satisfied. This is good politics.

So what are the steps of a good attack? The same steps used in a firing squad— Ready, Aim, Fire.

Ready! — Calm Your Spirit

The attack and defense of groups, the midgame, is the single most important topic in Go. If you have to develop a single skill area, let it be the midgame. Most games will be won or lost by how you handle groups. The more competent midgame player can easily make up for losses endured in the opening game, and a successful midgame can avert a tiresome endgame via resignation.

Some players attack just because they can, with no vision of how the attack is going to further their cause. No surprise that their attack peters out and they are left with nothing to show for it. Worse, since they don't know when to stop, they lose sente and their opponent gets the next big move. This is un-Machiavellian. Machiavelli made even the simplest moves work toward some goal of his. Pursue a goal when you attack. Have a plan.

Other players attack to kill. They will take any risk, suffer any damage, all in hopes of killing a group. Killing is hard to do and might backfire into killing you. Machiavelli was not one to take risks for himself. Let your opponent take all the risks. Your goal should be to find profit elsewhere while you attack. The purpose of the attack is to get the profit for free. As you attack and make profit, your opponent just defends, making nothing new. If your opponent fails to defend and you have no risk, trying to kill then won't hurt you. Attack with sente or profit. If you know your attack move is sente, you can proceed. If your move will possibly be gote, prefer ones that make immediate profit while threatening the target group. That way you guarantee some value from the attack, even if the attack can never be followed up.

Aim! — Who To Attack

Would you attack someone holding a gun, looking at you, and about to step into a waiting getaway car? I hope not. At least not unless you are wearing a bullet proof vest, have wired the car to explode, and substituted his ammo clip when he wasn't aware of it. That is, not without a lot of thought, incentive, and preparation.

If you are going to attack someone, you prefer them to be weak and have few or no options for defense. Attacking strong groups is a waste of your move. Attack only weak groups. A weak group is one that doesn't already have space for two eyes and has few shape-development moves it can play. Prefer committed groups (ones with many stones) and shapeless groups. The enemy has the most to lose and the least choice of moves.

Groups consisting of single stones are hard to attack. The enemy has little commitment. Before you can get an attack going, you often need to increase the enemy's commitment.

In Diagram 1a, Black would like to attack White's marked single stone.

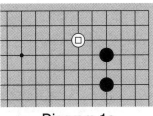

Diagram 1a

In Diagram 1b, Black 1 attacks at a distance, but White abandons the marked stone to invade the corner. When the dust settles, White is alive in the corner, and Black has not yet secured the attacked White stone. The problem was that White lacked commitment to that stone.

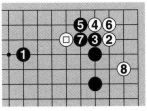

Diagram 1b

The way to increase White's commitment is to play contact. Contact strengthens both sides, so it is not normally the way to attack. But by increasing the number of stones involved, contact also increases commitment.

Diagram 1c shows a good way to attack White's single stone. The diagonal contact is a standard way to increase commitment while depriving White of the option of sliding into the corner. It does not "protect" the corner, however. White can still invade there later. White will not invade now because to do so would create serious harm to the existing outside group.

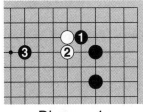

Diagram 1c

In Diagram 2a, Black 1 is a mistake. Of the two marked White groups, Black has attacked the less committed one. White naturally takes this chance to stabilize the bigger group with White 2 and then abandons the attacked stone further by dodging into the lower left corner with White 4 and on. Black really messed this one up.

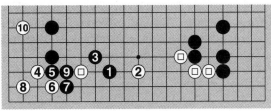

Diagram 2a

But if Black thinks that increasing White's commitment is the answer, Black is wrong. If Black plays 1 of Diagram 2b, White still ignores him to stabilize with White 2 and there is no big way to capture White's single stone. The problem is that Black is attacking White's less committed group.

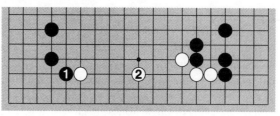

Diagram 2b

Attack big committed groups first.

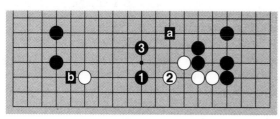

Diagram 2c

Black 1 in Diagram 2c attacks both groups at a distance. If White stabilizes his bigger group with White 2, Black jumps out with 3, continuing to pressure it. Black has *a* or *b* as follow-ups. Black got control by threatening the bigger unit first.

Fire! — How to attack

Attack Big Small and Small Big: Small groups should be attacked at a distance, and big groups should be attacked up close. If you attack a small group up close, your opponent can abandon it and you get little profit. If you attack a small group from far away, your opponent cannot afford to give it up with all of that surrounding space. Big groups, on the other hand, are profitable to kill but tend to have many development moves. Playing far away may not seriously reduce the available options and you have nothing to lose by playing up close.

Restrict Your Opponent's Options: The typical weak group has up to three broad options for defense. Move along the edge to the left, move along the edge to the right, and move toward the center. The first step in attacking any group is preventing it from living in one move. That may mean blocking an extension. Or it may mean stopping a connection. Or it may mean stopping two-eye formation. Along with stopping immediate life, you need to learn a few fundamental moves.

Side Squeeze

The first step in attacking a group is to block its expansion along the side (*side squeeze*). Do not let it make a two-point extension. Begin attacks with an side squeeze play (on the third or fourth line at a distance of two to four lines away from your opponent's stones). This prevents the target from immediately securing life-giving territory by extending along the side.

In Diagram 3, Black should make an sidesqueeze play at *a* (the default) or on a marked intersection. This keeps White from extending along the side to gain territory. The default squeeze prevents any useful extension without getting too close. Playing closer to White increases the likelihood of White sacrificing a stone or of White counterattacking soon after.

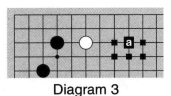

Diagram 3

Match Your Squeeze to the Opponent's Line: Play low for low or high for high.

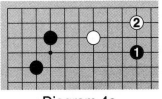

Diagram 4a

High squeeze plays against a third-line stone allow the enemy to slide underneath you. In Diagram 4a, White can easily slide when Black attacks. Unless Black's plan involves getting central thickness and allowing this slide, Black will not be happy.

Low squeeze plays against a fourth-line stone can be pressured by contact too readily. In Diagram 4b, Black plays low to attack White's marked high stone. White initiates contact with White 2. There are many variations. Black 3 on the outside is typical, but White can crosscut and sacrifice with 4 and 8. The result is White's original group becomes hard to attack.

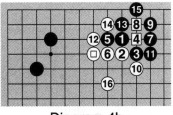

Diagram 4b

Avoid Redundant Squeezes: Once you have a wide squeeze stone in place, squeezing tighter wastes your initial squeeze.

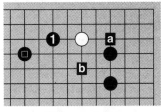

Diagram 5a

In Diagram 5a, if Black plays at 1, then the marked handicap stone is poorly placed. Black's handicap stone already squeezes White, so Black should attack differently. Maybe Black should secure the corner at *a*, or cap White at *b*. Either would be better than the redundant squeeze at Black 1.

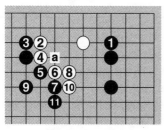

Diagram 5b

Perhaps Black was afraid White would make a two-point extension despite Black's squeeze. Contact extensions are rare. If Black attacks from the corner with 1 and White extends to 2 in Diagram 5b, Black will use the contact fight to build a massive wall. Remember, Black is not seeking to kill; Black is seeking to profit. Such massive thickness is good for Black, and White is still not secure. The key for Black in this sequence is Black 7. This two-step block is a standard tactic when the opponent launches a defensive contact fight. Black 7 threatens to cut at *a* and capture two White stones, so a White backdown with 8 is expected.

If White refuses to back down, then Diagram 5c results. Black captures two White stones and White needs to make two moves in succession (illegal). White needs to protect the connection near *a* and White needs to capture Black's stone with *b*.

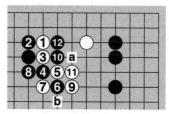

Diagram 5c

Press

The small knight's move is used to press your opponent against your wall and either enclose your opponent or build a new wall using your knight's move. If you can't enclose your opponent or use your new wall, then the knight's move is worthless.

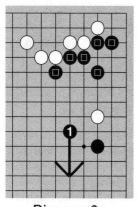

Diagram 6a

In Diagram 6a, Black 1 is the ideal pressing move against White's stone. It pushes it into Black's marked wall and, probably, White will never escape. Black 1 also starts a wall facing in the arrow direction. If this wall can be useful, then Black 1 makes sense.

Diagram 6b shows Black attacking with single skips. Aside from letting White out easily, the problem with this diagram is that Black gets no advantage from going first in this position. It doesn't matter whether Black plays 1 and White plays 2, or White plays 2 and then Black plays 1. Going first here makes no difference to the resulting position. That is wrong. If Black plays first, Black should expect extra. Machiavelli would never miss the chance to use an advantage. Neither should you.

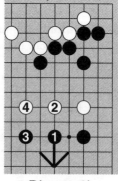

Diaram 6b

Diagram 7 is another great place to use the press. And if one press is good, two are better. White may or may not live, but Black will surely get nice thickness.

While your knight's moves can be cut, the enemy never has the time to spend doing so. The only thing to avoid is pressing your opponent against your weak group. That just makes it weaker and you may die.

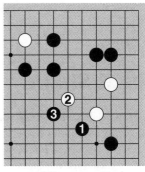

Diagram 7

Cap

In *Darwinian Evolution,* while discussing developing a single stone, I said the single skip was the optimal shape whenever playable. In attacking, when there are many possible skipping plays to prevent, the cap becomes optimal. A capping move occupies an opponent's potential single-skip in the direction of the enemy's open running space. Not only does the cap take a vital shape point, but it aims at enclosing the enemy group and forces your opponent to move in a new direction to get around the cap. Look for the cap and play it early.

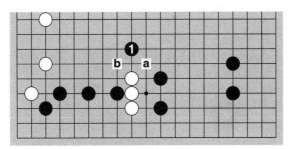

Diagram 8a

Diagram 8a shows a perfect Black 1 cap. It is where White would play a single skip to escape to the center. In this example it is an isolated cap, that is, it has no links to either side, so it leaves escape routes *a* and *b* for White. Notice that if White plays either of them, White can never complete any good shapes with them, because Black's stones are on the essential points. White will slow to a crawl and build no shape as he runs. Black, meanwhile, can play full speed toward building walls.

all the essential points. White will slow to a crawl and build no shape as he runs. Black, meanwhile, can play full speed toward building walls.

If White runs right, as in Diagram 8b, for example, Black can press with 3. White 4 requires a contact defense of 5. After White 6, Black DOES NOT use the knight's move below 7 to press White. That would be in contact with stones already strong. Instead Black settles for a single skip to continue his wall. When White sticks a nose out with 8, Black secures territory below with 9. White still has a long way to run.

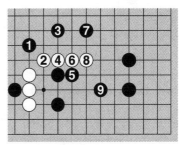

Diagram 8b

125

The cap would be Machiavelli's favorite Go tool. It leads to much ambiguity of purpose. That's good for keeping the opponent in the dark. Just don't lose sight of your own purpose.

Steal Shape

A group will try to defend itself by making eye shape (see *Darwinian Evolution*). If you allow this to happen, your attack will fizzle quickly. You must be sensitive to moments when the opponent has almost completed a shape, and then destroy it. That way the enemy wastes the maximum number of moves and you the minimum. The ideal shape-stealing move forces the defender to connect, using an empty triangle. Make your opponent do this and you cannot lose.

Remember the completed shapes: muffin, brownie, baklava, cupcake with cherry, and cream puff. Each of these shapes is used to analyze the perfect time to strike. If you can take an essential shape point while threatening to disconnect your opponent's stones, you will have played perfectly. If your move only ruins shape without threatening to cut, it is gote and probably no good.

Muffin: If your opponent defends with the hanging connection, peeping to ruin shape is almost a reflex.

In Diagram 9, White 1 is met immediately with Black 2. When White connects with 3, White has no good shape and one bad shape (the empty triangle). After this Black won't even care if Black 2 dies, though Black may save it.

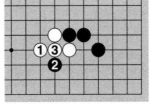

Diagram 9

Brownie: The only way to attack the shape of the brownie in sente is to double peep in the middle.

Diagram 10

Playing at *a* in Diagram 10 stops the brownie but may not be sente and leaves the cupcake with cherry still possible. Playing at *b* ruins everything but may not be safe for White. Usually you play at *a*, threatening to follow up with *b*. It's OK, but not brilliant.

Baklava: Stopping the baklava in sente is just not feasible.

Cupcake with Cherry: When you get the chance to ruin this shape, you can't turn it down. In Diagram 11, White's marked stone is trying to run out and White decides to contact Black's marked stone in the process. Blocking outside with 2 is standard and White 3 commits White to the cupcake with cherry shape. Black may be tempted to connect at *a*, but Black

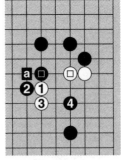

Diagram 11

4, taking the cherry, is devastating. If White played here, White would gets lots of potential shapes. With Black here, White can make no good shapes and White is threatened with being cut apart. Any White defense will result in a White empty triangle. White has no time to cut at *a* right now, as Black can abandon 2 if need be.

Equally devastating is the play in the center of three marked White stones of Diagram 12. Working with Black's marked stones, Black 1 insures that the only shapes White can make are false eyes. Black 1 is the cherry of two cupcakes and threatens to cut White apart, this time in two places. Machiavelli would turn over in his grave if you missed this opportunity to eat your opponent for dessert.

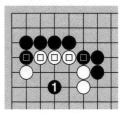

Diagram 12

Cream Puff: You can't threaten a cream puff in sente.

When trying to ruin the shape of a group bear in mind these rules:
1. **Force your opponent into bad shape.**
2. **Block the most completed shapes first.**
3. **Block multi-shape moves.**
4. **Retain a link back to safety.**
5. **Attack in sente.**
6. **Avoid unstable contact.**

In handicap games as White, many of my moves will be dictated by the shapes of my opponent's moves. If my opponent creates a mistaken configuration, I will immediately try to ruin it. I'm a bully at heart.

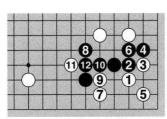

Diagram 13a

Diagram 13a is something I did to a 2-dan who took three stones. White 1–7 is a standard 3–3 invasion joseki. Black cannot block White 7 at its left without getting cut off. Being a 2-dan, my opponent realized this and chose a "good shape" connection. His good shape was an illusion. I needed no more invitation to launch a shape attack with White 9. His required defense of Black 10 sets up three of the four points needed for a muffin. White 11 destroys it while threatening to cut. Black 12 connects, forming an empty triangle. Black has been severely wounded. He is committed to saving a lot of stones and has only Black 8 to provide a basis for outside shape development. All of his other stones are worthless. Well — not quite, but almost. White's outside stones are quite flexible, with many shape and sacrifice options.

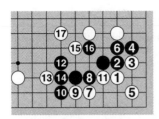

Diagram 13b

Diagram 13b is an alternative for Black. If Black changes his 8 of Diagram 13a to the 8 here, White proceeds with another logical shape trash. Black is not going to like this sequence any better.

Where did Black go wrong? Let me count the ways. First, consider that Black has allowed his options to extend from either side of his group to be blocked. Follow that with the danger of an invadeable corner territory. Complete the picture by being within White's sector line and it being White's turn. Black deserves whatever happens to him. He must have had chances earlier to extend, secure his corner, or run out. He didn't take them.

The Machiavellian Way

It is time now to focus on coordinated attack strategies instead of single moves. Machiavelli delighted in devious strategies. As you become skilled, so will you. There are two general ways to attack a group. You can enclose it, forcing it to live, or you can steal its eyespace and force it to run. Enclosing it is instant gratification; you profit strategically immediately whether or not the group lives. Forcing a group to run is the way of Machiavelli. You get complete control over where it moves and what damage you cause during the attack. In the hands of a competent chaser, the game is over as soon as a group is put on the run, though the runner may take a while to realize this.

Enclosing Attack

For all the reasons put forth in *Call of the Wild,* you should avoid being enclosed. Now the boot is on the other foot. If you have the opportunity to enclose a weak group, you should rush to take it. The strategic value is enormous. Enclosing a weak group is always a good idea. How to enclose was taught in *The Wolf Pack* so I won't spend time on it here. It's so advantageous, you might enclose even if it is a bluff. You can always let your opponent escape if it turns out there is a way out. If you are giving a handicap, you should ALWAYS enclose Black. With Black's weakness it is never a bluff.

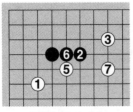

Diagram 14

Diagram 14 is something I often do in low-handicap games. When Black plays away and fails to run in reply to White 3, White 5 and 7 instantly enclose Black's corner. This looks pretty feeble, but it almost always pays off big.

Diagram 15 is really extreme. Black 2 was played somewhere else (or even as a squeeze against White 1). When Black ran with Black 4, Black never dreamed White could play 5. Black will surely break out of here, but breaking out will strengthen White, and there's always the chance Black will really mess up.

Combination Fights

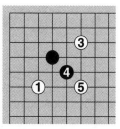

Diagram 15

There is only so much you can do with one enemy weak group. If, however, your opponent has two weak groups, or some weak stones in an important area, you can do almost anything. All you have to do is make the two sets of stones interact. Typically this means running the weak group toward the other stones, then either playing a separating move between both groups (if the other group is weak) or playing contact against the weak stones (if the second group as a whole is not weak). This is also called a roundabout attack.

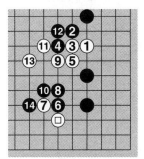

Diagram 16

In Diagram 16, White dared invade at 1. Upon seeing a weak White group below, Black began to push White 1 toward it with Black 2 and 4. When White got near enough, Black contacted White's marked stone with 6. To ignore the contact would be to suffer a loss on the lower side, so White responded, but Black 8 set up sector-line and link potential, damaging White 1. White can't keep everything safe at once.

Please note that playing contact does not mean following contact fight rules. You are not in contact to build a wall or have a fair fight. You are in contact as a distraction that allows you to get a stone in the path of some other weak running group.

In Diagram 17a, Black can safely play Black 3 in either of the two contact situations shown to place stones in between White's weak group (shown as a marked stone) and White's contacted stone. The cutting point is completely safe.

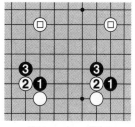

Diagram 17a

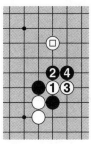

Diagram 17b

If White dares to cut, as in Diagram 17b, Black sacrifices and interposes even closer forcing stones between the marked weak stone and the contacted stone. This will be even more severe on the weak marked stone. Remember, Black is only giving up a stone. White is risking a whole group that was previously under attack. Always try to remember that you don't have to save every stone you play. Discard a few to simplify the situation or distract your opponent.

Chasing Attack

By far the most devastating attack is the chasing attack. The question is: *devastating to whom?* The chasing attack usually leads to a resignation, but whose will it be? In skilled hands, the chaser will destroy much of the opponent's position — and then kill the group as an afterthought. In clumsy hands, the chaser will run the group throughout the chaser's own potentials and then fail to kill it, or the runner will become too strong and the hunter will suddenly become the hunted.

A chasing attack usually begins by stripping an opponent's group of its eyespace. This is immediately profitable, depriving your opponent of territory and giving you some, and forces your opponent's group to run for eyes. It takes a l-o-n-g time to make eyes away from the edge.

Diagram 18a shows a typical Black group with edge territory that can be stripped. It's even easier if the right-hand White stone is at *a*.

Diagram 18a

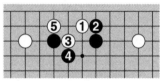

Diagram 18b

Diagram 18b shows one such strip. Black cannot stop White from connecting out, and Black will have cutting points to worry about.

Diagram 18c shows a different Black defense, equally ineffective. Black 6 will not survive. Diagram 18c is White's most severe play, but it involves good tactical ability.

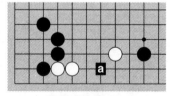

Diagram 18c

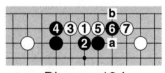

Diagram 18d

Diagram 18d is a simpler way for White to connect out. After White 7, White can play *a* or *b*.

Another common eyespace stealer is a Black play at *a* in Diagram 19. It will steal all of White's eyespace.

Diagram 20a shows a full chase from a pro game. White has just played White 1 to save his upper right group by running out. White has many marked weak

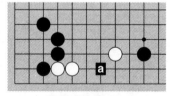

Diagram 19

groups on the board, each inside various Black sector lines. Black has just one marked weak stone. Since Black can devote full attention to saving the marked Black stone, while White must be concerned about saving several White groups simultaneously, White is in trouble.

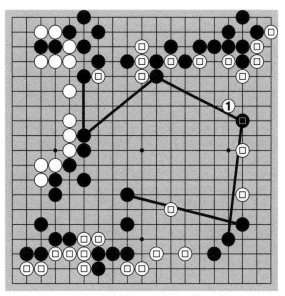

Diagram 20a

In Diagram 20b, Black launches a chasing attack. Combining chasing with shape stealing, Black runs White's group out into the center starting with Black 1. Periodically White has to protect other marked groups that fall into danger (with White 18, 22, 24, 30, 36). Appreciate, at the end of this diagram, the shapeless wreck of White stones that is about to crash into Black's left central wall. Machiavelli would have loved the feeling of power and control that Black must have enjoyed.

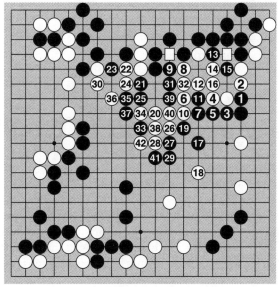

Diagram 20b

Dominos

The American justification for being in Vietnam revolved around the *domino theory*. According to this theory, as a nation went Communist, the adjacent nations would also start to fall, leading to a classic chain of falling dominos. I won't say how effective this was in the international arena, but it is extremely effective in high-handicap Go. A favorite White strategy is to enclose and assault a corner as soon as possible. White does not expect to kill it. White expects sente and strength from which to assault the adjoining side. From there White will topple the next corner, and soon the board has turned into smoking ruins.

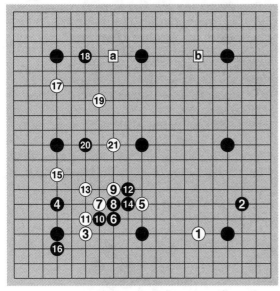

Diagram 21

Diagram 21 is a splendid example of Dominos. I gave a 2 kyu two more stones than he should have needed, and I used the domino strategy to achieve a big win. White 1, 3, & 5 are a standard attack, but my aim was to enclose the lower left corner. By White 15 I had done so. I then attacked the left side handicap stone with White 17 through 21. I can next enclose the upper left corner with *a*, and from there the upper side with *b*, etc.

The Machiavellian Go Player

Go & Politics caricatures political types by describing how they would play Go. Here is the Machiavellian caricature.

The Machiavellian is ruthless and clever and believes he should have total control. You don't play him directly, however, you play his front man. While you are nominally playing with your opponent, the Machiavelli is advising and assisting invisibly. Perhaps he has invited an old friend of yours to drop by the board for a visit, suitably distracting you from your play. Nothing is ever what it seems.

The Dark Side

In these days of dominating technology, *Magic – the Gathering*® rules the nation. A mere card game to some, to others it is a complete fantasy world of magical conflict. There are black and white decks (as well as other colors). Richly ornate, the cards depict a magical realm called Dominia. Each color has a speciality. Black, for example, specializes in strong death-dealing ability, while Blue is the power of transformation and illusion. Players accumulate Lands (which possess mana, the power needed to cast spells), Creatures to attack and defend with, Enchantments to control the actions of others, and Artifacts to enhance magical powers. The object is to remove all life from your opponent before your opponent can do the same to you. This is not a benign game for the well-intentioned. It is an out-and-out battle to the death between evil wizards who delight in playing the "Drain Life" card or placing a curse upon enemy creatures to prevent them from fighting.

Go is a magical contest, too, though more in the domain of light. Players accumulate lands (territory or eyes) to immunize themselves from spells, place creatures (stones) to attack and defend with, and use artifacts (shapes) to enhance their powers. You cast spells to paralyze groups of stones (prevent them from making two eyes). For the remainder of the game "dead" groups remain buried in enemy ground, yet at any moment they may be summoned by other stones to become undead. But the game's object is not the complete death of the enemy wizard, it is a sharing of the domain.

Magic – the Gathering® is a trademark of Wizards of the Coast, Inc.

Basic Spellcasting

To become a sorcerer, as in all master crafts, you must first become an apprentice and learn the fundamental skills. You must learn how to pronounce your spells and what different talismans can do.

Ring of Containment

The first thing the master sorcerer does, before attempting to conjure demons from the other world, is draw a pentagram on the floor. This "force field" will contain the evil power, preventing it from spreading out and wresting control from the sorcerer. The sorcerer will also probably wear a ring of containment as insurance, generating an extra protective field. You can never be too careful with the dark forces.

Likewise in Go, before you attempt to vanquish an enemy group, you must first enclose it so that it does not spread out and harm your other positions. Doing so is described in other chapters and it is assumed in this chapter that the target group is already enclosed. However, you need to contain more tightly in this chapter because you need to stop the group from growing external territory even while it remains enclosed. Any extra mana acquired by the target will seriously endanger your death spell.

In particular, stop the enemy's skip along the second line.

In Diagram 1, White is contained, but can still grow by skipping from the marked stone to *a*. Black must play at *a* to contain White tightly enough. Sometimes Black can play one line closer to White, but this brings Black into contact and can only be managed if Black stones are nearby (e.g., diagonally up and left of *a*) or super strong. Black does not want to spend time warding off evil magic caused by playing too close.

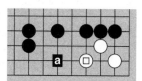

Diagram 1

Curse of False Vision

As you have already learned, an eye must be surrounded by exactly one defender string.

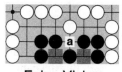

False Vision

If you can arrange it so that the defender can only become one string by joining on the eye itself, then the eye is false and the defender will go blind. If Black plays *a* in the False Vision diagram, Black joins three strings into one and has two safe shaded eyes. If White plays at *a* first, Black can only join by filling in Black's own eyes, and Black is dead.

Spell of Drain Life

To make life a group needs two eyes, that is, two empty intersections touched on all sides by friendly stones or the edge. The fundamental principle is no enemy stone can sit next to an eye point.

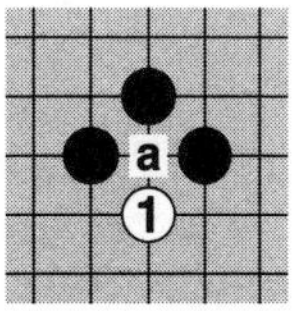

If one does (Diagram No Eye), then that eye is ruined. The defender would have to fill in the eye to try to capture the intruding stone.

No Eye

But wait! One stone can drain much life. In Diagram Big Drain, White's single stone

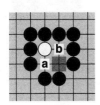

drains life out of *a*, *b*, *c*, and *d*. The stone itself, however, is still trapped by the enemy and remains as a source of mana for Black. When it is captured, all other intersections will be filled, and the stone will be alchemically transmuted into a golden eye.

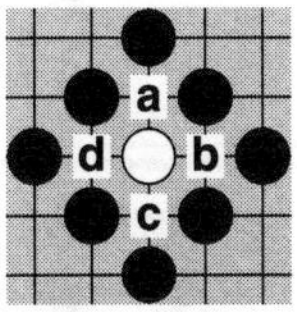

Big Drain

In Diagram 2a, Black has three points of territory. It is conceivable that Black could make two eyes if White did nothing.

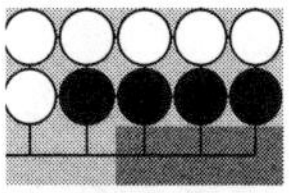

Diagram 2a

After White 1 in Diagram 2b, Black will never gain life. White 1 has drained one unit of territory away. Since White 1 is safely connected to living outside White stones, it can never be captured by Black. Even if it could, it would just be a false eye. By implication, you can drain life in small amounts any number of times by playing moves connected back to safety, but only once can you drop a stone deep into enemy territory to pull off a big drain-life trick. This is the basis for much of the black art of killing groups.

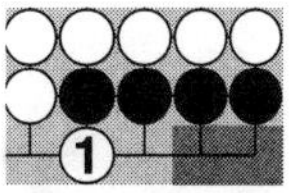

Diagram 2b

Diagonal Drain Life: It is also possible to drain life from an eye by placing a stone diagonal to it. This works because although capturing a two-stone string creates two points of territory, that territory can never be split apart into two eyes.

In Diagram 3a, White's stone ruins eyes at *a* and *b*, apparently leaving the shaded intersection as a possible eye. But because that intersection is diagonally related to White's stone, White has two ways to extend toward it, and Black cannot stop both.

Diagram 3a

Once White has extended one way, as in Diagram 3b with White 1, the potential of empty intersections has all been drained, and Black can only get one eye where White has two stones.

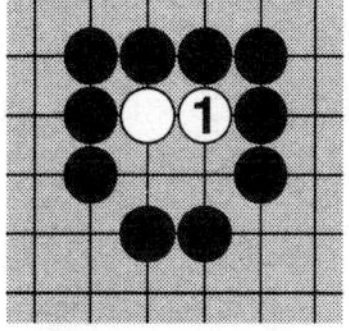

Diagram 3b

Diagonal drain life only works if there are two open intersections leading to the diagonal point. Also, it only works once. If you try to drain life diagonally twice, your resulting string consists of three stones, which provides the potential for two eyes or seki.

Creatures and Artifacts

The spell of drain life is intimately involved in what are called the *dead shapes*. These are shapes of territory which can all be destroyed by a single life-draining move, sucking the life out of potential eyes adjacent to or diagonal from the attacking move.

Traditional Go books use names like bulky-five or rabbitty-six to help you remember the shapes. We have never found those names particularly memorable and in the context of learning how to kill someone, a rabbitty-six shape sounds pretty inocuous. So we have chosen to create more vivid names for the empty points involved in dead shapes, names which are more in keeping with this chapter's theme.

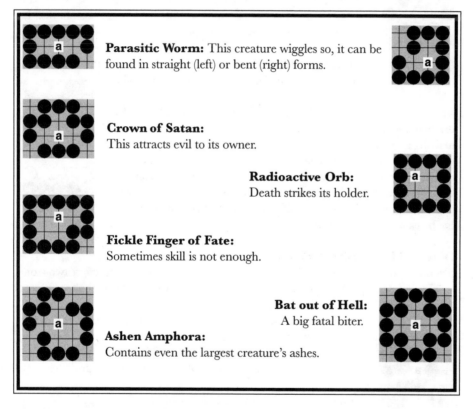

Parasitic Worm: This creature wiggles so, it can be found in straight (left) or bent (right) forms.

Crown of Satan:
This attracts evil to its owner.

Radioactive Orb:
Death strikes its holder.

Fickle Finger of Fate:
Sometimes skill is not enough.

Bat out of Hell:
A big fatal biter.

Ashen Amphora:
Contains even the largest creature's ashes.

Death lies in each of these shapes of *terror-tory*. White can play at *a* and drain the life from all remaining intersections. The shape of the Radioactive Orb is so bad, White doesn't even need to play at *a*. White can just wait until Black plays within the territory, and then strike. In all other diagrams, if Black plays at *a*, Black divides the territory into two or more pieces capable of becoming eyes, whereas a White play insures the death of the shape's owner. In Ashen Amphora *a* drains the maximum amount, four adjacent points and one diagonal point.

In all other possible shapes, playing the life-draining move does not remove all potential for life in one move, so the defender gets a turn to cast spells. Usually this is unacceptable to the attacker.

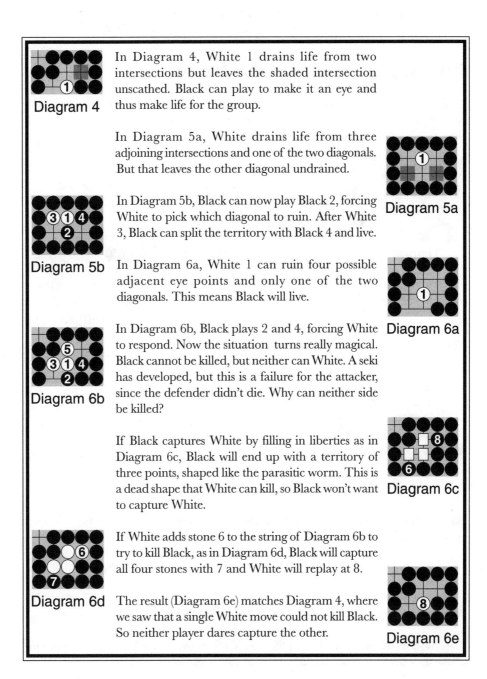

In Diagram 4, White 1 drains life from two intersections but leaves the shaded intersection unscathed. Black can play to make it an eye and thus make life for the group.

Diagram 4

In Diagram 5a, White drains life from three adjoining intersections and one of the two diagonals. But that leaves the other diagonal undrained.

Diagram 5a

In Diagram 5b, Black can now play Black 2, forcing White to pick which diagonal to ruin. After White 3, Black can split the territory with Black 4 and live.

Diagram 5b

In Diagram 6a, White 1 can ruin four possible adjacent eye points and only one of the two diagonals. This means Black will live.

Diagram 6a

In Diagram 6b, Black plays 2 and 4, forcing White to respond. Now the situation turns really magical. Black cannot be killed, but neither can White. A seki has developed, but this is a failure for the attacker, since the defender didn't die. Why can neither side be killed?

Diagram 6b

If Black captures White by filling in liberties as in Diagram 6c, Black will end up with a territory of three points, shaped like the parasitic worm. This is a dead shape that White can kill, so Black won't want to capture White.

Diagram 6c

If White adds stone 6 to the string of Diagram 6b to try to kill Black, as in Diagram 6d, Black will capture all four stones with 7 and White will replay at 8.

Diagram 6d

The result (Diagram 6e) matches Diagram 4, where we saw that a single White move could not kill Black. So neither player dares capture the other.

Diagram 6e

Intermediate Spellcasting

The novice spellcaster only kills groups whose territory looks like one of the dead shapes. The intermediate spellcaster casts a broader range of spells and kills more.

Summoning a Dead Shape

The intermediate spellcaster can conjure forth the dead shape from groups whose territory is not completely sealed. This is done by draining life around the edges and then zapping the group with a final Big Drain.

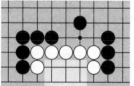

Diagram 7a

In Diagram 7a, White's shaded territory of six points is not a dead shape, but neither is it completely sealed.

In Diagram 7b, Black drains life around the edge with Black 1. White 2 stops Black from draining more life. The resulting shape of five territory points is the dead shape of the Fickle Finger of Fate, however. From here you should be able to drain all the remaining life from White.

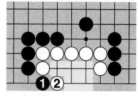

Diagram 7b

Worried that White might capture your Black 1? Fear not. It's a minion that has served its purpose and can be sent back into the void.

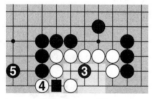

Diagram 7c

If White captures Black 1 as in Diagram 7c, it's a false eye. Black 5 stops White from escaping without forming an empty triangle or risking ko. Directly blocking next to White 4 would risk ko, so Black should back down. Black can block later when White has more stones to capture than just one, so Black's capture doesn't lead to ko.

Reduce from outside, then strike at the vital point. This is what an intermediate spellcaster knows is the most common incantation to kill a group. It has the advantages of covering many situations and being profitable even when it fails. That is, reducing from outside is sente and worth endgame points even if you fail to kill the group.

Beware the Eye of the Newt

Care must be taken when draining life from the outside. If you force the defender to create the eye of the newt, you may force life. Instead, poke it out.

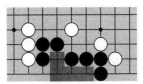

Diagram 8a

In Diagram 8a, Black has a four-point shaded territory that is not currently a dead shape.

Following the rule **Reduce from outside, then strike at the vital point**, Black might play 1 of Diagram 8b.

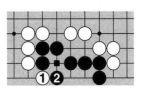

Diagram 8b

Unfortunately this forces Black to form an eye of the newt. Whenever your play on the boundary would force the enemy to finish an eye you must poke it out instead.

In Diagram 8c, White pokes directly into Black's eye with 1. Black is forced to stop White's escape with 2, after which White can play 3 to drain the remaining life from Black. This is an advanced technique in Magic the Gathering called **banding**. Multiple creatures *band* together to attack as one. I will elaborate on this later.

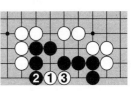

Diagram 8c

Houdini's Key Ring

A master of escape, Houdini could escape from anywhere. With the right shape you can play inside of enemy territory, yet escape. All you need to find is a place with two doors near each other.

In Diagram 9, White can play at *a* and escape past one of Black's marked doors to a waiting White marked stone. In doing so White destroys two points of Black territory and the group as a whole.

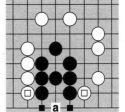

Diagram 9

Sacrificial Minions

Many times stones you play are not expected to survive. They are expected to be captured, but only in the form of a false eye. Typically this happens at the edge, but not always.

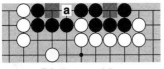

Diagram 10a

In Diagram 10a Black has three points of territory, but only the two shaded ones can ever be eyes.

White plays 1 sacrificially as in Diagram 10b. It drains the life from one of Black's potential eyes and, even if Black captures 1, it will never become an eye.

Diagram 10b

It is even possible to capture two stones and still retain a false eye.

In Diagram 11a, White has a marked stone draining the life from all adjoining intersections, yet it itself still retains vitality for Black because it can become the core of an eye.

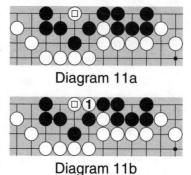

Diagram 11a

Diagram 11b

In Diagram 11b, White plays White 1, which can never become an eye for Black, plus it drains the Black life potential from its neighboring White stone. If Black captures the two stones, White can send in a single sacrificial minion to keep Black from making an eye.

Can you sacrifice three stones and still keep the eyespace false? Three stones, when captured, can usually be made into an eye. There is no need to consider trying to sacrifice three into a false eye. The same is true for four stones.

Advanced Spellcasting

The tricks of the master defy belief and can take years to master.

Amulet of Reanimation

The Master Sorcerer summons the dead and, if that creature gets hacked to pieces, those pieces meld into a new creature. In Go, weaker players lack that persistence. They stop reading out a situation as soon as they lose several stones. They figure the opponent must get an eye from it and will live. Wrong. As long as defects remain in the enemy's boundary, do not stop reading. Your captured stones may be reanimated.

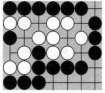

Diagram 12a

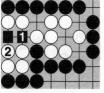

Diagram 12b

In Diagram 12a, White clearly has one eye, and it certainly looks like White can get an eye out of Black's stone caught in White's territory. Many players would stop thinking right now.

Those that wouldn't, imagine poking in with Black 1, using **Sacrificial Minions**, and visualize White 2 capturing two stones as in Diagram 12b. Most of those players would break off their reading here.

The Masters keep going in their reading. Black reanimates a sacrificial minion in Diagram 12c.

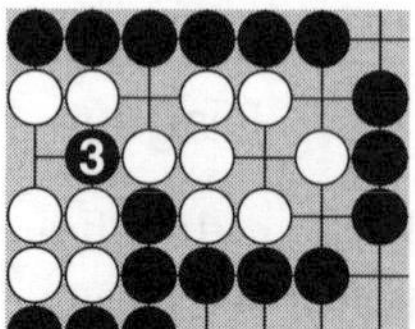

Diagram 12c

White captures it, but in Diagram 12d we see that White has fallen victim to the **Curse of False Vision**.

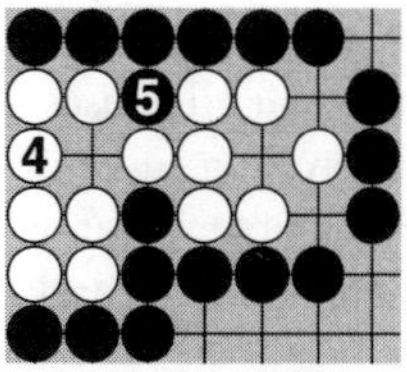

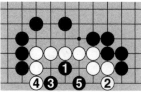
Diagram 12d

Banding Attackers

In Magic — the Gathering, you can only attack with one creature at a time unless you "band" several together to form a composite attacker. In Go, if you place more than one stone in enemy territory, it must band together with your other stones into a single string. Otherwise, the enemy gets two separate eyes. Furthermore, this string must form one of the dead shapes. Otherwise, the enemy will form two eyes over its ashes.

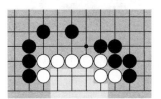
Diagram 13a

In Diagram 13a, Black wants to kill White (no surprise) but the techniques presented so far are insufficient.

Black 13b shows Black's true mastery of the black arts. Black 1 ruins many eyes. White 2 threatens an eye, but Black 3 threatens to escape. White 4 stops this, but Black 5 creates the ability to form a Crown of Satan. If White fails to attack, Black can fill all outside liberties and then make an internal eye. If White plays inside to stop the eye, Black can expand to a Fickle Finger and eventually to a one-eyed group. White dies in all cases. Each Black move retains connection to the last, thus banding together.

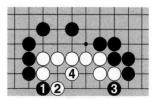
Diagram 13b

Making an almost-eye oneself is a common feature in banding. It forces the opponent to falsify the eye, but it means that the defender fills in territory.

By the way, **Intermediate Spellcasting** (reduce from the outside and then strike at the vital point) doesn't work here. Diagram 13c shows one failure. If Black plays at 3 first (instead of 1), White will still respond at 4 and the result is seki.

Diagram 13c

Casting Future Prophecy

Spending five to ten minutes reading out all variations only to discover you can't kill a group is both exhausting and depressing. Before you spend all that effort you would like to know if you will succeed. While you *can't* foretell that you *can* kill someone, you *can* foretell that you *can't*, and it only takes minimal reading. Here is how.

Assume Primitive Defender Replies to Attacker Moves: If you can't kill when the defender uses obvious responses, further reading is unnecessary. If something interesting turns up, then further reading may be needed to see if the result is truly attainable. What moves should the attacker make and what simple responses should we assume the defender will make?

There are two things to adjust: gaps in the boundaries and diagonal cutting defects in the joints. We must remove them to get a suitable impression of the future.

Drip Sealing Wax in the Gaps: Usually the territory is not completely sealed; there are gaps in the boundary. Imagine what the final shape would be if the attacker pushed or poked on the boundary points and the defender obligingly blocked on the adjoining territory points.

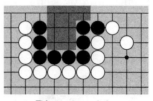

Diagram 14a

Diagram 14a shows a Black group with boundary gaps.

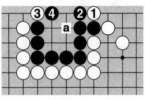

Diagram 14b

Assuming the play shown in Diagram 14b, the resulting shape is a dead one (the Fickle Finger). This is a favorable prophecy, advising you to read out the problem more carefully. It does not insure that you will succeed in killing Black.

Diagram 14c shows a way to mess up and let Black live. This is not the correct answer.

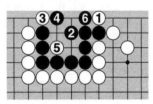

Diagram 14c

Prophesying is not about finding the correct line, but I'll show it to you. Diagram 14d is one correct line. White 9 replays at White 1, and Black is dead.

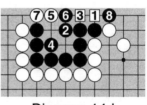

Diagram 14d

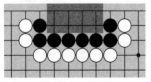

Diagram 15a

Diagram 15a shows another Black group with an incomplete boundary.

After the reduction of Diagram 15b, the shape is unrecognizable, so the group must be alive.

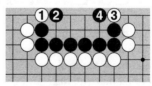

Diagram 15b

Still Beware the Eye of the Newt: Don't play a reducing move that forces the defender to make an eye.

In Diagram 16, White should not play the White 1 for Black 2 exchange, forcing Black to make an eye. White must play at 2 and make Black play at 1.

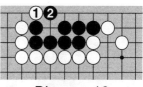

Diagram 16

Tighten Up the Joints: In addition to gaps in the boundaries, there may also be diagonal connections needing to be resolved. The open diagonal connection and the cutting point are the two forms of this. With the open diagonal, merely assume the attacker plays on the outside and the defender obligingly plays the solid inside connection.

How long could you spend reading out variations of Diagram 17a?

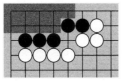

Diagram 17a

Think of all the time saved by casting future prophecy to generate Diagram 17b and discover that Black is unkillable. (The open diagonal exchange was White 1 for Black 2, though the order in which the three exchanges of White moves for Black moves is unimportant.)

When the joint in the boundary is a cutting point, assume the defender fills the cutting point and the attacker gets an extra interior move to drain extra life (as though playing the life-draining point threatened the cut).

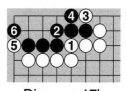

Diagram 17b

Black wants to see if White can be killed in Diagram 18a,

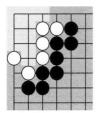

Diagram 18a

In Diagram 18b, Black makes a gap reduction exchange with Black 1 for White 2. Black then plays a **Drain Life** move with 3, and White simply fills in the defect with 4, as though 3 threatened to cut. Black does not recognize the resulting shape of six territory points as a dead shape, but Black has the extra draining move (4) to play, along with Black's normal next move (5). With two drain-life moves in a row, Black can suck out all of White's life into Black's two-stone string, which will kill White. So Black concludes maybe White can be killed. In fact, White can't.

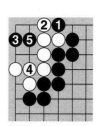

Diagram 18b

But, in Diagram 18c, which is similar to 18b, White can be killed.

Diagram 18c

Killing enemy groups may seem to require magic, but in reality it is just a matter of following the two basic principles of limiting the eyespace and occupying the essential point that would split a region into two eyes.

I'm a Roku-Dan*

Tune: I'm a lumberjack   Lyrics: Copyright 1985 by Francis Roads

I'm a Roku-dan and I'm all right,
Play Go all day and I sleep all night.
Chorus: *He's a Roku-dan and he's all right,*
      Plays Go all day and sleeps all night.

I'm learned in joseki, so I know just where to play,
My brilliance in byoyomi makes my games last all the day.
Chorus: *He's learned in joseki, so he knows just where to play,*
      His brilliance in byoyomi makes his games last all the day.

I know all my tesuji so I'm never in a mess,
And when I'm tired of playing Go I play a bit of chess.
Chorus: *He knows all his tesuji so he's never in a mess,*
      And when he's tired of playing Go he plays a bit of chess.

I play along the second line and then I count the score,
If its too small I jerk the board and then I've 19 more.
Chorus: *He plays along the second line and then he counts the score,*
      If its too small he jerks the board and then he's 19 more.

My pocket's full of Go stones from opponent's view well hid,
If I find out that I'm behind I slip some in my lid.
Chorus: *His pocket's full of Go stones from opponent's view well hid,*
      If he finds out that he's behind he slips some in his lid.

And if you wonder how I keep my grade, remember that the man
Who runs the grading committee is your roku-dan.
Chorus: *And if you wonder how he keeps his grade, remember that the man*
      Who runs the grading committee is our roku-dan.

I'm a roku-dan and I'm all right,
Watch birds all day, play Go all night.
Chorus: *He's a roku-dan and he's all right,*
      Watches birds all day, plays Go all night.

*This sample Go song is from "The Official BGA Song Book." Roku means six.

Territory

Fools Rush In

Natural Principles

Quibbling

New Age Go

"He who possesses most must be most afraid of loss."

Fools Rush In

A bitter cold wind gusted through his T-shirt as he climbed up the slopes of Mount Everest. He could barely move; his arms were bleeding and sore from hours of scraping his flesh along the craggy surface. He gulped for air but could find little at that height. He was ravenous, having not eaten for five days after getting lost following an unmarked path. Suddenly his sneakers slipped on a patch of ice. Flailing his arms uselessly, he arced out into space, fell sixty feet, and crashed into the rocks below. Death was instantaneous.

If you were going mountaineering, would you fare better than the poor soul above (may he rest in pieces)? Would you be adequately dressed, carrying food and oxygen, attached to a belaying line with a team of other mountaineers? Would you have first researched maps of the area before embarking on the climb? Probably. But that's because you know the consequences of failure are so high. Yet many a Go player who sees an enemy potential territory forming, rushes in with no research, inadequate preparation, and no friendly stones to help. Their stones are easily smashed into the stony walls bounding the region and trapped forever in the cairn of the enemy position. Don't let that happen to you. Learn the lessons herein.

A *potential territory* is a region of empty points bounded by strings, links, maybe the edge, and at least one sector line. This sector-line boundary marks the outer limits of the potential territory and is the major focus of strategic decision making.

Diagram 1a shows a modest potential territory, with its links marked and the sector line drawn. To the left of the potential territory is enclosed corner territory that White can reduce by a knight's move slide.

In the opening players sketch out areas of potential territory. In the midgame these areas and the groups bounding them become the focus. Players strive to expand and secure their own potentials and to reduce and destroy their opponents'. Weak groups are created, become attacked, and live or die. By the time the dust settles and the endgame begins, most games are already won or lost (though weaker players may not realize this.)

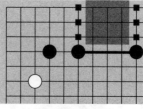

Diagram 1a

Of the two tasks, attack or defense of potential territory, defense is much simpler.

A Mountain Out of a Molehill

Anyone can take a potential territory and secure it. All you have to do is add stones along the sector line to convert the line into links.

In Diagram 1b, Black 1 seals the sector line, converting the potential into actual territory. Nothing to it. But it's small. White hardly cares.

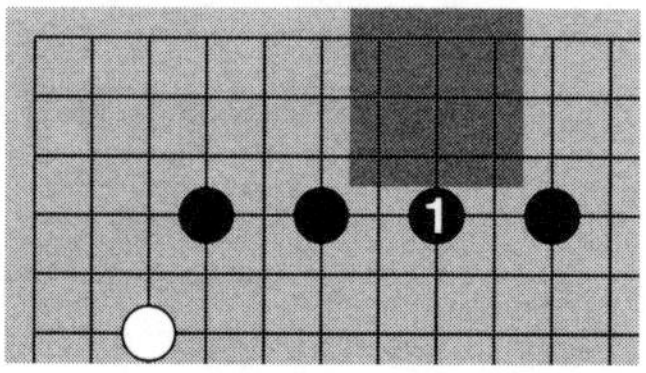

Usually sealing potential territory immediately is the wrong way to play. Instead what you want to do is make it bigger. Build a natural wonder, an imposing

Diagram 1b

mountain with sharp cliffs and a deep valley. This will attract tourists from miles around who will pay you to visit it. Your opponent will be unable to resist climbing this place with his stones. While your opponent does this, you can charge for the privilege, taking pieces of enclosed territory in sente. And, who knows, maybe your opponent will slip and fall like our luckless traveler at the beginning of this chapter.

Growing bigger has several advantages. First, you might get what you claim, so claiming more is better. Second, the bigger your claims, the more urgent it is for your opponent to deal with them. This means your opponent will have to stop playing elsewhere and play on your ground, giving you control. Third, even if your opponent reduces your claims by some percentage, you get more territory if you have more potential.

Raise with Single Skips

A single-stone group bounding a potential territory is subject to being easily pressured. Reinforcing it drastically changes the value of that potential. The usual reinforcing move is the single skip toward the center.

Black 1 in Diagram 2a is a huge, reinforcing single skip. It is much bigger than it looks. Superficially, it seems that all Black has done is shift the sector line boundary from the diagonal one to the horizontal one.

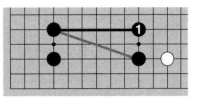

Diagram 2a

Benefit 1: The skip controls more potential. Instead of bounding 17 points, Black now bounds 20 points. By itself this would be small. But there are other benefits.

Benefit 2: The skip makes the area less invadeable. Before Black reinforced, White might have invaded with 1 as in Diagram 2b. White's invasion threatens to connect underneath Black's stone (explained by Diagram 10a later), so Black must stop this. Black 2, diagonal, stops the connection and slowly moves to surround White. Too slowly. White runs loosely with 3 and escapes and Black has an isolated weak group. Black can cut off a single White stone, but this is piecemeal so a big WARNING FLAG should pop up in Black's mind. Trust me. This is a bad idea (see *Buy Wholesale, Sell Retail*).

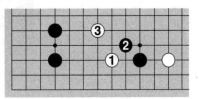

Diagram 2b

To see the effect of skipping to protect the boundary, consider Diagram 2c. If White invades at 2 after Black has skipped with 1, Black can cap at 3. This cap, in conjunction with Black's single-skip stones, neutralizes White's threat to bridge underneath at *a* (tactics proof omitted). Now White is in serious trouble because he cannot run out or connect. Black's single-skip reinforcement has done more than just increase the size of Black's potential slightly. It is no longer safe for White to invade.

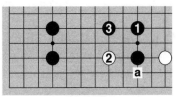

Diagram 2c

Benefit 3: The skip provides greater threat. The reinforcing skip can be used as a base to safely reduce the opponent's neighboring potential territory.

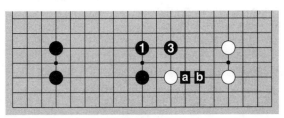

Diagram 2d

In Diagram 2d, if White ignores Black's jump to 1, Black can turn and cap with 3, broadening Black's central control while reducing White's prospects. It also aims to play *a* or *b* to attack White's stone.

Don't Jump Again: As you have seen, the first single skip from a boundary conveys immense benefits. Successive ones from the same side do not, primarily because the major benefits of stopping the invasion and threatening to harm the opponent's boundary stone happened from the first one. After that, jumping further only shifts the sector line and maybe provides a base to reduce the enemy but without threatening the enemy's stones.

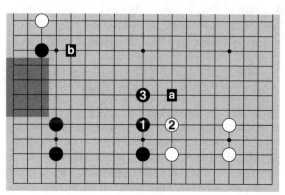

In Diagram 2e, White 2 matched Black's jump, so Black jumped again to 3. This move is not so valuable. Black's threat to turn at *a* lacks punch and Black 3 does not make the Black area on the bottom significantly less invadeable.

Diagram 2e

Alternate Sides: The general way to defend a potential is to balance the strengthening of the two sides instead of constantly reinforcing one side.

In Diagram 2e, playing at *b* instead of 3 would be much better. It would protect Black's shaded potential from a direct invasion.

Don't Use the Double Skip: The single skip is good but the double skip is not. Using a double skip from a single stone is like building a steep embankment. It is subject to rapid erosion.

In Diagram 2f, Black 1 is a poor way to expand. It does not prevent White from invading at *a*, and if White plays any of *b* through *f*, Black will have to spend a move patching the link. Black won't have the time for this.

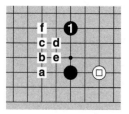

This warning notwithstanding, double skips are fine from multiple-stone strings facing the skip. Skipping from a wall of stones gives you time to rejoin the skip to a stone of the wall when the link is attacked. In general, you can make a double-skip toward the center from a two-stone wall, and you can make a triple-skip toward the center from a three-stone wall.

Diagram 2f

Previously you learned that in extending along the edge, count how high the wall is and extend over that same distance to make a safe extension. When extending toward the center, you don't need complete safety, since the cost of losing the stone is less. Therefore you can extend one farther than the width of your wall. From one stone, extend two spaces (single skip). From two stones, extend three spaces, and so on.

The Scenic Overlook

One of the safest ways to attack an opponent's potential territory is to limit its growth (misleadingly called reduction). This is done by standing on top and looking down into the deep valley of the potential. It's an awe inspiring view, but one that can be seen from safety.

Reduction stops the growth of your opponent's potentials, granting most of them. In doing so, you have made a judgement about the whole board. If you can match your opponent's claims, then limiting them is reasonable and doing anything more risky is unreasonable. If you are behind, then you must be more aggressive and invade (described later).

To reduce (or limit) a potential territory is to prevent it from getting bigger. The move is on or outside of the sector line defining the potential. Your opponent generally responds by playing a stone somewhere between your move and the rest of the potential territory, thus securing it. In general with light reductions:

1. **The actual territory becomes somewhat smaller than the potential.**

2. **The attacker's group is temporarily safe** because it is not within enemy sector lines. It is best if the attacker extends from a previous group instead of creating a new one.

3. **The attacker's move forms new sector lines** that can be used elsewhere.

4. **The attacker retains sente.**

There are two kinds of places to play the reducing move: one is near the middle of the sector line, the other is near either of the two ends of the sector line.

Suspended in Mid Air

Placing a reducing move near the middle of the sector line gives maximum threat to the potential territory. You are in a position to lower yourself straight into the valley. On the other hand, your support is shaky since usually you are forming a totally new group. If your flying platform runs out of energy, you may crash. Or the sides of the mountain may continue to grow and you may not have the power to fly over them, so you get swallowed up.

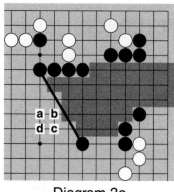

Diagram 3a

In Diagram 3a, Black has the indicated potential territory. If White wants to lightly reduce it, White will play somewhere like a, b, c, or d. Each of these will induce Black to secure much or all of the potential territory, but at least it will not get any bigger.

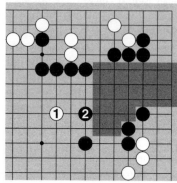

In Diagram 3b, White played 1, inviting Black to seal the potential into a fully enclosed territory with Black 2.

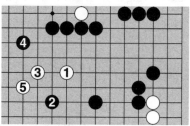

Diagram 3b

Playing near the middle has its risks. Your opponent might try to extend one of the flanks and threaten to swallow you up.

In Diagram 3c, White tried to reduce lightly with 1, but Black decided to chase White with 2 and 4. Without seeing the rest of the board, who can say what this chase will lead to? This is the danger of creating a new flying group.

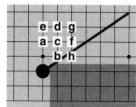

Diagram 3c

Stand on the Peak

While flying over the valley provides a magnificent view, it is safer to pull out at one of those scenic overlooks along the road near the top of the mountain. In Go, the safest place to play a reducing move is near a single-stone endpoint of the sector line. You are closest to your friends and the mere presence of your weight on the peak prevents the ground from shifting higher.

Stand on the Third-Line Boundary: Third-line stones are easy to pressure from above. Against fourth-line stones one generally invades because their link to the edge is weak.

Diagram 4 shows a solitary Black stone at the end of a sector line bounding the shaded potential territory. The intersections a-h are all possible places White might play to reduce the area by threatening this stone. They all threaten to follow up with an attack on Black's outpost.

Diagram 4

Which one to choose depends upon many things. First, how safe is the move? *h*, for example, is within Black's sector line, so it will be highly risky. Second, how much does White have to reduce? The higher up or the farther left, the less it reduces. Third, how can White use the reducing move on the rest of the board?

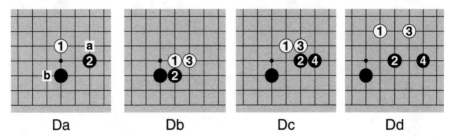

Da   Db   Dc   Dd

Diagrams Da through Dh (D is for Defense) show the likely sequences for each of the attacker's reducing moves *a* through *h* of Diagram 4. Assuming Black wishes to keep any potential, Black must back down as shown, and White retains sente.

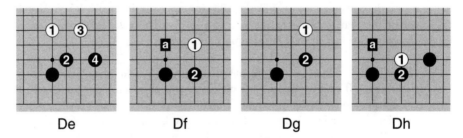

De   Df   Dg   Dh

The Cap is the Number One Choice: Diagram Da is the most common reducing move. White will continue with *a* or *b*, depending upon whether White wants to continue reducing (*a*) or try to create a side area of his own (*b*). Other choices don't offer that second option, which is why capping is so popular.

The Shoulder Hit is the Number Two Choice: The other most popular choice is shown in Diagram Db. Provoking a contact fight forces both sides to play some extended sequence (not shown), which rapidly settles how the area will be played out. While capping is very flexible, Black has many possible responses, so the situation can remain highly ambiguous. The shoulder-hit of Diagram Db forces the situation to finish out immediately, reducing future ambiguity.

Diagrams Df and Dh have the weakness that Black might counterattack at *a* instead of backing down. Dd, De, and Dg are generally too high up for Black to try counterattacking. In Diagram Db, the stone is not too high, but Black would have to initiate contact on the left of the stone to counterattack, and attacking with contact is a bad idea (strengthening the opponent instead of attacking him).

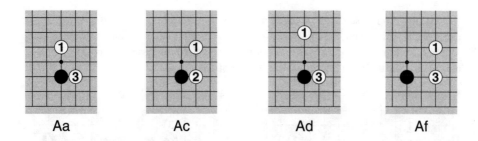

All of White's reducing moves on an endpoint threaten to follow up by isolating that endpoint. The A (Attacker follows up the corresponding initial move from Diagram 4) series of diagrams demonstrates some of the threatened continuations if Black fails to respond.

Deep In the Valley

Jumping deep in the valley of enemy potentials constitutes an invasion. An invasion destroys everything in its path, sort of like lava flowing down the mountain. It is dramatic, but fools rush in where even dan players fear to play. Star Trek's *To boldly go where no one has gone before* may be heroic, or it may be just foolishness.

The usual goal of invading is to live locally, but you face the risk of landslides or avalanches that can crush you. If that happens, you have given your opponent thickness (the wall surrounding your group) and profit (the territory of your dead stones). Living locally limits the effect of your invasion to the here and now, keeping the rest of the board uninvolved. If your invasion is badly considered, you may not be able to keep it local. Your group might be forced to run, and the whole board suddenly becomes involved. You might cause a cascade reaction, generating tectonic shifts that demolish the entire landscape. Invading is not a simple choice.

Preparation

If you were going to scale the Himalayas, would you just fly there and start climbing? No. (Or, at least, I hope not.) For example you shouldn't start this trip in winter. Spring is a much better time. In Go, you don't just invade anytime either.

Wait Until After the Opening: One of the big costs of invading is the tremendous wall you give your opponent in sente (you live in gote). If this wall can be used profitably, your opponent may get more territory later than your invasion currently destroys. Before the board is fully sketched out, almost any wall can be used, so invading is a hazardous operation. Don't invade until the opening is nearly over.

Wait Until the Potential Can't Extend Farther: Don't invade if your opponent can extend along the edge from one of his stones and acquire new territory.

In Diagram 5, Black shouldn't consider invading at *a*. White will just extend to *b*, acquiring territory and leaving Black with a worthless weak group. Black should play *b* first.

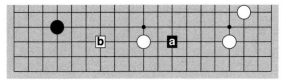

Diagram 5

Wait Until You Have No Weak Groups: Having one weak group can be managed (usually), but having two or more weak groups is a sure ticket to the cemetery. Make sure you really need to invade or that invading is easy.

Attitude

Mountain climbers have attitude. They know they are undertaking something risky, but they do what they can to minimize that risk. They keep safety in their mind at all times. They want to survive. If equipment needs to be sacrificed to stay alive, they abandon it whenever necessary.

Whenever you invade, you are going to be outnumbered and caught within opponent sector lines. This is not the time for frontal confrontations. The Charge of the Light Brigade into the jaws of enemy strength was celebrated in poetry — but they didn't survive. You want to survive. If stones need to be sacrificed to keep the rest alive, abandon them without compunction.

Where to Start

If you want to get to the top of a mountain, you first look for the easiest route, usually a roundabout route. Failing to find an easy path, you look for natural handholds in a direct climb. Failing that you drive pitons into the face of the cliff and brace for a difficult climb.

Invade at 3-3: In Go, the easiest route is a 3-3 invasion under a corner handicap stone. It is so easy that it usually keeps sente.

In Diagram 6, Black has a massive potential territory, but White can still easily invade with 1 and live. Black made a mistake. Normally extending with single skips into the center makes sense, but not with a corner handicap stone. After extending along the edges, the next step for Black must be to secure the corner. Extending the sides into the center allows White to invade and ruin 40 points *in sente* (actually, ruin 30 and gain 10).

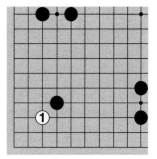

Diagram 6

If you can't invade and live in sente, you'll need all the help you can get. You want to distract the opponent by finding an invasion that is also some kind of threat.

Threaten to Slide: Playing on the third line near a fourth-line stone aims to slide for additional life space.

In Diagram 7, Black 1 invades. It can run out (the primary threat). It also threatens to slide to *a* or peep at *b*, either of which will ruin White territory as well as help stabilize Black.

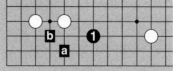

Diagram 7

Threaten Two Areas: Playing on the pivotal point of two adjacent areas is another good choice of threats. When your opponent blocks you on one side, you have already made a supporting move for use on the other.

In Diagram 8a, White plays on a pivotal point between the two Black areas, *a* and *b*, rather than invading in one of them explicitly.

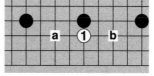

Diagram 8a

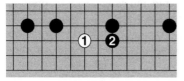

Diagram 8b

If White invaded at *a* directly, as in Diagram 8b, Black would probably block at the pivot. Black gets maximum territory to its right, and the lone White must now flee with no start on life.

By playing on the pivot, as in Diagram 8c, White gets a guaranteed reinforcement in some area. If Black 2, White plays 3. Black must now defend a defect with 4. White 5 threatens to expand right, and Black 6 blocks. White then runs with 7, having built a substantial base on the side.

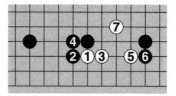

Diagram 8c

Another favorite pivot point occurs with the small knight's corner enclosure. White 1 in Diagram 9 may look like the start of a light reduction, but White fully intends to invade. White will play *a* or *b* as a follow-up, depending upon which side Black leaves unprotected.

Threaten to Tunnel Out: Another useful threat point is to play a move threatening to escape to friendly stones on the other side by diving under an enemy's edge link.

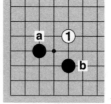

Diagram 9

The most common tunnel-threat move is shown in Diagram 10a: the third line single-skip (Black 1) inside a third line White boundary stone, with a corresponding Black single-skip marked outside stone. This exact pattern threatens to connect underneath, and White will have to spend a move deflecting this, giving Black time to get settled or run.

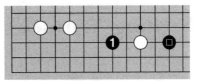

Diagram 10a

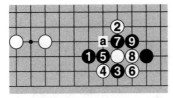

Diagram 10b

If White ignores this threat and skips out with White 2 as in Diagram 10b, Black 3 begins the attempt. If White resists, Black can sacrifice Black 3 and break through another White link. At the end of this diagram, White must play at *a* to separate Black, but the range of tactics and sacrifice options for Black is enormous, and White is in danger of losing his enclosed stones. Usually White cannot try this.

Diagram 11a is another situation, one often encountered in a handicap game. White would like to invade an enclosed territory. This is much more difficult than invading a potential territory. With a potential territory, you always have the threat to run out. Here, you must find other threats and keep threatening until you get life.

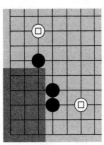

Diagram 11a

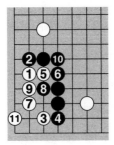

Diagram 11b

In Diagram 11b, White makes the attempt. White 1 and 3 both threaten to connect out, and Black blocks the attempts. White 5 is played to create a defect in Black's wall to concern Black. White 7 links up White's forces and aims to make eyes. Black 8 forces White 9, but now Black is concerned that if White cuts where 10 is played, Black might lose two outside stones before killing White. Black backs down and connects with 10, letting White clearly live with 11.

Notice in Diagram 11b the value of having the White flanking stones where they are. Were they on the fourth line, they wouldn't help threats from the inside. Were they farther away, they wouldn't endanger Black enough to worry Black. Flanking on the third line, a single skip away, is a powerful move with many threats inherent in it. Extend this close if your aim is to invade later.

Settling Yourself

Having begun scaling the mountain, you try to keep to a schedule. Delays can be fatal. You only have so many supplies and so much endurance. In Go, once you have made the initial invasion, you need to get settled or escape quickly. The longer it takes, the more danger you are in and you enable more consequential damage to your other positions. There are several keys to getting settled quickly (*sabaki*).

Stay Near the Edge: It takes fewer moves to make an eye along the edge than anywhere else. Expand along the edge as long as you can before running to the center.

In Diagram 12, White invades with 1. After Black 4, White must choose between running to *a*, *b*, *c*, or *d*, or moving along the edge with *e*, *f*, or *g*. (Contact extensions, like playing right of *e*, are bad and playing left of *g* fails to break Black's link.) If White wants to counterattack Black's marked stone, White might run, but usually White will move along the edge first, trying to get the best life base possible.

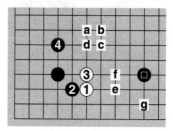
Diagram 12

Play Contact: Contact involves your weak stones in local fighting, where your attacking opponent doesn't get to take advantage of global superiority. Your opponent has to spend time defending cutting points and liberty counts, instead of attacking your invasion severely. Playing contact does NOT mean you should follow contact fight principles. This is not a fair fight. You are outnumbered. You are willing to sacrifice a few stones for the good of the many. So you pay much less attention to keeping your stones securely connected.

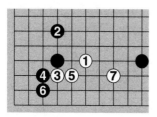
Diagram 13

In Diagram 13, White has invaded with 1 and launched contact with 3. This forces Black 4. When White draws back with 5, Black is still unstable, so Black needs another move to defend the cutting point. Black 6 is the most ambitious defense, protecting the cut and undercutting White. White then extends to 7 and has a shaky base. In this diagram, White has played normal contact fight moves, since White believes there is time enough to dig a base for the White group.

In Diagram 14a, White does not have room to make a reasonable base, so White launches contact with 3, but follows up with messy instability. White can be slit into pieces, but White is inviting this.

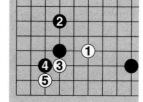
Diagram 14a

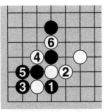

Diagram 14b

If Black cuts off White's second-line stone with 1 as in Diagram 14b, Black will lose a stone and a link also.

On the other hand, if Black cuts off White's original invasion with 1, as in Diagram 14c, Black must continue with Black 3 and lose the corner stone.

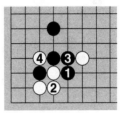

Diagram 14c

In any event, White doesn't care about losing a stone. White's goal is the easiest life achievable with *some* White stones in the area.

Link Loosely: This is a broader continuation of **Play Contact**. You need to move rapidly, acquiring potential eyespace or getting out of the area while retaining the potential to be a single connected force. To this end, each move you play should be linked, but not securely. You even want your opponent to cut you apart. Your opponent would then be piecemealing you (see *Buy Wholesale, Sell Retail*) and you would have opportunities to make useful sacrifices.

White 1 in Diagram 15a is played as a threat against two Black areas. When Black decides to protect the lower side, White 3 initiates contact with a loose link. Does Black dare cut it off? Rarely.

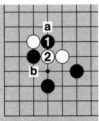

Diagram 15b

In Diagram 15b, Black has cut it off with 1, and White has played the obvious White 2. Now Black is faced with being laddered with *a*, or having the corner territory broken up with *b*. Black won't play 1 this way.

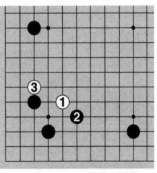

Diagram 15a

If Black still wants to cut White apart, maybe Black will play 1 in Diagram 15c. Problem is, by the time this diagram is finished, White has many marked good plays for later, and Black has only cut off a single stone. Black is not likely to play 1 this way either.

Play Crosscut: Anytime you can play crosscut against single stones, you probably should. It creates a messy multiple-contact fight where you can surely sacrifice something.

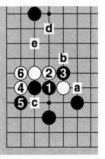

Diagram 15c

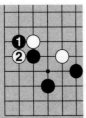

Diagram 16a

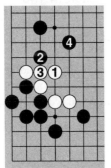

Diagram 16c

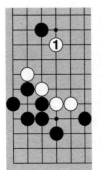

Diagram 16d

In Diagram 16a, Black has given up trying to cut White apart. Instead Black responds in a wholesale fashion with Black 1, a normal contact-fight move. White immediately crosscuts with 2, ready to sacrifice.

Diagram 16b

If Black buys the sacrifice and plays 1 in Diagram 16b, White forces Black to eat it with White 2 and 4. Black gets to keep the corner, only slightly bigger. But look at what is happening to Black's marked stone. It is getting more and more isolated.

Now, White will often screw up. White sees links that can be cut and decides to defend them in the honest, contact-fight fashion.

In Diagram 16c, White defends both cuts with 1. Black peeps with 2 and White connects. Now Black attacks wholesale with 4, and White is under strong attack.

Knowing What You Have to Defend is a Burden: It is clear what stones have to be saved, so White has few choices. White should have continued to play loosely.

White 1 in Diagram 16d is much better. What could be looser? Which stones will White defend? The temptation to cut must almost overwhelm Black, but Black must not cut.

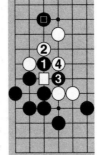

Diagram 16e

If Black cuts off another White stone with 1 in Diagram 16e, again White gives it to Black. After White 4, Black is in atari and will have to connect where White's stone used to be and White will get sente. Black cannot afford ko, so Black must connect (see below for an explanation). Black's marked stone continues to wither. Before, the danger was distant. Now, it's almost on top of poor Black.

Play Ko: It is nearly impossible to kill an unenclosed group with ko because the group can use its ability to continue growing or running as ko threats. This provides a large number of threats. Furthermore, if the group wins the ko, it can often threaten to continue destroying territory or enemy strings. Therefore, ko favors the invader. See *The Road Less Traveled*.

If Black failed to connect, and instead cut with 1 in Diagram 17, White would capture the ko. If White gets to win this ko by playing at *a*, White will be almost completely alive, and Black's marked stone will be up against a wall of White. If Black makes a compelling ko threat and retakes the ko, White has a local threats at *b*, and can just play *c* to ignore the ko. White has still not committed to much of a loss here if White loses the ko. White could even just invade somewhere else.

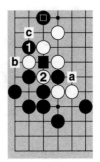

Diagram 17

When Black retakes the ko, White cannot play *a* to ignore the ko. Trying to save two stones misses the point. Black wins the ko with *b*, and Black's attacked stone is suddenly connected to safety and White has many committed weak stones.

To summarize, when you invade an area, keep flexible by playing sacrificable connections, and keep it local by embroiling your opponent's stones in contact..

The Proper Defense against Invasion

The owner of the territory must end contact-fight instability immediately to take advantage of numerical superiority.

In Diagram 18, when White plays contact with 1, Black ends it immediately with 2. Now, even if White tries a follow-up contact move against the corner, Black will be stable and can ignore it.

Will White play *a*? White shouldn't. That implies White cares about the connection and will commit to saving specific stones. White should play any of *b*, *c*, or *d*, to maintain a loose connection and continue growing.

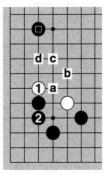

Diagram 18

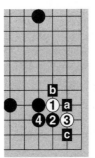

Diagram 19

In Diagram 19, after White 1 and 3, Black may be tempted to play a, b, or c. The sensible thing to do, however, is stop the contact as soon as possible by connecting at 4. Now the burden is entirely White's.

In general, attacking is both dangerous and rewarding. It requires the greatest skill. Attacking is where you can display your creativity and inspired play. Defense is generally easy.

Natural Principles

Here's how to find value in your defeats.

Non - resistance
— be like a palm bending in the wind

There are four ways to deal with the forces of life:
- Surrender to them as one doomed from the start.
- Ignore them and live a random life full of accidents.
- Resist them and dwell in turmoil and disease.
- Embrace them, use them, and blend with nature.

"Turn problems into opportunities and stumbling blocks into stepping stones."

Development
— be like water cutting through rock

Demand leads to development of a skill. Demand requires motivation in order to sustain the effort. Motivation needs to be given meaning. Development comes from a string of little failures; you learn from your mistakes. See failures as stepping stones to progress. Reaching your goal takes time and persistence.

Balance
— in extremes find the middle way

You win some and you lose some. To find the middle ground explore the extremes. Play with different styles and approaches: be an aggressive player, a hoarder of territory, a lover of influence, and a coward, so you may better understand what it is to be a samurai and know where your balance lies. Progress is a function of time and intensity of effort. The two must be balanced or you risk burnout — aim to keep your sense of pleasure in the game.

"What counts is not the number of hours you put in but how much you put in those hours."

Natural Order
— grow with the cycles of the seasons

There are transitions between stages of growth. Expect plateaus in your strength. There will be times when you need to consolidate and absorb the learning you have already undergone. To try to force your way through these times is pointless. When the time is right, you will continue your growth. Learn to value the in-between times, and use them as preparation for the next step. A warm-up is a transition ritual: a physical warm-up prepares you for exercise; a mental warm-up can help before a game by providing focus and energy for the new task.

In order to grow, you must be able to learn from your mistakes. Whenever possible, go over your game with a stronger player. You will not see your own mistakes, or at least you will only be aware of the short range tactical error, not the strategic error twenty moves earlier. If you cannot do this, it is better to play another game than to learn the wrong lessons. Others further advanced in the cycle are there to help you. Amass experience until you are ready to move on to the next step.

Quibbling

W*e have four percent of the world population. We have eighteen percent of the world economy. But we have fifty percent of the lawyers. ... Everybody suing. Everybody disputing. Everybody in court. After all, three quarters of a million American lawyers have to do "something."*
Rising Sun by Michael Crichton.

They should play Go. They'd be perfect during the endgame, quibbling about each and every territory boundary.

Unfortunately, the law has nothing to do with justice ...It's merely a method for dispute resolution.
Disclosure by Michael Crichton

Court battles take forever and cost a fortune, just like the endgame in Go. The grand visions being created in the opening game may last thirty moves. The battles of the midgame are eventually resolved — all areas are well-defined and all groups are alive or dead, in about seventy moves. But the endgame — the endgame will last for almost one hundred and fifty moves with both players haggling over boundary placement until no profitable moves are left. If justice were to prevail in Go, then the player who was leading at the end of the midgame would win. Don't count on it. While each boundary quibble is only worth a few points, the sum of all such disputes can result in a huge shift in score. Victory in many games will go to the best endgame lawyer, who tirelessly argues the case, wearing the opponent down with adroit questioning and subtle innuendo. It is easy to go numb under constant pressure from one's opponent and fail to realize the moment when one should raise an objection or begin cross-examination.

During the endgame, territories must be secured against two weaknesses: gaps and defects. Then, both players should occupy any remaining neutral points. Finally, each player passes.

Gaps

In the annals of legal history, no gap is more famous than the "18-minute gap" in the Watergate tapes. The Nixon administration claimed that the erasure of 18 minutes of recorded government tapes was accidental. Most think that story is full of holes.

In Go, gaps arise all the time. Gaps are holes in a territory boundary, links instead of stones. Gaps are the usual source of endgame moves.

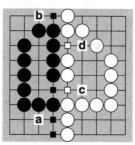

In Diagram 1, *a* is a gap, *b* and *c* are defects, and *d*'s are neutral points.

The Bigger the Gap, the More to Lose or Gain: In Diagram 2, Black's double-skip gap exposing *a* is more important than the single-skip gap on the upper edge exposing *b*. With a single move on the upper edge, White can destroy one point of territory. With a single move on the lower edge, White can destroy six points.

Diagram 1

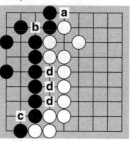

Opposing Gaps Double their Value: Attacking one gap implies plugging the other. In Diagram 2, the gap leading to *c* is worth more than the gap leading to *d* because dealing with *c* implies dealing with both Black's and White's gaps there.

Diagram 2

Big Gaps Facing Each Other Generate Magnificent Endgame Moves, so huge they are often played in the midgame. If not, then the first thing you should play out in the endgame is all fourth-line link boundaries. Next, find all edge boundaries where both players' stones are on the third line and play them out.

In Diagram 3, both players will want to play *a* or thereabouts when they can find an excuse.

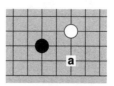

Diagram 3

The biggest and most valuable gaps invariably occur around the edge of the board. Here, it is possible to do more than merely poke on a gap; here, one can often jump all the way across the gap and into opposing territory. This is much bigger than merely pushing on a door and having the opponent build another one slightly farther back.

Single Skip: When a stone on the second or third line is next to an open link, it may jump freely past the boundary, provided it doesn't end up adjacent to an enemy stone.

In Diagram 4a, White is on the second line and adjacent to Black's link to the edge. White can destroy much shaded Black territory with a single move.

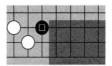

Diagram 4a

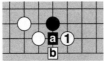

Diagram 4b

White 1 in Diagram 4b is just the move. Black's territory evaporates and White can use White 1 as a base for further destruction. If Black plays *a*, White will play *b* to retain connection to safety.

Things are not as clean in Diagram 4c, where White's skip touches Black's marked stone. White can safely escape, but White does not destroy as much territory because White cannot keep moving deeper into Black's territory. Furthermore, White might lose sente.

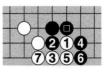

Diagram 4c

Large Knight: When you cannot skip freely, either because you are not next to the boundary link or because skipping will end up touching an enemy stone, you can still take advantage of being closer to the edge than the enemy by sliding underneath with a small or a large knight's move.

In Diagram 5, the single skip would not work well, so White slides all the way on the first-line to 1. This cannot be cut off.

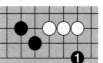

Diagram 5

Sliding to the second line from the third can be an important way to get stability for a group (or deprive one of stability). In such cases, the slide may be played in the midgame or even as early as the opening! Making or depriving a group of a life basis is an urgent move, not merely a profitable one.

Diagram 6a

Diagram 6a shows another large knight's slide. Black is not close enough to skip across the fourth line link, but Black can safely slide there. In which game phase this can be played depends upon the safety of the Black and White stones involved. If either one is weak, the move can be played as early as the opening.

Slides cannot be stopped easily.

If White blocks immediately in front of Black 1, as in Diagram 6b, Black simply goes around with 3. White must cut with 4 to retain the barrier, but Black 5 kills White 2. White can separate Black from Black's friends with the next move, but Black will be able to live almost immediately without staying connected back to safety.

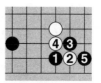

Diagram 6b

Attachment: The preceding moves all required that both players' stones be on different lines from the edge. When both player's stones are on the same line, you still have big endgame values when those stones are on the third or fourth lines.

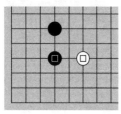

Diagram 7a

In Diagram 7a, Black and White marked stones stare at each other along the fourth line.

In Diagram 7b, White attaches to Black's stone just underneath it. This is a big endgame move. Black 2 stops further White advancement, and after White defends with 3, Black must make some defense also.

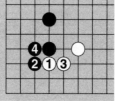

Diagram 7b

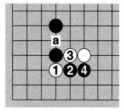

Diagram 7c

The only risk is that Black might counterattack with 2 of Diagram 7c. White 3 is forced. Black cannot sacrifice Black 2 now or Black will be worse off than in Diagram 7b, so Black saves the stone with Black 4. The problem for Black is that White can either fight it out with Black 2 and 4, or cut through Black's link above at *a* and destroy territory that way. The question will be who loses more by this diagram. If it is White, then playing the attachment was too aggressive.

Diagram 8a is an example of marked tones staring at each other along the third line.

Diagram 8a

Being first to attach, as White 1 does in Diagram 8b, is big because, after both sides protect, White has gained points and still has sente.

The danger, as always, is that Black might counterattack.

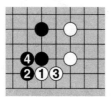

Diagram 8b

In Diagram 8c, Black does this in a mild fashion. The damage to White is not so severe, and White pierces through Black's upper link and into Black's territory. Black must capture with 8, otherwise there was no reason to go after White in the first place.

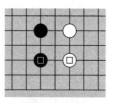

Diagram 8c

The real risk is Diagram 8d. Black moves into White's territory, and White moves into Black's territory. Who will die? White had better have a favorable answer or have planned a trade of territories.

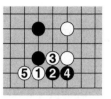

Diagram 8d

Once again, these moves may be played early on if they involve the life basis of the group initiating the contact. You cannot, however, use these moves to attack a group because they imply the willingness to sacrifice the initial attachment if need be. You cannot attack someone by making them a present of an eye. It just doesn't make sense.

Clamp: Sometimes the link is tiny, but it can still yield a big penetration because of a nearby defect. The clamp is the appropriate tool in such cases, though it can never be used to gain a life basis.

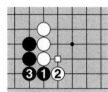

Diagram 9a

Diagram 9a shows the setup for a clamp. Black has played an apparently gote endgame sequence, but White is left with the marked cutting point as a bad aftertaste. Usually White will treat this sequence as sente and defend the cutting point. If not, ...

Black 1 in Diagram 9b is the clamp. White's single stone is squeezed on opposite sides, and Black threatens above and below simultaneously. White has to play 2 to stop a major incursion. Now Black has many moves that can be played. If Black can cut at *a* and capture one of White's two cut strings, Black will be ecstatic. Even if Black can't cut, all of the other marked moves threaten to cut, and maybe Black can start an invasion. If this invasion is successful, White's stones will become isolated and probably die.

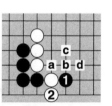

Diagram 9b

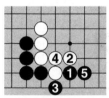

Diagram 9c

If White doesn't like the results of cutting Black off, the only thing White can do is back down with 2 of Diagram 9c. Black 3 connects underneath, and Black 5 marches straight into White's territory. This is a major loss for White.

Defects

In the law a defective title means one's connection to something can be disputed. In Go, this is represented by the diagonal link, which can be threatened easily with being split. If your opponent plays on your diagonal link, you will need immediate legal advice. Below is our public defender's cheap advice on whether or not you own your claim.

If the opponent's play on a diagonal link threatens to capture one of your stones, then you have a problem and you must defend that defect before your opponent gets there. If your opponent can't capture you, then the defect doesn't matter and playing a defense costs you a point.

Reprising Diagram 1, *b* and *c* are defects. Since this is the endgame, when the opponent cuts, the move will be within your territory. That is, the cutting move will be enclosed and it will be your turn. Applying principles from races to capture (*The Dinosaur's Hind Brain*), if you have as many as or more liberties than the cutting string has, you will succeed in capturing it. So... imagine your opponent cuts and count liberties to see if you need to defend before the cut occurs.

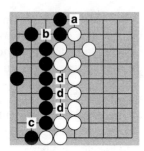

Diagram 1

In Diagram 1, if White cuts at *b*, White will have one liberty and Black's worst liberty count is two. Black will win and need not defend in advance. If White cuts at *c*, White will have two liberties and Black will have only one for one of cut-apart Black strings. This is fatal, so Black must defend at *c* as soon as possible.

Free Advice

The rule of thumb with lawyers is that you get what you pay for (or at least you will always pay for whatever you get). The more expensive the lawyer, the better the defense. In Go, paying for things does not improve their value. The biggest moves are always those that are free. Even if a move is only worth a point or two, if it's free, take it. Below are classic crimes you can get away with on the Go board.

PickPocketing: Reach sideways into your neighbor's pocket. Black 1 in Diagram 10 threatens to reach deep into White's territory, so White must stop it with 2. Black 3 saves a stone and threatens to cut and capture White 1, so White must defend with 4. Black has gained two points in sente. Furthermore, if White had gotten here first, White could have done the same thing to Black.

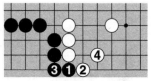

Diagram 10

Black avoided losing two points in sente also. Since it's free, it's big. If Black 3 didn't threaten to capture White 2, it would be gote and hence not big.

Illegal Entry: If you are standing on the threshhold, walk on in. Simply pushing in with Black 1 in Diagram 11 threatens to walk all over White's territory, so White stops this with 2. Net gain: one point in sente for Black. Since pushing results in your liberty being filled, just be sure you don't need to defend after pushing, or you lose sente and it's not free.

Diagram 11

Gerrymandering: Adjusting political boundaries to shift demographics was popular before it became illegal. In Go, it is still legal. To gerrymander in Go when stones are on the same line, think of attachment. If that seems risky, settle for the diagonal play.

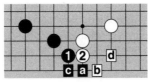

Diagram 12

In Diagram 12, Black decided not to risk attaching at 2, and so played diagonally at 1, moving Black's territory boundary and threatening to jump past White's. White blocked with 2. Later Black can **pickpocket** (*a-d*) in sente and White can't. Therefore, Black 1 is directly worth four points (Black gains two, White will lose two) and, since Black stops the reverse from happening in sente, the final value is counted as eight points.

Don't Get Caught! These moves aren't particularly valuable when played in gote. How do you know something is sente? It's not easy, as it depends upon a relative scale of values and who will need to defend last after the move is played. In general, it's sente if it threatens to kill or save a group. Otherwise, it's sente if it threatens to damage the biggest territory around. And against weak players, it's sente if it threatens to damage a territory bigger than ten points. (A weak player doesn't do comparative analysis, just defending what is owned if it looks big.)

The only excuse for not taking a sente move immediately is saving it for a ko threat or preserving options in a position.

In Diagram 13a, White can play 1 and 3 in sente, but White should wait. Playing 1 and 3 damage White's marked stone thoroughly, so White must be certain that it is truly doomed already.

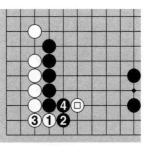

Diagram 13a

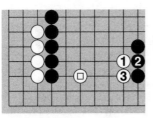

Diagram 13b

White might want to try to live, as in Diagram 13b. Until White knows otherwise, White should wait on taking sente endgame moves here.

Right now Black cannot play in the area in sente. If Black plays 1 and 3 in Diagram 13c, Black takes gote because Black is not threatening to continue damaging White's territory significantly. This means White can wait and see. If, however, 1 and 3 become sente in the future because White's corner group becomes too weak, White must rush to play out Diagram 13a before Black plays out Diagram 13c. Otherwise, White loses free moves and Black gets them instead.

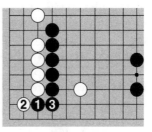

Diagram 13c

Unreasonable Doubt

A good lawyer will always find a way to cast "reasonable doubt" in the minds of the jury. No matter how overwhelming the evidence, a lawyer can always find a way to confuse the truth. Maybe the lawyer will create the illusion of a potential second killer, or perhaps convince the jury that this sane murderous defendant led a troubled childhood and became temporarily deranged after losing three games of Go in a row. Whatever it takes to cast doubt the lawyer will do, since that's the goal.

Sides are Bigger than the Center: In Go, there is no need for anyone to work at confusing you. The board has a natural illusion waiting to deceive you. The typical endgame mistake of weaker players is to perceive center moves as big. In fact, the biggest endgame moves are invariably on the side. Sometimes this is true because there are often several ways to reduce a center territory. That means there is no rush to do any of them. Other times it is true because the move to attack a center territory often does not come from a territory. That means it is uni-purpose, reducing without securing. Moves along the side that attack and defend territory simultaneously will be worth more. Finally, more exotic tactics happen using the properties of the edge, so otherwise bland areas around the side are often hiding clever trick moves that can make the attack bigger or more sente than it would first seem.

Diagram 14 is going into the endgame. It may seem that much of the board is unplayed, but all groups are alive and there are no invasions to try. It is White to play. If White is a weak player, White will see a vast open center and want to take a piece of the action there with the next move. White will be tempted to play *b*, *d*, or *g*.

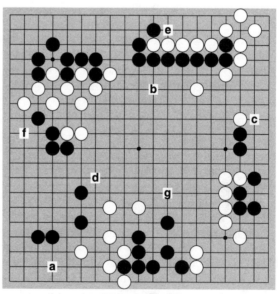

Diagram 14

Consider, however, the value of the sides. White at *e*, for example, is actually worth about twelve points in gote (six points in sente if Black responds). If Black played *e* first, White wouldn't respond, so Black would play a second move in sente and White would have to connect. *e* is gote for both sides, and the difference between each playing there is twelve points. It is hard to imagine White playing a gote center move that assures White of twelve points. *b* certainly won't. Black can reduce the center from four different directions. There is no hope of a significant territory in the center.

Weak Groups are Biggest: The slide to *a* is a big move that threatens to follow up with more damage. *f* is another big move we've seen earlier. The biggest move, however, is at *c*. This move, if played by Black, would damage White's territory just as much as White playing *a* would damage Black. Critically, White playing *c* threatens to attack Black's group. This adds a big premium to the move, making it sente.

Threaten to Kill

One of the perverse things about the law is that the police cannot generally take action when they know someone wants to kill someone else. Instead, the police must wait until murder is attempted. Of course, they might have waited too long and the murder gets committed. Go is better in this respect. You can and should respond to threats. If a move threatens to kill a group, respond to it. If a move does not threaten to kill a group, no crime is about to be committed and you shouldn't automatically respond.

Respond automatically to life-threatening moves only.

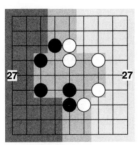

Diagram 15a

Every time you respond, you are losing points. Do that often, and you will lose.

In Diagram 15a, the score is twenty-seven to twenty-seven.

In Diagram 15b, Black threatens White territory with 1 and 3, and White responds logically with 2 and 4. Then Black plays 5, 7, and 9, and White gets control. Yet at the end of this diagram, White has lost by five points.

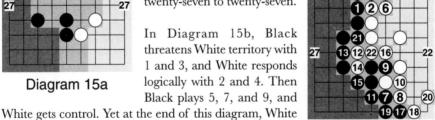

Diagram 15b

The key to avoid losing points is to play tit-for-tat. Find a move that is like the move just played against you. Even better, find a bigger move. Don't think of responding to your opponent's move unless it threatens your life or you have hunted for a better move and can't find one. In Diagram 15c, White plays tit-for-tat. Both lose territory equally, so the score remains tied.

You can become strong without computing endgame values if you can just recognize the big obvious moves.

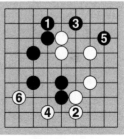

Diagram 15c

New Age Go

Competition is increasingly seen as a bad thing, leading to a self-seeking, violence-promoting attitude, which is at the root of many of the problems in society and in the world. Management training courses now encourage cooperation and group problem-solving by changing the victory criteria or inventing puzzle games. There is a new approach to games and sports, which aims to do away with the single victor while retaining the individual's will to succeed.

To take a simple example, look at the party game of musical chairs. As the group of children walk around the row of chairs, which seated all of them, one chair is removed. When the music stops all must try to sit down, but one will fail. This is repeated until there is only one chair left and the winner is sitting in it. Meantime the ones who are out (failed to find a chair) have to stand and watch. The New Age version would be to remove the chairs as before, but the challenge is now to all fit on the remaining chairs. At the end, everyone must try to fit on the last chair if all are to win a prize. This game keeps everyone involved all the way through and produces no losers. Similar mutations have been produced for many winner-oriented sports and games.

Go is around 4,000 years old and so it is hardly a New Age game, yet it contains an unusual approach to competition. The underpinnings of Go lie in Oriental philosophy, which is based on a sense of balance and harmony. In Go, excess is discouraged because it leads to disaster: greed is overreaching oneself and it produces a weak, thin position that is easily destroyed. To claim all the territory is not necessary, only one point more than the opponent is needed to win.

Despite the innate balance of traditional Go, there have been attempts to produce a version of the game that has no single winner or where the winning is not the point of the game. Penny Ante Go is played for money in exchange for territory points — it is essentially a way of introducing children to the idea of territory. Quality Go is played as a cooperative effort to make the sum of all territories exceed a preset limit. Skirmishes and captures will result in smaller territories and a lower score. Team Go and Pair Go do involve some cooperation but there is still a winning team, so the result is akin to that in a relay race.

But is it really necessary to change the way we play Go, or do we just need to try to understand the way we should be playing it? In China the proper way for a weak player to ask a stronger player for a game is to say: "Please teach me". The game is seen not as a battle but as an opportunity to learn. This attitude presupposes a blending and harmonizing of people — no opponents or enemies — just teachers and students.

High Concepts

Yin & Yang
Go & Sin
A Question of Balance
Winds of Change
Computer Go
Sacrificial Lamb

*" A craft can only have meaning
when it serves a spiritual way."*

Yin & Yang

A small atom buzzing furiously to and fro around the universe collides with another small atom spinning merrily along. **BOOOOOM!** Such is the result of matter hitting antimatter, a tremendous release of energy resulting from the destruction of the initial participants. This is the Western way to harness opposites. The Oriental way of harnessing opposites preserves their unique existence. The opposites, Yin and Yang (see *Philosophy & Go*), are more like the North and South poles of a magnet. They can be made productive by incorporating them into a generator, yet they remain essentially unchanged throughout this experience. This chapter is about high level opposites and how to view them cooperatively for your advantage.

Strategy & Tactics

The ancient Chinese considered schemes and strategy to be female, Yin, and action or tactics to be male, Yang. Some people are good strategists; some are good tacticians. But most people can't really tell you the difference between the two. Basically, tactics is the mechanics of doing something, while strategy is the why you are choosing to do it. Strategy is being able to tell yourself a story. *I am going to do this, to get this, because this will further this, which will result in my having whatever happen that I want to happen.*

Just what is tactics and what is strategy depends upon what you know. When you first learn Go, there is no strategy. You don't know why you choose one move over another. As you get slightly stronger, you learn the tactics of killing stones. At first, you kill anything you can, just because you can. There is still no strategy here. Later you correlate killing with making points, so you may attack bigger things first. Your story (strategy) is: *if I kill a large number of stones I will get many points and this will mean I win later.*

As you learn to leave small worthless stones alone, you pick up some higher strategy. Killing is now in service of some goal like making life for your stones. Making life is the reason (strategy) and killing is a tactic for accomplishing it. Running is another tactic you learn for living. So your story becomes: *I will try to kill these stones and get two eyes for life instead of running because if I run, I will only get temporary escape but if I kill, I will get two eyes and be alive permanently.* Living is the goal. It never occurs to you that some groups are better left to die.

When you learn to let groups die, then living becomes a tactic, and running and killing subtactics, and so on. That is, as you master higher and higher purposes and integrations of things, what was once strategy becomes tactics. Yin transforms itself into Yang because Yang was present all along. Tactics become reflexes one can choose. You learn to override primitive reflexes in service of strategy. The essential fact is that no matter where you are in your ability to see and do something, there is always a bigger picture that can be viewed, in which all of your clever schemes and abilities are merely taken for granted in playing out the higher level.

The game progresses in cycles from strategic to tactical and back to strategic. The old adage "Plans are nothing; planning is everything" means that rarely will a plan be carried out uninterrupted from beginning to end. However, planning helps you coordinate movement through successive periods of activity. Planning gives way to action, and the results of action suggest new plans. The game exhibits cyclical behavior, with the germ of the next phase present in the current one. Both strategy and tactics must be present to play well. Exquisite tactics without consideration of strategy will result in successful but useless actions. Grand strategy without the ability to execute it will come to naught.

Tactics and Strategy Principles

When you are a weaker player, the distinction between tactics and strategy is usually made based on the object of focus. If you focus on a string, link, or territory, then you think tactically. Your focus is at the bottom level of board perception. There are few choices for each unit of focus, though there are many choices because there are many units. If you focus on a group or a potential territory, then your focus is strategic, near the top of board-perception hierarchy. There are still relatively few choices, but now there are also few units. Actions in the strategic plane become major choices that have vast future impact on the rest of the game.

As a quick guide to strategy and tactics in Go, I offer the following broad principles:

Play Multipurpose Moves: This rule applies to everything. The wealth of ideas to be carried out each move is enormous, and you get only one move per turn. A move that works toward only one goal is a wasted move. Whenever possible a move should do two or more of the following:

> defend your groups
> attack your opponent's groups
> enhance your territory
> reduce your opponent's territory
> set up a follow-up move enabling one of the above

Defend Links: This is a tactical defense rule. Since containment is at the heart of Go, and links are your primary tools for containment, you must defend them. Otherwise, the positions you have carefully built in the opening will disintegrate under your opponent's attack. This was a basic reflex taught in *The Dinosaur's Hind Brain* and it is the basis of good play.

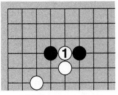

Diagram 1a

In Diagram 1a, White had threatened Black's link as a ko threat. Black won the ko and White continued with White 1, attacking Black's link. What should Black do?

Many Black players would fear for their corner stone and play as in Diagram 1b. Black 2 backs down and tries to live because directly blocking White would leave two cutting points and appears indefensible. Black succeeds in living, but Black's outside position is now a shambles. Black's marked stone is worthless and the territory in the corner is nothing to boast about. There is even some danger left from a White play at *a*.

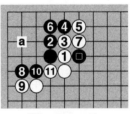

Diagram 1b

Better play is shown in Diagram 1c. Black defends the link with Black 2 and then awaits White's assault. When White cuts with 3, Black abandons the corner stone and grows strong on the outside. Black gets a strong outside position, and White's territory is only a little over ten points. Black's outside wall and having sente should make that up easily.

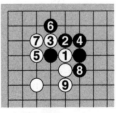

Diagram 1c

Avoid Enclosure: This is a strategic defense rule. If you get contained, your groups run a high risk of being captured, and your other positions are implicitly weakened because they have one less group to connect to. See *Call of the Wild*.

Attack From a Safe Base: This is a tactical offense rule. Keep yourself linked to an existing group to ward off counterattack and to minimize the number of groups you have to defend. You get only one move a turn. With many unrelated units on the board, some will have to wait patiently for rescue that may come too late.

Attack and Defend the Weakest Units First: In local tactics, the weakest units are those with the fewest liberties.

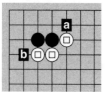

Diagram 2

In Diagram 2, for example, Black can play at *a* or *b* in the contact fight. Both moves are on the second line, but *a* is a better choice because it is played against the weaker White stone.

For groups, the weakest units are those with the fewest options for survival.

In Diagram 3, moves *a* through *d* should be the ones that spring to your mind as Black's next choices. *a* and *b* are good attacks on weak White stones. *c* expands in front of Black's corner enclosure. *d* safely wedges within White's potential, preventing White from making a big framework.

c and *d*, while good moves, are uni-purpose. They only destroy or create territory. *a* and *b*, creating territory while stabilizing Black groups and attacking White groups, are better choices. White's weak upper right-side group has three options for defense; run toward the center, extend to the left, and slide into the corner. White's weak central right-side group has only two options: run toward the center and extend upwards.

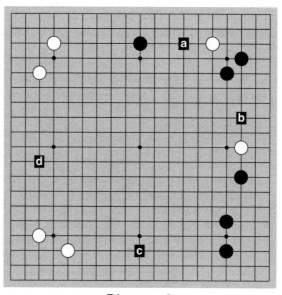

Diagram 3

From an offensive viewpoint, therefore, *b* is clearly a better move. It leaves a White group with only one option, instead of leaving both White groups with multiple options. Furthermore, Black's upper right corner is within White's sector-line, whereas Black's upperside stone is not (the line is too long). From a defensive viewpoint Black should defend the upper right corner first. *b* is perfect, defending, attacking, and making territory.

Keep your Opponent Divided: This is a strategic and tactical offense rule, similar in spirit to *attack from a safe base*. The more groups and strings your opponent has, the harder it is to manage them simultaneously. It is best if you can divide your opponent without creating new units yourself.

Play with the Future in Mind: Every move you play must contribute toward the future. Have a follow-up in mind. If you cannot find an interesting follow-up, then don't play this current move.

Never Have Two Weak Groups: This is strategic defense. If you have two weak groups on the board at the same time, one of them will probably die. If you have three weak groups, one of them will surely die.

Abandon Long Fights over Small Stones: This tactical defense rule allows you to spend your moves where they are most needed. Stones are stable if they cannot be saved. Even if they can be saved, if the effort of saving them is large or you have other more important things that need saving, declare the less valuable stones dead in your mind. Any enclosed string is a candidate for being declared dead. Think before you defend it. If you do decide to declare something dead for this turn, wait at least ten turns before trying to save them again. Wavering indecisively is the *worst* thing you can do.

Medicine has a related principle called triage. When overwhelmed by patients, divide them into those who will survive with no treatment, those who will die even if treated, and those for whom treatment will make a difference. The difference between Go and medicine is that in Go it is conscionable to let stones die when they could be saved. Medicine is still struggling with the issue of when extraordinary efforts should and should not be applied to saving someone.

Save It for Later: Don't fight where you can't win. Don't even play it out to see if your opponent is paying attention. This is a tactical offense rule. Just because something doesn't work now doesn't mean that it won't work later, or that you can't use it for ko threats later. The Japanese use the word *aji*, meaning taste, to describe these situations that have *lingering potential*.

In Diagram 4a, Black has captured six White stones in the corner. They can't be saved, but White has a forcing move at *a*, which will threaten to revive them. Playing it now, however, is wrong. Since Black can't jump out beyond *a* anyway, there is no rush to play there, and *a* makes a great ko threat. Also, White might prefer to play *b* someday, sealing off that side instead.

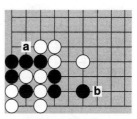

Diagram 4a

Normally White couldn't seal Black off with *b*. But due to the lingering potential of White's dead stones in the corner, Black cannot easily resist.

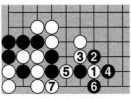

Diagram 4b

If Black resists, Diagram 4b happens. Black captures the barricading White 1 stone, but White's corner stones revive by capturing some Black stones.

Strong players avoid plays that would destroy their good aji and, instead, strive to make the game play out in such a way as to make the aji come to life. Even if it doesn't ever get used, its potential may make the opponent play less aggressively, seeking to avoid triggering the aji.

Avoid Aji Destruction: Aji-destroying refers to your forcing move that uses up your options without accomplishing anything significant. Peeping when you can cut is a typical example of aji destruction.

In Diagram 5, White will be overjoyed to connect at *b* if Black peeps with *a*. *Never peep if you can cut.* That doesn't mean that Black should necessarily cut here. It just means that Black should cut instead of peeping or maybe do something even bigger in scale than cutting.

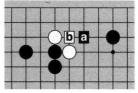

Diagram 5

A more subtle example of aji destruction is playing one of two alternatives before a realistic choice can be made between the two lines.

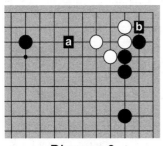

Diagram 6

In Diagram 6, Black can attack White with *a* or *b*. Without knowing how the rest of the board will develop, it is impossible to make a choice now, so Black should wait. Even if it is clear which line of play should eventually be chosen, playing any move prematurely uses up ko threats. And you never notice this until when? When you are in a ko and it is too late. So you want to find the moment just before White would have a reason and the time to play one of the two moves, and then you attack.

Don't Attack a Link If You Won't Cut: White 1 in Diagram 7 is wrong. White doesn't expect to cut. At best Black will respond at *a* and White 1 does almost nothing while *a* helps Black. At worst, Black will pick another defense (*b-e*) or take sente.

Diagram 7

Black 1 in Diagram 8 is another bad move. Black has no intention of cutting. Black just knows 1 is sente. By playing 1 now, Black: loses a big ko threat, loses a liberty, and loses opportunities for other choices (Diagrams 9 & 10.)

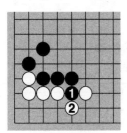

Diagram 8

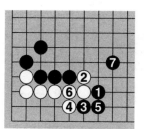

Diagram 9

In Diagram 9, Black 1 threatens to enclose White. When White resists with 2, Black builds a position that keeps White from expanding to the right.

In Diagram 10, after Black 1 Black follows with *a* or *b*, depending upon White's response.

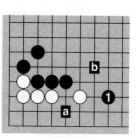

Diagram 10

In Diagram 11, Black 1 is only good if Black intends to cut at *a*. Continuing with 3 is a mistake for Black. Either cut or don't play Black 1. Play a different move.

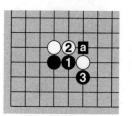

Diagram 11

Think you can see it now? Don't attack a link you are not planning to cut!

Past & Future

There is an old saying *What have you done for me lately?* which points out that past laurels are nice, but the important thing is continued performance. In Go, what you did earlier is nice, but not important. Nor, for that matter, is what you are doing now. The important thing is the future! The game of Go lasts for about two hundred and fifty moves. Even after one hundred moves are played, less than half the game has been played out. Therefore the real value of a move lies not in what it does now, but what myriad futures it supports.

Beginning Go players play the game on a move-by-move basis, thinking only of what they are currently doing. They are viewing but the tip of an iceberg and playing poorly. A strong player seems to be capable of time travel and places a stone at a seemingly random point, which turns out to be exactly where it is needed ten moves later. A well-placed stone lays the groundwork for a multitude of possible futures, which may be only dimly seen from the present.

You must strive to be prescient and always ask yourself *Does this move have any potential for affecting the future?* If not, don't play it. To affect the future, a move must seriously change the safety status of a group or face the unplayed center or sides of the board. Moves that do not affect the future should be avoided until the endgame, when the future is about to end. A twenty-point profit move with no future impact is small stuff compared to a move that affects the rest of the game.

In Diagram 1c, repeated here from earlier, Black could play Black 10 to the left of Black 6. It's worth over six points. Black shouldn't play here, however, because it has no effect on the future. It doesn't destabilize White, and it doesn't significantly secure Black. It is buried in the corner with Black and White stones closer to the outside than it is. Therefore it is not going to change many future scenarios and should be avoided until the endgame.

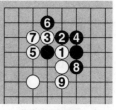

Diagram 1c

In Diagram 12, should Black defend the upper left corner or the upper right corner? Invading area 1 is easier than invading area 2. You should defend the upper left corner because your defense supports the more probable future invasion.

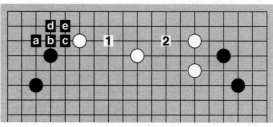

Diagram 12

Thus the future affects your strategy as Black of which corner to pick. The future also affects your tactics for defending the upper left. You could pick any of *a-e* to secure your corner. Which to choose depends upon what you might do with each in the future. *a* just secures the corner. *b* and *d* aim to invade into 1 (with different tactical sequences). *c* and *e* aim to secure a bigger corner (but it is harder for the weaker player to keep it). Black expects White will defend in response. This means *c* and *e* do *not* plan to invade.

The past cannot be ignored completely. You made moves in the past that color the present and future. New moves must account for old.

Perseverance & Immediacy

Japanese businesses are masters of the concept of long-range planning. They think and act on plans running decades into the future. What is more, they are willing to pay large amounts of money to buy marketshare or future technology without expecting a return on investment in the near term. The Oriental tradition, as manifested in the I Ching and the sayings of Confucius, calls for perseverance. An apprentice in a sushi shop is expected to spend three years delivering goods and cooking rice before he is considered ready to hold a knife. Bonsai trees are an art sculpture; it takes years to produce the small plant shaped *just so*.

The American tradition, reflected in its people and its companies, favors immediate gratification. You see it reflected in our dependency on credit cards. You see it in the fast-clip video montage of children's programming, like Sesame Street. You see it in

American companies that focus their efforts on next quarter's profits and view six months as a long planning cycle.

In Go, you need to have both perseverance and immediate gratification. You must aim your plays into the distant future, but they must also accomplish something now. Go teaches you to think in multiple time frames. You act in the present, as a result of situations created by your past moves, trying to create possibilities for favorable situations in the future. You can only aim for possibilities, since you cannot see far enough into all possible futures to know how your opponent will react.

For example, the ability to attack a group arises from moves played in the past. Whenever you attack a group, you want an attack with immediate tangible results. You cannot guarantee your opponent will defend, and you cannot guarantee you can punish your opponent for not defending. This means you always want to know your move has some value in addition to its attack value. What you hope is that the attack value is strong enough that your opponent does have to defend. This means you get your profit for free, since usually a defensive move only keeps what it has and makes nothing new. Your opponent will choose to defend a group if it looks like allowing you an even more severe attack in the future will be worse.

Global & Local

Knowing the best local move is not enough; the entire board must be considered. Many times an exquisite local play, found after much laborious reading, is wasted by being played prematurely. On the other hand, simple moves played at the correct global moment are often regarded as brilliant.

If you have been paying attention, you'll realize that in some sense there are no local moves. All moves must mind the global scene and the future, though they are played in some locale in the present.

Winning & Losing

You can walk with your eyes closed, but your steps will be hesitant and you will have difficulty going any distance in a straight line. In Go, playing moves without being aware of the score is like walking with your eyes closed. To make sensible choices you should always have some awareness of how you are doing. Strategy and tactics will vary based on this.

In games like chess, when you get a significant advantage, the game is all but over. This may be true for chess, but it is not true in business. Go, being more fluid, is a better model for business. There is no clear way to play to convert an advantage into a win. All you can do is continue playing well. Often an early advantage results in losing because you play too conservatively in order to protect your win. Being behind prompts you to do something daring and either one of you can make a mistake in the situation created.

Winning Big: When you are winning big, you don't want surprises and you can afford to pay for insurance. Make sure your groups are secure and respond locally to every enemy move lest you miss the impact of some move. Many players are tempted to ignore enemy moves to try to increase their win elsewhere. This is a way to lose.

Matching the opponent when leading is a standard tactic in one-on-one sailboat racing. When the trailing boat tacks, so does the leading one. No matter whether the trailing boat executes good strategy or bad, the leader matches it so as to retain the lead. Failure to do so can result in surprises. In the 1983 America's Cup finals, Liberty was leading when Australia II's skipper choose to shift to the opposite side of the course. Liberty failed to match, and the wind suddenly shifted slightly. Australia II won, but it's more accurate to say that Liberty lost by failing to execute a matching strategy.

Imitating the follower can be done immediately or you can wait to see whether the alternative approach is worthwhile. Whenever a weak company innovates, the strong company can wait to see if the market is valuable, and then jump in only in cases where value is shown. It costs money to imitate immediately, and it costs risk to imitate later. In Go, you should always imitate immediately. In business, you need to make trade-off judgements. Usually the risks of waiting can be properly managed, but it is possible to screw up. This happened to IBM. When the microcomputer first came out, IBM tried to ignore it. Then they overpriced and underpowered their product. Their position blew up, forcing them to lay off tens of thousands of workers.

Winning Small: This is the most difficult situation. You know you are winning, so you have a lot to lose, but only continued good play will preserve your win.

Uncertain or Close: This might arise either because you cannot determine what is happening or because the signs are mixed. Maybe you are ahead on territory but behind on influence. Play to clarify what you are uncertain about.

Losing Small: Here you have the most options. You can continue to play well and wait for small mistakes from your opponent or you can try something outrageous, trying to provoke your opponent's mistake. This is being "Number Two" in business. Avis, the car rental company, used to trumpet their number two position to advantage in their ad campaigns: *We're number two. We try harder.* That being number one leads to complacency was the understood meaning. This is equally true in Go. Having a significant advantage can make your opponent complacent.

Losing Big: You cannot continue to play normally. You must either do something radical or resign. Even then, the odds are not good. You do, however, get an opportunity for creativity. You will be willing to try things you would never normally consider.

You don't play Go in isolation. Instead, you bring with you habits and attitudes from a lifetime of existence and game playing. This, in Go, is the source of "original sin" as well as lesser transgressions.

Bad Habits

The Hawaii Drivers' Manual lists five bad driving habits: Laziness, Impatience, Inattention, Arrogance and Ignorance. Can you see them in *your* Go game?

Laziness *is not checking your situation before you move.* On the Go board this would be not counting your and your opponent's liberties in a race to capture. Or assuming your opponent's move was just an ordinary ko threat and not a trick play.

Impatience *is failing to come to a complete stop at a stop sign, the driver who weaves about tailgating and pressuring other drivers until something goes wrong and the rush becomes his undoing.* On the Go board this is the unthinking reflexive move that gets you into trouble. Speed reduces your field of vision in a car or on the Go board.

Inattention *is exhibited by the relaxed driver chatting so hard on the phone or to a passenger that his mind is not on the road.* On the Go board this is seeing only the local situation, not the rest of the board. Maybe you are looking at the rest of the room, watching people get coffee, seeing everything but the board in front of you.

Arrogance *is seen in the competitive driver who has little respect for other road users.* In Go this style of play is greedy and overreaching. You assume your opponent is incompetent or beneath consideration.

Ignorance *is seen in drivers who do not know the meaning of all traffic signs, regulations and safe driving procedures. This ignorance may result in the "they're all out to get me" state of mind.* Presuming you do know the basics of how to play, ignorance can be not understanding the implications of your opponent's move or not seeing how future concerns can be dealt with by a move played in the present.

Just as bad driving habits are hazardous on the road so bad Go-playing habits are hazardous on the board.

The Seven Deadly Sins

The seven deadly sins in medieval thought have their place in Go as well.

Pride: You know you are better than your opponent, either because you are giving a handicap or because your opponent's recent play stank. So you take sente instead of making the sound defensive play, assuming your opponent will follow you elsewhere. You play a forcing move without considering if it is really all that forcing. You try to see just how far you can really swindle your opponent, trying to convert a mere win into a demonstration of how thoroughly you can defeat your opponent. ~ Disrespect or foolishness — it is caused by pride. And pride comes before a fall. Not only does it cause you to lose games, but it makes them less enjoyable. Expressing contempt in your play makes you look bad and your opponent feel bad.

Anger: Your opponent just succeeded where there was no right to succeed: maybe it was an invasion or maybe your group died. Now you must even the score in a display of macho strength and attack. Your opponent didn't deserve success. ~ A hasty and angry response will only make things worse. Pause to reconsider your strategy and reevaluate your opponent. It may be wise to punish your opponent's mistake but it is foolish to try to take revenge for your failure. Chill out.

Lust: Until more women play Go, it is lust for battle we are talking about here. His group is so weak looking, the temptation is to play to kill it at all costs. ~ Most Go players love a good fight, but generating complexity for its own sake makes you lose track of the overall situation. The Klingons have a saying: "It is better to win the war than win every battle." Winning that battle may lose you the war.

Sloth: You can't be bothered to read out the tactics, thinking you can probably live with the move you play. Given a choice between invasion and light reduction, you invade, not bothering to count the score to see if you need to be so severe. ~ The resulting carnage may make you wish you had bothered to think it out. Allowing a habitual reaction rather than figuring out whether it's really relevant is lazy. Once a joseki has stepped from its path, the next move needs thought — or at least the application of EZ-GO principles.

Avarice: You are already ahead and it's the endgame. Your opponent's move doesn't seem all that important, so you ignore it and try a tricky tactical play to gain extra points. You make a potential territory and try to keep all of it. You take sente instead of defending your weakness because you want a bit more of the board. ~ Your opponent can exploit your greedy play, and you may start to regret your overreaching action. Know what is enough.

Gluttony: You cut off and capture small stones just for the local success of it. This is piecemeal taken to excess. Maybe you even fill in all the liberties and remove them just to see them removed from the board. ~ Eating up stones just because you have the opportunity to do so is pointless piggery. Think about big moves and the future of the game — not how many prisoners you can stuff into your lid.

Envy: Are your eyes bigger than your stomach? Does your opponent's territory always look bigger than yours? Do you want it all? Your opponent's potential territory looks so big, you want to destroy it all. You invade deeply instead of playing a light reduction. ~ Envy can get you into deep trouble. The lead may only have been an optical illusion — you didn't need such drastic action. Deal with envy by counting the score. If you are really badly behind, consider resigning. It is polite and, remember, you learn more the more games you play.

Bad habits and sins come from not playing the specifics of the situation in front of you and allowing the past to creep in and control your play. If you want to play better, identify your weaknesses and work to correct them.

A Question of Balance

I n the past, American fighting heroes were boxers like Jack Dempsey and Muhammed Ali. They epitomized our national military paradigm — stand up front, block those punches, and hit 'em hard until they fall down. Then a paradigm shift happened from our interactions with the Orient. Now America loves karate. The movies *Karate Kid* and *Under Siege* glorify karate skills, and the leading video games *Streetfighter* and *Mortal Kombat* teach our young to jump and kick (by the proxy "karate thumb punch" on the video game hand controllers).

Karate is not in your average street fighter's repertoire because a host of new skills and understandings are needed to utilize it. It takes dedication and training to learn those skills, which puts it beyond reach of your average thug. Just what are these new skills?

First, you don't block or absorb punches as much as you move out of their way or deflect them. The assumption that you need to directly stop the blow is not there. You may even make use of the enemy's attack, because to attack implies losing some degree of balance. This is the entire basis of judo, where the off-balance attacker's momentum is used to throw the attacker over an ankle, or thigh, or shoulder.

187

Second, the rest of your body's end points are also weapons. The feet become important striking tools, so the blow can be launched from a variety of places to reach a broader target. Before, punching never went below the waist. Now kicks can pinpoint the ankles and knees. Even the head is a weapon. Weapons are everywhere.

Third, the skills have a spiritual side. You learn that they are not to be used indiscriminately and that you need to be calm and peaceful within yourself in order to use the skills best. While the skills are violent, the user is not. Of course, like anything else, the original values get perverted. Judo was the first imported skill, but it never really caught on. Judo means *the gentle way* and is strictly a defensive skill. It does not have the offensive punches and kicks found in karate. It wasn't violent enough for our culture.

These new skills require lots of balance and coordination. It's not easy placing a kick all the way up to head height, much less maintaining your balance while doing it. Deflecting a blow takes more precision than sitting in the way of it. Often martial arts moves are combinations of simpler moves, a symphony of orchestrated behaviors intended to open the way for a successful blow. Schools of martial arts emphasize particular styles of actions.

So how does this apply to Go? The same skills, balance and coordination, come into play in Go. The chess player looks to overpower the opponent by swarming pieces on some particular side of the board and blocking the opponent's threats one for one. The Go player disperses forces all over the board, in an ever-changing pattern of emphasis. Balance and coordination among stones are essential. Style is a way to achieve this.

Balance

The I Ching teaches that there is a place in all of us where opposing forces are in proper balance — that in balance lies true power. An analogy is a pan of water on a stove. If the heat is too high the water will boil away. If the heat is too low the water will not boil. Only at the balancing point will the water be useful for cooking food. Balance can be static or it can be dynamic. Balance is an expression of Yin-Yang. It is impossible to stay stationary at the center between two extremes, so you are always moving between those polar opposites, first one way then another. Over time try to spend equal time on each side of the center.

In Go, balance seeps into every crack and crevice on the board. Every stone played has some implications toward attack, defense, influence, and territory. Your job is to find the appropriate balance so that all of your stones work well together and all of your opponent's stones do not. Each move you play, if played well, will utilize forces created by your previous moves. All will work together, as though this game had been preordained and you knew when you played your earlier moves just what moves would be made later. (Even if that is not true, making it look like it was true is sure to scare your opponent.)

You can balance with your opponent's moves and/or balance with your own.

When considering your opponent's moves, you can do:
1. **the same as the opponent** (*matching*).
-or-
2. **the opposite of what the opponent did** (*countering*).

When considering your moves, you can do :
1. **the opposite of what you did before** (*evenning*).
-or-
2. **the same as you did before** (*emphasizing*).

I will discuss each of these below, enumerating Go rules that apply.

Matching

Matching (*keeping up with the Joneses*) maintains the status quo by replicating the value your opponent got. Its weakness is that the enemy gets to control the agenda.

Matching Endgame Moves: As I say in the chapter about sente (*Winds of Change*), responding to an opponent's move means you lose points. In the endgame, since there is no future influence or safety to worry about, points are all that matters. Rather than lose points, make an equivalent endgame move against your opponent's territory, playing tit for tat. You may both lose points, but at least you will lose them equally.

When Black plays 1 in Diagram 1, the correct move for White is not to block with *a*, but to make an equivalent threat with *b*. This matches Black, so no gain has been made.

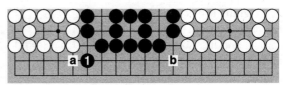

Diagram 1

Matching High with High and Low with Low: When the enemy approaches a symmetric corner stone (3-3 or 4-4), play the corresponding symmetric point on the other side. This gives you territory and safety, and balances the effect of your opponent's move. If the move was close to you, play close for safety. If the move was high for influence, play high for counter-influence.

In Diagram 2, White 1 approaches far and high, so Black 2 responds far and high. Similarly for any other White approach on the right labelled *a* through *c*, Black would normally respond on the left on *a* through *c* to balance White's approach.

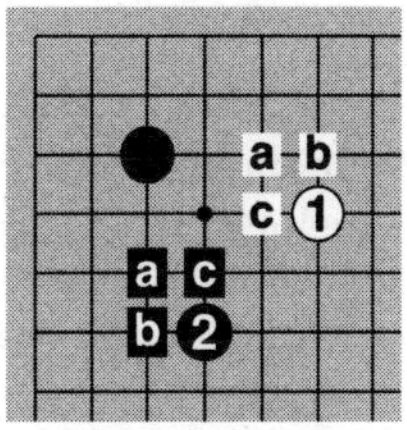

Diagram 2

In Diagram 3, White has approached Black's handicap corner with a low and close 1, and Black has responded with a low and close 2. If White had played any of the other approach moves shown, Black would have responded with their matching responses.

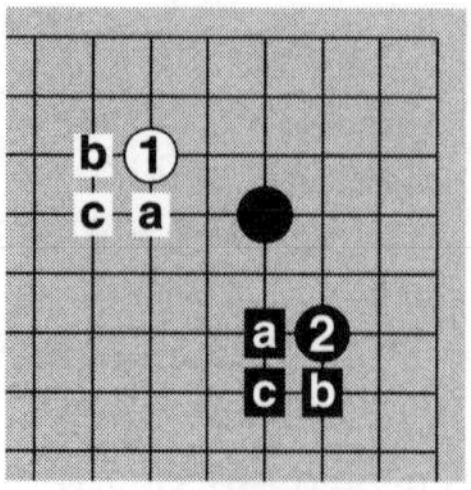

Matching Strength with Strength and Weakness with Weakness: When you extend from a stone toward the center, you must consider the surrounding enemy position. If the enemy is close to your stone, you must play close (in-line or diagonal) to keep safe. If the enemy is farther from your stone, you can play farther (small knight or single skip). If the enemy is extremely far from your stone, you can play extremely far (large-knight or double-skip).

Diagram 3

Countering

Countering (*tug of war*) maintains equilibrium with your opponent by accumulating value that is the opposite of your opponent's. Countering is self-reinforcing for both players. Once the two of you get locked into the situation, it is hard to break out and do something different without experiencing a sudden loss of control.

Countering Alternative Defenses: If you have a weak group with two different ways to make safety, you don't need to play either of them yet. But as soon as your opponent takes one, you should immediately take the other.

In Diagram 4, Black is safely ensconced between two White corners and has two ways of making a two-point extension, *a* and *b*. As soon as White plays near one of them, however, Black must immediately counter by taking the alternative.

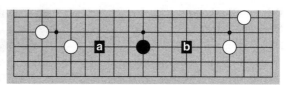

Diagram 4

Countering Style with Opposing Style: This has to be started early. If your opponent is playing for territory, play for influence. If your opponent is playing conservatively, play aggressively.

By selecting the opposite strategy, you get your opponent's cooperation. Sometimes your opponent will panic and change style in order to try to neutralize your position by matching. This makes some of your opponent's moves inconsistent with each other.

Evenning

Evenning (*a little of this, a little of that*) is used to redress an imbalance in your position by going in the opposite direction. It keeps you close to the center but may result in aimless random play. It lacks excitement but is highly flexible as the situation changes.

Evenning Third and Fourth Line: *Metaphorical Go* demonstrated the value of the third and fourth lines and the need to maintain a balance of moves on both of them.

Evenning Strength with Weakness: Play far from your strong stones and close to your weak ones. *Stay away from thickness*, goes the proverb, *be it your opponent's or your own.*

Evenning Far with Near: When you extend from two positions simultaneously or make two extensions from one position, play a mixture of far and near. This is a different form of evenning strength with weakness.

In Diagram 5, Black makes several near/far balancing errors. Black 5 is a long extension from Black 1. Since Black already has a long extension to Black 3, Black 5 is wrong. It would be better played at Black 7, making a short extension for balance.

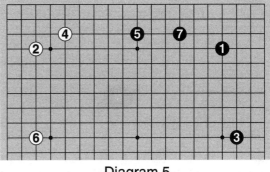

Diagram 5

White 4 and White 6 are well balanced. They could be played in either order, although usually White 4 is played first, because of the solid profit and strength created in the corner. Black 7 is exactly in the middle between Black 1 and Black 5, leaving two weak links. Instead of being exactly the same, it is better to balance by having a strong and a weak link. Black 7 should be one line to the right, making a strong link to the corner and leaving a wider gap to Black 5.

Evenning Influence: In the opening game you need to disperse your forces to equally address the board. If you spend all your moves in one area, you fall behind everywhere else.

Evenning Liberties on Link Endpoints: In defending a link, balance means trying to even up the liberties of the two endpoints, rather than defending so that one end has many liberties and the other few.

In Diagram 6, Black's double-skip link is threatened by White's two stones. While Black *a* and *b* seem equivalent defenses, *a* is better because it evens the liberty counts of Black's two stones.

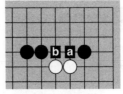

Diagam 6

Emphasizing

Emphasizing (*single-minded focus*) is easy to do consistently. Rarely, however, is extremism its own ultimate reward, so the difficulty is knowing how and when to cash in on an extreme position to even out the attribute mix.

Emphasize Your Advantages: Emphasizing is best in the opening, to create a position utilizable in a specific way. For example, if you are good at fighting, you can emphasize influence over territory in all of your corner encounters. If you are good at endgame, create lots of small positions in the opening. Conversely, if you are bad at endgame, either create the fewest groups you can or try to kill a big group in the midgame. If you are good at tactics, confront the enemy or invade often. Conversely if you are bad at tactics, make sure your position contains few weaknesses and avoid challenging the enemy.

To stand out amongst your competition in business it is important to have an emphasis to distinguish yourself. If areas of innovation, price, and service are important factors, doing moderately well at all of them (evenning) is less likely to get you customers than being best at one of them and weaker on the other two (emphasizing) . People notice the extremism and those who value what you do best will flock to your door.

You must be careful when emphasizing, lest you miss the moment when evenning is important. A company typically needs management, sales, and financial controls. Going all out for sales may seem good at first, but a company lacking sound financial controls and/or management is going to collapse sooner or later.

Coordination

Coordination means using many parts as though they were one. In Go, it means using many moves to achieve one goal. Coordination equals consistency. You cannot coordinate inconsistent moves.

Good moves utilize as many previous moves as possible. Imagine pulling your right arm back to punch someone and then striking with your left arm instead. This is inconsistent. There is no power in your left arm punch, since it travels almost no distance to strike. You moved your right arm back as part of a plan to use it, and then ignored it. Coordination is essential. Failing to follow that plan is inconsistent.

When you review a good game of Go, you will see a series of moves in one area, followed by jumping to some other area or two, followed by a new series of moves. The series of moves all coordinate around some focal issue and stop when that issue has been resolved. The best way to learn from professional games is to review them as follows. Try to define what was at issue in each series. Determine why the player who left the series did so. Was it a trade completed? Did one side lose it? If the move was an interrupt and the fight resumed immediately afterward, why was it done then?

The easiest way to achieve coordination is to make plans and then execute them. If your moves arise independently each turn, any coordination with prior moves is accidental. Coordinated play will lead to a series of moves. You should know what you are trying to do and when it has succeeded or failed. You should have an expectation about who will leave the series first (sente).

Plans arise from two sources, internal (style) and external (tactics). Using who you are and what you are good at, you select a style of play and begin the game. As tactical opportunities arise on the board, additional plans will suggest themselves to take advantage of the moment. I will not discuss plans derived from tactics.

Style

The board begins empty. You can play anywhere. How can you decide where to play? Take a moment to settle yourself. Pick an overall style for the game. *You just make it up!* It can be based on your emotional inclination or your particular skills. It can be tried on just for practice or fun. Don't get locked into only one style. Experiment. Learn what other styles are like. Styles help you keep your moves consistent.

Below are styles available in our software Go program EGO. They are a good starting point for your consideration. You can pretend they are like the astrological signs, predicting your personality.

Earthy: The earthy player goes after territory from the beginning. You prefer third line moves and corner territory. You are a farmer, growing your own food.

Airy: The airy player goes for influence, playing fourth line moves or higher. Your goal is to pick a fight later, when your influence will be useful, or end up with a large side territory because your opponent declines to invade. You are a politician.

Fiery: The fiery player wants a fight now. You hope to mix it up and land a knockout punch in the confusion. You are quick to take offense, always involved in an argument. You are a trial lawyer.

Watery: The watery player plays solidly, avoiding weaknesses. You expect to wear your opponent down by patiently playing the whole game and leaving no chances for tactical mistakes. You put 50% or more of your money in a savings account. Low interest and low risk. You are an accountant.

Leaper: The leaper switches focus rapidly, rarely staying in a series of moves long. This wears out the opponent who is not flexible. You are a child, with a low attention span for boring moments.

Pirate: The pirate thinks the way to victory is to make sure the opponent has no territory. If the opponent has none, then the pirate will win by having some. You are a corporate raider.

Samurai: The samurai plays with a sense of honor and balance. You seek to overcome your opponent by skill, not trickery. You neither seek a fight nor shrink from one. You are methodical and patient, reviewing all your options. You are a Federation starship captain.

Psycho: The psycho player wants to bewilder the opponent. In bridge you make bids not sustained by the cards. You rob banks using a water pistol. You are a magician.

Trying out different styles is a useful learning experience. One person who did this wrote *In a recent game, I resolved to play earthy, not pirate. I stepped back and closed defects, instead of stepping out into the attack. I played more prudently at times when I was uncertain. And, I was still aggressive, and played for territory. My fighting skills were still useful, and I knew what I could do with them when I needed to. I was able to see several times where I was operating from a solid secure footing, and could therefore make bigger moves, because I had healed the defects as I went. The results of the style in this game were increased strength and territory. And, I wasn't able to keep the style the entire game. Several times I found myself moving like I always have. The embodied moves of the past continue to be automatic for me.* This person's normal style in life and in Go is pirate. By taking on a different style in Go, he got to try out an alternative viewpoint in a safe domain with rapid feedback. The point is not that earthy is a stronger style than pirate, it may or may not be. The point is that styles guide play, can be chosen to serve strategic needs, and that consciously trying different styles improves one's overall repertoire.

The Great Wall

My usual styles are airy and psycho. I am good at strategic fighting and hate playing out the endgame. In both airy and psycho I create positions that can lead to strategic fights that will cause the resignation of one side or the other. When my opponent is of equal strength, it is a 50:50 proposition who will resign first. When my opponent is weaker, I play much stronger than my rank suggests.

I am infamous for my *Great Wall Opening*, which appears to be totally psycho. It violates the classic tenets of playing corners before sides and using the center only as an escape area for running. I said "appears to be psycho" because it is not. It is based on understanding Go at a more fundamental level than my opponent.

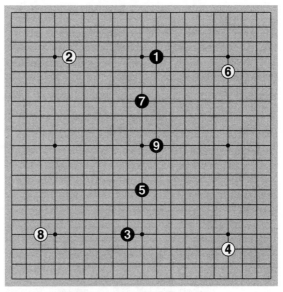

The Great Wall Opening

Conventional opening theory teaches one to utilize two edges to make territory efficiently. Great Wall theory teaches one to utilize all of one's stones efficiently.

Use of the Great Wall Opening immediately unbalances an unknowing opponent psychologically. Because I violate usual play so blatantly, my opponent loses respect for my ability after only a few moves. My opponent loses understanding of the game at the same time — but never realizes it. The Great Wall can be used as Black or White.

A long time ago I used the Great Wall in a best-of-three playoff series to determine who would represent the United States at the World Amateur Championships. In the first match I came out of the opening and midgame with an advantage, but my opponent's superior endgame play won him the game. I knew that if the second game got to the endgame in a similar vein, I would lose. I pulled out the Great Wall. After my first six moves, all strong spectators knew I had lost. My position made no sense to them. At the end of the game, they couldn't understand how I had won. They spent hours trying to find my opponent's mistake in game replays. They never did understand that my opponent had lost quickly. They didn't understand the Great Wall.

I used the Great Wall again while on a US Goodwill Go Team touring Korea. In one game my opponent was a rank stronger than I, but that didn't save him. I won the game by resignation. A partial game record and some commentary on my theory of play are provided below. After the game, a professional player commented on our game.

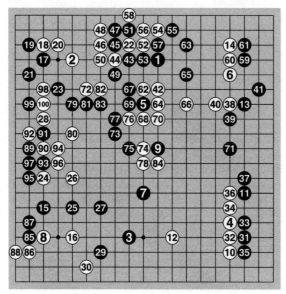

Korean Friendship Game (1-100)

Of Black 1 he said: *I have never seen anything like it.* No surprise there. Whoever plays on the side for their first move? Of Black 3 he said: *At least it's consistent.* That's it!

The whole point of Go is utilizing stones most efficiently, which means coordinating them and being consistent!

The Great Wall allows one to play consistently utilizing *every* single move played. The opponent takes each of the corners, but the moves are all unconnected and don't get used consistently.

The professional concluded that the Great Wall is a legitimate opening, but that it takes much mental effort to make proper use of it. The pro spent most of lunch the next day discussing it on napkins with his fellow pros.

The order of the initial moves of the Great Wall is not critical. Sometimes I just march from one side to the other instead of weaving back and forth.

One of the keys to using the Great Wall is to build a large potential territory on the side, using the wall as a roof. This dictates some unusual corner attacks. Black 11, 13, and 15 stem from trying to control the sides where the wall directs its energy.

Another key is to view your initial side moves as strong, not weak. Welcome an invasion. White 24 is a typical mistake. White is tempted to invade Black's loose sides. This is exactly what I want and allows me to use all my stones in an attack. While trying to save this side invasion, White can lose adjacent corners.

The best counter-strategy to the Great Wall is to reduce the sides by pushing from the corners. Give up side territory, but take no risks and lose no corner territory. This takes patience and vision usually only associated with really strong players. The temptation to panic and invade the huge-but-weak-looking side is almost irresistible.

Black 43 is another key. Instead of directly defending a threatened large knight's link, one should sidestep and attempt to reform the link at a distance. This keeps pressure on everywhere and doesn't directly strengthen the weak opponent stone by responding locally with a contact fight. Black 45 was a sacrifice. Since White's corner was already alive, this sacrifice builds useful strength for Black's weak group and redundant strength for White's strong one.

By turn 100, two of White's four initial corners had become significant Black territory, one was neutralized, and the fourth was subject to severe endgame reduction (the lower left corner reduced to just seven points). White's center group was safe for now, but not completely secure, and White's left side group was currently under attack.

The Great Wall is not something that only I can utilize successfully. Since its presentation many kyu players of different strengths have tried it during some of their tournament games. They also report good results using it.

Center Blocking

When I was developing the Great Wall theory, I played many games using it against a player one rank stronger than I. He came to one conclusion — don't let the wall be completed. He eventually rushed to take the center point before I got there, to disrupt the wall. Even though he was a rank stronger than I, he felt a completed wall was too powerful for him to handle. I have since worked out ways to cope with that preemptive defense.

Diagram Great Wall Block is such an example. As soon as Black has declared a Great Wall strategy, White tries to stop Black by taking the center point with White 4. White figures Black will now be stopped from playing the wall. Black 5, however, continues as though White 4 weren't there. If White replies per usual to the contact fight created,

Black happily plays out the contact fight in its most aggressive form, cutting with Black 7. By cutting, Black is able to again involve all Black stones in the fight. White 8 is needed to protect White 4, which is in danger of being ataried and driven toward the rest of Black's stones. When Black extends with 9, White must now protect White 6 with 10.

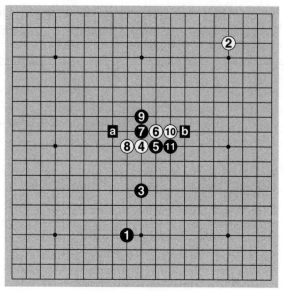

Great Wall Block

At the end of this figure Black has two ways to proceed, *a* and *b*. Either will allow Black to fight advantageously. The game will now be played out with a massive central battle, which will eventually seep down to the sides and over into the corners in defiance of the traditional order of play. White's inclination will be to prevent *b*, since it is such a locally great move for Black. However, Black at *a* allows Black to push White into the Great Wall.

The Great Wall is hard to refute, but it also takes a lot of thinking to make use of it. If you apply the thinking involved in making the Great Wall work effectively, you may not need the Great Wall. You will play good Go with any opening configuration.

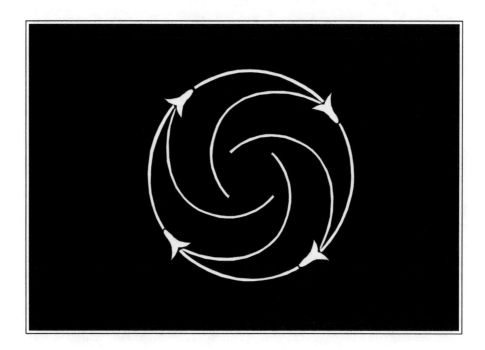

Winds of Change

Have you ever seen a log rolling contest? Two men stand on a long cut tree floating in the water. They run in place on the tree, starting it spinning. The goal is to make the opponent lose balance and fall off. Spin it too fast, and both fall off.

Have you ever used a hang glider? You carry wings above you, jump off a cliff, and coast through the air. Catch a rising wind (thermal updraft) and you gain altitude. Climb too rapidly at the wrong angle and you stall. Beware of wind shears and downdrafts. They may dash you into the ground.

At issue in these analogies are the existence of forces of motion set into play initially under one's control. Knowing when and how to stop or change the force, or when it will stop or change without your control is essential. The key is *anticipation*.

To anticipate sudden change you need a mental model of how things will normally progress, and the forces acting on it that might cause it to change. In Go, sudden change results from either tactical surprise (you didn't see that your opponent could do that) or the application of sente and gote. I can't help you with tactical surprise, but I can teach you about sente and gote.

Sente & Gote

Sente (sen-tay) is the initiative, the starting of a new sequence of play, literally *the leading hand*. *Gote* (go-tay) is having to respond, being last, literally *the trailing hand*. Strong Go players strive to control the immediate future by maintaining sente. A move is sente if it requires an answer by the opponent. It keeps the initiative. Gote refers to playing last in a situation. Whoever has sente sets the agenda for the next encounter and gains the most from the local situation initiated. Naturally one would like to have sente and avoid gote.

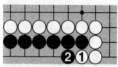

Diagram 1

In Diagram 1, White 1 is defended by Black 2 and then White plays elsewhere. White 1 was "sente" and Black 2 was "gote", but did it have to be this way? No. Sente and gote are relative and depend upon the size of moves and threats available on the entire board. If you threaten to kill a group worth ten points, your move may seem like sente. But if your opponent finds a move threatening to kill a group of yours worth twenty points, your move is not sente, because you will respond to your opponent's move instead of continuing with your threat.

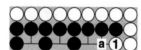

Diagram 2

In Diagram 2, the same White 1 is played as in Diagram 1. But in Diagram 2 clearly Black already has two eyes for the Black group, so responding at *a* is optional. It is only worth one point for Black to defend there and it will be gote if Black does so since White will not have to respond to Black. Black should play at *a* only in the last stages of the endgame, when no other moves are bigger than one point in gote.

Bear in mind that sente and gote depend not upon the value of the move, but upon the value of its follow-up. In Diagrams 1 or 2, the value of White 1 is only one point. Whether or not White 1 is sente depends on what will happen to Black if Black fails to respond. Since sente moves are "free", it does not matter whether they are big or small in terms of immediate profit. Gote moves, on the other hand, are not free. You must get significant value from your gote moves. Otherwise you might as well just pass.

To have or keep sente you must anticipate what is happening. When will the current sequence end? Whose turn will it be? To weaker players the answers to these questions might as well be sought in Delphic prophecy, but to stronger players the answers are usually known well in advance. They know rules about who deserves to end in sente or gote in different classes of situations.

If you deserve to end in sente but end in gote, how much will that cost you? What does it matter? The answer is that losing sente unnecessarily costs about six points in the final score. Considering that in professional games the winning margin is often less than five points, you can see that a slip in keeping sente can spell instant defeat to a pro. Another way to think of it is that sente twice wasted is like passing. If Black loses sente six times, Black has lost three handicap stones.

Sente/Gote Rules

Here are some rules of thumb in Go to help you know what to expect. Many of them revolve around the same theme involving weak groups.

Attack in Sente: The expectation is that when you attack, your opponent will defend, and then you will make some other value from your attack using your sente. If you attack, your opponent defends, and then you have to defend yourself from your opponent's defense, you lose sente and accomplish nothing for your attack.

Diagram 3 comes from a game between reasonably strong dan players. But White paid no attention to the rule of attacking in sente. White 30 and 32 were OK, because Black's weak group running out of the lower right corner was still inside of White's sector-line (shown). White 34-40 were wrong, because White ended the sequence with a defensive move at 40, and Black was no longer under attack.

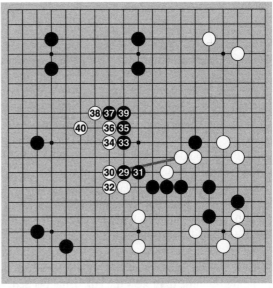

Diagram 3

The fault was White 34. The remaining White moves were needed to stabilize the contact fight that White started with 34. White should have stopped attacking after Black 33 and taken sente. White 34 attacks with contact in violation of rules in *4.3.2.1.Contact*. The result was a loss of sente.

Live in Gote, Die in Sente: In the normal course of events, once a group is alive, the attacker has no reason to continue attacking it and should take sente. Likewise if a group is dead, for the defender to add another stone to it that doesn't threaten to make it live again is as bad as or worse than passing. This rule gets violated whenever players lack the tactics to realize they are already alive or dead, or get so caught up in the local play that they forget to get sente and play elsewhere as soon as possible.

As the defender, be extremely careful that your move at least threatens to maintain life. Dying in gote is horrible! Seek out your attacker's weak points. Try to end up with sente (don't expect to succeed). As the attacker you must be cautious not to play too aggressively. It is easy to become overextended playing to kill, and this frequently results in the group gaining life in sente, as you go back and fix a weakness created during your overenthusiasm.

Invasions Lose Sente, Light Reductions Keep It: This is merely an extension of "living in gote." When you invade you get a weak group that falls under attack. The attack ends when you get life, so you live in gote. Light reduction (see *Fools Rush In*), on the other hand, threatens to destroy a potential territory but stays outside of the sector-line. When the owner defends it, the reduction stones are usually already safe from attack, hence the reducer has sente to do something else.

3-3 Invasions Keep Sente: This is an important violation of **invasions lose sente**. Because groups invading here get immediate territory, they live unusually easily. This makes 3-3 invasions a high priority in the early midgame.

Diagram 4 is a stereotypical example of a 3-3 invasion. Black doesn't want White to escape containment when White invades, so Black is forced to keep playing whenever White moves. Black would like to take sente after White 11, but Black must defend the cutting point or a White cut endangers Black's stones. After White cuts, if Black sacrifices a stone, White is out, contrary to Black's wishes. But if Black tries to save a stone after White cuts, Black must crawl on the second line, which is also bad. So Black must defend the cut now.

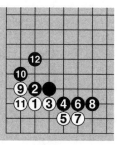

Diagram 4

Peep in Sente: When played correctly, a peep requires a defending response to protect the link being peeped. After that, the originator should be free to play elsewhere. Threats to cut and the resulting defensive connections rarely have any global impact. They are strictly local moves. They are played for their local implications, and only if sente can be kept in the process.

In Diagram 5a, Black 1 peeps White, who defends with 2. The problem for Black is that now Black's stone is still weak in a contact fight and needs further defense and no matter how Black moves, White will still be contact stable. The usual follow-up move is for Black to play at *a*, but White will play *b* and Black's marked stones then need defense.

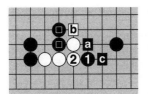

Diagram 5a

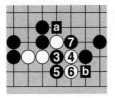

Diagram 5c

Trying the unusual c instead of a doesn't help. Black loses sente either way. Black should either not peep or find a way to peep while retaining sente.

Diagram 5b shows a better peep for Black, one that keeps sente.

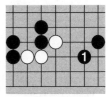

Diagram 5b

If White ignores Black's peep, Black 3 cuts as in Diagram 5c. By the end of the sequence, Black can capture by playing at a or b, so White is dead.

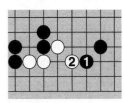

Diagram 5d

If White defends with 2 as in Diagram 5d, Black has no need to defend further, so Black gets sente.

Beware of the 2 Inch Rule: Weaker Go players almost invariably play within a small distance from the opponent's last move. Even if they don't need to directly respond to the opponent's last move, the weaker player feels the need to add some stone in the area to balance out the extra weight of a newly placed enemy stone. If you don't need to respond directly to an opponent's move, be sure to look over the board as a whole and not become fixated on a small area by viewing the opponent's move through tunnel vision.

Good Gote, Bad Sente

When players only understand why sente is valuable, they lust after sente and often try to avoid all gote moves. Not only is this impossible, it often leads to disaster. Not all sente is good and not all gote is bad. These terms fail to take into account the future impact of a move. A gote move that implies a powerful follow-up is quite different from a gote move that is a dead end. A sente play that leaves many weaknesses is not worth playing.

In Diagram 6a, Black has played Black 1 in sente. Black's goal was to secure the corner. Unfortunately Black still has a weakness at a. Worse, Black has converted White's position into a wall with a perfect extension. This was bad sente. It leaves weakness.

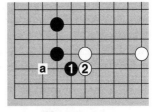

Diagram 6a

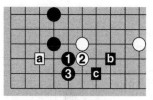

Diagram 6b

In Diagram 6b, Black protects against the weakness at *a* by accepting gote with Black 3. At least now Black can aim to invade at *b* or *c*. However White is stronger than initially, and Black's corner still looks somewhat loose.

Black's best choice is Black 1 in Diagram 6c. This move is gote, but secures the corner completely. It has follow-ups to *a*, *b*, and *c*, and White is no stronger than White was before. This is good gote because it solves Black's problems and has excellent follow-ups.

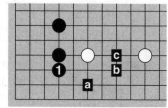

Diagram 6c

If White decides the danger from those follow-ups is too great, White may defend. If White does, Black will get sente, since nothing White can do will require a Black defense. Black will be happy with sente.

Big Points Make Good Gote: In the opening the gote occupation of a big point is of fundamental importance. Big points are not sente but are almost as valuable, being gote plus large future impact.

Defend Now, Attack Later: One is often tempted to ignore one's own weakness to attack. This is usually a bad idea, whether the weakness is a strategic weakness or a tactical one. The exception is when a tactical attack is launched for the purpose of defending a weakness. Just make sure it succeeds!

Faced with White's attachment at 1 in Diagram 7a, Black made a reasonable contact

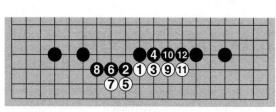

Diagram 7a

response with Black 2. When White played 3, Black was left with a cutting weakness to 2, which Black ignored. Black thinks White is being pressured, and by the end of the sequence Black sees a thick Black wall and is pleased with it. How little Black knows.

First, Black's wall has been built in gote (White is already alive). White can play to neutralize the wall. Second, Black's wall faces toward the center. Would you be surprised to find living White groups hidden just above Black's wall along the edges? The wall is probably already useless. Black has given away most of Black's territory for a solid but useless wall; White has sente and both players are pleased. Poor Black.

Black got into trouble by attacking before defending. Had Black thought that attacking would kill White and thus that the defect would never need defense, that would have been acceptable strategy but erroneous tactics (since White cannot be killed). But Black didn't think that.

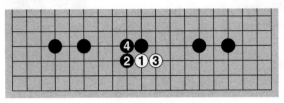

Diagram 7b

The correct Black move for 4 was to solidly connect as in Diagram 7b. Now Black has no more weakness and can attack White without worry. Black loses less territory because Black keeps the territory to the left of Black 2. White does not yet have any territory so it is still weak, and Black has wasted no stones building a wall facing worthlessly upward. As the diagram stands, White seems to need to play here further to survive, so Black should be able to get sente.

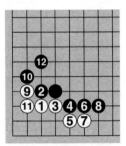

Diagram 4

If you are really sharp, you will notice a discrepancy between the advice of defending now (e.g., defending defects now), and the joseki play of the earlier Diagram 4, where Black 6 and 8 do not defend the defect directly. Even if you did not notice this discrepancy, notice it now and think about why it exists.

The difference is that if Black connected with Black 6 as in Diagram 8, White could escape containment. Once you have someone enclosed, you don't want to let them out. Since White 1 invaded into an enclosed space, Black should keep White enclosed. Hence Black 6 and 8, which defend the defect indirectly and keep White enclosed.

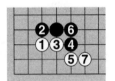

Diagram 8

Run First, Attack Second: This is another instance of **Defend now, Attack Later**. If you counterattack someone before you escape the sector-line, you run the risk of becoming enclosed during the fight. Worse, because you initiated the fight, you may feel committed to your attacking stones and neglect to stop attacking and make life when you do get enclosed.

Sacrifice to Gain Sente: If you have to defend two or more things at once, not only will you probably do a bad job with one of them, but you will surely lose sente. If you choose to sacrifice one of them, you gain sente after your opponent accepts your sacrifice and spends moves capturing it. (See *Sacrificial Lamb*.)

"May you achieve your goals"

This is one ancient Chinese curse that is unlikely to worry Go programmers. Getting a Go program to the strength of a dan player is still a distant goal. Beating a Taiwanese professional and hence winning the Ing prize of over a million dollars is even more remote. Achieving either of these goals would be worthy of a Nobel prize in computer science.

Don't hold your breath. It's been twenty-five years since the first programs were written. The best today's programs can accomplish is maybe 8-kyu. That's not bad against a human beginner, but after a few years of serious play a dedicated human will surpass any Go program.

"But there are Grand Master-level Chess programs" you say. "Why aren't there dan-level Go programs?" As Chess is to tic-tac-toe, Go is to Chess. It is a mistake to lump Chess and Go together as games of equal complexity. Although the information processing capabilities of the human brain make it look like an equally 'easy' task to learn Chess or Go, these are different animals when it comes to programming.

Bill Robertie in *Inside Backgammon* (Vol. 2, No. 1, Jan-Feb, 1992) compared the complexity of various games by dividing the players of each game into classes such that in each class a player has about a 75% chance of beating a player of the next lower class. This is a way of measuring how many ranks of skill there are in a game. Here are his results:

Go	40	Backgammon	8
Chess	14	Checkers	8
Scrabble	10	Hearts	5
Poker	10	Blackjack	2

Notice how far Go is above Chess. Some people think a 9x9 game of Go is comparable to a game of Chess. Imagine fitting six 8x8 chess boards on a 19x19 Go board and then playing those interacting Chess games simultaneously!

Chess programs look ahead millions of moves each turn. This allows a program to see ahead all combinations of moves for seven to nine moves deep in the search tree. (The latest Chess machine, Deep Blue, computes a hundred million moves each second! And while it won one game, it lost its match against Grandmaster Kasperov.) Most humans lose track of where the pieces are after that many moves and will make a tactical mistake. Also, Chess is primarily a tactical game. Evaluating who is winning is usually a matter of counting up who has more of which pieces. In the top Chess programs, the sum of all positional values is often worth no more than a pawn and a half.

In Go, there are too many choices to consider and no easy way to evaluate the results. A game of Go lasts about three times as many moves as a Chess game. Looking ahead millions of moves only goes three to four moves deep in the search tree.

Nothing useful has happened. Also, Go is a positional game and no position can be evaluated easily. You must spend a lot of effort to determine whether stones are alive, dead, or capturable.

Bruce's History in Computer Go

I began programming Go in 1972. I had been working as an Artificial Intelligence researcher for Prof. Walter Reitman at the University of Michigan's Mental Health Research Institute. Prof. Reitman was an amateur Go player who felt Go would be a good thing to computerize as a model of how humans think. At that time the best Go programs were written as Ph.D. theses by Al Zobrist or Jon Ryder. Their performance was terrible; they would lose to humans who had just been taught the rules of Go.

I did not know Go, so I learned the game specifically for this project. This resulted in a situation unique in all the millennia of prior Go play. Normally people learned Go for the fun of it, to play. As they got better, they internalized and forgot consciously what they learned. It became reflex. I learned Go to program it. I knew that everything I learned needed to be programmed, so I kept in touch with what I was learning. This lead to my creating a new Go perception to support analysis, the sector-line, as well as a new human theory of Go play called "Instant Go", from which this book eventually descends.

The goal of Reitman's project was to create a good Go program, written in LISP, on an IBM mainframe. After seven years I had written a program that could play around 18-kyu, able to give nine stones to beginning players and still win. This was a significant first. In 1979 the project

ended. Playing cost over $2,000 a game and, given the costs and risks of failure attempting to build a 12 kyu program over the next three-year grant period, I recommended we stop. (In fact, 12-kyu programs did not appear for over a decade later.) I went on to other things.

In the early 1980's, however, IBM shipped its first 16-bit PC. I could now buy a computer for the cost of one of our previous games! This was the first microcomputer that I felt had a reasonable chance of powering a Go program, so I began work on a home version, called NEMESIS. It was released in 1984, the first program ever to play in a human Go tournament. In 1986 it was the first commercial Go program in Japan.

Current Computer Go

The existence of NEMESIS and the published Instant Go articles had predictable side effects. Others who had previously thought programming Go was impossible were shown otherwise, so they began their own programs. Japanese pride had been wounded by having a foreign Go program being best in their software market, so when the Japanese launched their Fifth Generation Initiative, a 10-year project to leap ahead of the US in Artificial Intelligence technology, they included millions of dollars in funding for a Go program of their own. (This program didn't succeed in taking the lead.)

The existence of computer Go programs paved the way for the Ing Wei-chi Foundation to sponsor an annual tournament with serious prize money attached. They chose this as a vehicle to promote their own version of the rules of Go. Every year in November roughly 16 programs compete against each other to determine the victor. The winner receives nearly $10,000 and a chance to play against strong humans in a challenge match worth additional money. At the low end (taking a 17-stone handicap from a strong amateur) the prizes are only a few thousand dollars. At the high end, if a program can defeat a professional player in an even game in a best of seven series, the prize is over a million dollars.

Annual no-money tournaments are held each summer in Europe and the US in conjunction with their Go Congresses, and in 1995 the Japanese launched a monied ($20,000+) tournament called the Fost Cup. In the past, most programs have played using human operators to place the computer's move on the board and to enter the opponent's move from the board. (Many Faces of Go and NEMESIS support a standard called the Go Modem Protocol and so generally played their games directly via serial connection between machines.) In 1995, however, the Fost Cup required all programs to play via serial cable using the Go Modem Protocol, so the major world programs now support this standard.

An informal Computer Go Ladder exists to foster ongoing Internet competition and practice. *http://cgl.ucsf.edu/go/ladder.html*

Computer Go programs exist on a variety of machines, including IBM PC, Macintosh, and UNIX, but since the PC is the most common machine, I will mention only programs that are commercially available for the PC and that are 8-kyu to 12-kyu in strength.

The 1995 world champion is **HandTalk** (by ZhiXing Chen). **Many Faces of Go** (by David Fotland) was the second strongest program, which has a mature interface with many features. **Ego** (by Bruce) has the distinction of having multiple styles of play. **Goliath** (by Mark Boon) used to be the world leader but has been invisible for several years and is presumed to be planning a major resurrection at any moment. **Star of Poland** (by Janusz Kraszek) is not easy to find. **Go4++** (by Michael Reiss) is due out shortly (presumably under a different name).

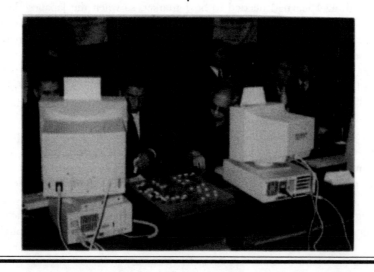

Sacrificial Lamb

In movies and TV shows the central character always goes back into an impossibly dangerous situation to save the life of some comrade. And in the movies they always survive. This may be courage, but its not sacrifice: the heroes don't expect to get killed. In real life most of the time heroes would be blown to bits, burned to a crisp, filled full of bullets, or crushed under an entire building — and so would the victims they went in to save. Sacrifice is the abandonment of a hopeless cause or the desperate ploy of a suicide bomber or a gecko losing its tail in order to survive. It's not a nice thing — going out to knowingly get killed or being abandoned. No wonder Go players are so reluctant to sacrifice any of their stones.

You will be strongly tempted to struggle to save every last stone of yours, heedless of cost or risk. But you can tell a strong player from a weak one by seeing how readily the player sacrifices stones. Sacrifice means deciding to abandon something early and making use of its death to accomplish some other purpose. Some of the most unexpectedly brilliant tactical plays come about when you suddenly conclude you are doomed and cast about for something else to accomplish. Be ready at any moment to sacrifice what you are for what you could become.

Perhaps we should change the paradigm. Sacrifice means to lose something. It's all very well to exhort you to learn a Buddhist sense of non-attachment so you can give things up, but it's an alien way of thinking for most. So instead let's teach you the American sense of semi-attachment called trading. You give up something to get something else. Learn to be a Yankee trader. Your goal is to give a little and gain a lot.

If you are psychologically prepared to give, you can easily outplay an opponent who is not. This goes right to the heart of American materialism. When we go after something, we expect to get it and then keep it. If someone tries to take it away from us, we will resist automatically. But this puts us at two severe disadvantages.

First, when our opponent attacks anything of ours, our opponent knows we will resist. And in resisting, we must lose ground because initially our focus is on keeping what we have by making concessions. And if concessions don't work, then and only then we fight, on terms defined by the attacker. Western Europe kept making concessions to Hitler to avoid war. Hitler knew this was in their character and so he kept pressing.

Second, when we go after something, our opponent knows our focus is limited to that goal. A flexible opponent may use judo on us. The opponent uses our own momentum against us or gives us what we seek while taking something of greater value during our distraction. Hence the title *Sacrificial Lamb*. When attacked, think of ways to trade your way out of trouble by making a sacrifice, as well as of ways to resist. Be flexible.

Q: What can you trade?

A: Among the things you can trade away are stones, groups, territory, and influence.

Q: What can you afford to trade?

A: Anything you have already lost, anything that has no future strategic value, and anything that is obviously worth less than what you are trading for.

Q: When should you seek a trade?

A: As soon as you realize you are going to lose something, any time the opponent plays an endgame move against you, any time the opponent cuts or threatens to cut off some stones of yours, any time you have a heavily outnumbered weak group, and any time you are trying to defend multiple things simultaneously.

Q: What can you get for your trade?

A: The sky's the limit. Stones, groups, territory, safety, and control. There are so many ways to sacrifice or trade that I can't possibly teach you all the patterns. All I can do is show you the flavor and idea. Learn how to look and when to look.

Trade Stones for Security

Trading away stones is the easiest. You're probably going to play a hundred and twenty-five of them in a game, so giving away a few isn't that expensive. There are two kinds of stones you can trade; ones you have already played and ones you have yet to play.

Stones you have already played are the easiest to sacrifice. You can see them now. They are particularly easy to sacrifice if you have realized you can't save them. Even if you can save them, whenever you have two things that need defending at the same time, you should immediately consider sacrificing one of them.

Fatten the Lamb: When you have a stone or stones that are already doomed, often if you add an extra stone or two you can significantly prolong the life of the sacrifice, giving you extra outside moves. Look to see if adding a stone gives you at least two more liberties than you have now and see if the move threatens to revive your stones. You need two more liberties because your opponent can fill one of them next turn, and you want to end up harder to kill.

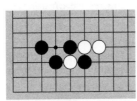

Diagram 1a

In Diagram 1a, White's single stone is doomed, but the correct way for White to play is to fatten the sacrifice.

In Diagram 1b, White adds a stone to die. Black 2 is a clever trick to leave behind a weakness in White's position, but it is only a minor irritation. White 3, 5, and 7 threaten to revive White's stones, and the result is some useful White influence.

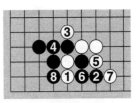

Diagram 1b

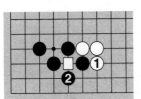

Diagram 1c

The influence of Diagram 1b can be contrasted with that of Diagram 1c, where White fails to fatten the lamb first. White's influence in Diagram 1c is much less.

Create the Lamb: Stones you haven't played are harder to trade away. You have to find a useful place to put a stone you know is going to die. You need a good mastery of tactics for this. The most common place to throw away a stone is inside the opponent's existing territory. Since the territory is there already, it's just a question of a few points more or less. A few more points for your opponent is well worth a change in strategic safety value for you.

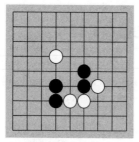

Diagram 2a

Diagram 2a shows Black with a link that needs defending. White also has a link, but Black has read out that if Black cuts White, the cutting stone will just be captured. That doesn't mean that Black shouldn't cut.

In Diagram 2b Black cuts anyway with Black 1, and even extends with Black 3. These are both sacrificial lambs. White cannot try to cut Black's original stones apart. If White

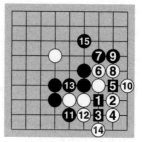

Diagram 2b

does try to cut, White will instead be captured. White must react now to kill Black's cutting stones. Black 5 is yet another lamb for the slaughter and the sequence through White 14 is entirely forcing upon White. Black has protected the original weak link, and with Black 15, has built an impregnable fortress engulfing White's lone stone. The cost? Almost nothing! In Diagram 2a, White had a sketch of eleven points. In Diagram 2b, White has completely secured ten points, and has an option to pick off Black 11 in gote for three more points. This was on a 9x9 board but Black's thickness would be equally impressive on a 19x19 board and White's lone stone almost worthless.

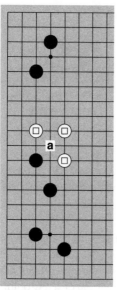

Diagram 3a

Consider Diagram 3a, where White has three stones in serious danger since they lack eyes and are threatened with a double peep. Black is strong all around, so planning to attack Black would be foolish. White should just be concerned with becoming stronger quickly.

White looks for nearby Black links to sacrifice onto. White's solution is to sacrifice into Black's existing territory, as shown in Diagram 3b. White builds an eye and solves the threat of the double peep, while retaining sente. All for a few extra points given to Black. This would be a bad thing to do if Black were also weak, since it would have strengthened Black enormously. But Black is already strong, so further strength is merely redundant.

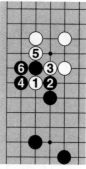

Diagram 3b

Trade Stones for Insecurity

Stones can also be sacrificed to keep your opponent from achieving security.

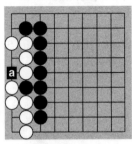

In Diagram 4, if Black plays at *a*, it can be captured. But sacrificing a stone here means White can only get a false eye in this area, so White's group will die. Sacrifices on connection points to destroy eyes are called *pitch moves*.

Diagram 4

Trade Links for Links

When you create a link, you imagine your stones are connected and usually can't bear the thought of them becoming separated. Usually they can be. If your opponent tries to cut you apart, remember that to attack you, your opponent probably also has nearby links. Rather than futilely resisting being cut, see what you can do to your opponent in exchange. Instead of focusing on saving your connection, focus on giving up a stone of your link, and either damaging opponent links in return, or rebuilding a wall around the stone your opponent captures. (Also see the chapter *Buy Wholesale, Sell Retail*).

There is a proverb "single skips are never wrong". They build excellent shape and though the connections aren't guaranteed, they sacrifice well.

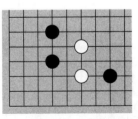

Diagram 5a

Diagram 5a shows a White group with a link that Black *could* attack. Black shouldn't.

Diagram 5b shows why. Black succeeds in cutting off and capturing a White stone, but loses a Black link and stone in the process. Black 9 was essential if Black was to keep the cutting stones, but with White 10 Black lost a corner that was much bigger than what Black got.

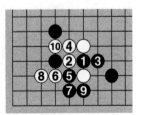

Diagram 5b

Consider the Black line of single skips in Diagram 6a. (Ignore the fact that it is strategically useless.) Black might be concerned that it can be cut. But would White try? What would White hope to accomplish? At best White can hope to cut off a single Black stone, but White is already safe on both sides.

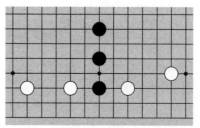

Diagram 6a

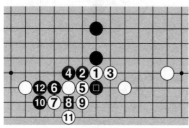

Diagram 6b

If White tries to cut with 1 in Diagram 6b, Black can force with 2 and White must defend with 3. Black then decides to sacrifice the marked Black stone and plays 4. White must cut with 5 (taking the offer). Black 6 threatens to cut White apart or kill stones, so White 7 is forced. Black then sacrifices with 8, forcing 9. After Black 10, if White captures with 11, Black connects with 12. Black is much better off than White.

But wait you say. White might play 11 differently. If White cuts with 11 instead (Diagram 6c), Black captures with 12. White must now cut with 13, and Black 14 makes it a huge ko. If White loses this ko, it's a disaster. If Black loses this ko, Black really only lost the original stone that Black chose to sacrifice.

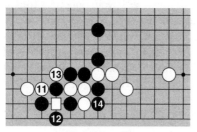

Diagram 6c

If Black doesn't like the ko, Black can offer up a different sacrifice of the other endpoint as shown in Diagram 6d. This time Black connects at 4 on the bottom and White must cut on the top with 5. Black 6 threatens to kill White along the edge, and White 7 defends. Black 8-12 threaten to kill White 5 again. After this, Black is that much stronger and White has gained little. Will White now try to cut above 10? Not on your life, even if it works!

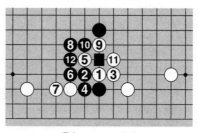

Diagram 6d

The thing to notice is that the person who makes the sacrifice gains a lot of control over the opponent, who is trying to steal something in the first place. Resist, sacrifice this, sacrifice that, these are all options for the "defender".

Trade Links For Influence

Trade Single Skips: Diagram 7a shows a Black single skip attacked by White. This is a perfect opportunity to sacrifice to build influence.

Diagram 7a

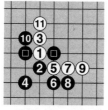

Diagram 7b

In Diagram 7b, Black threatens to rejoin with 2 and protects one side with 4. White 5 completes the cut, and now Black begins a sacrifice technique. Black 6, 8, and 10 all force White to swallow the cutoff stone. At the end of this diagram, Black has an influential wall and sente. Black had control. Depending on where Black needed the influence of the wall to radiate, Black could have built this formation in any of 4 directions, by changing 2 and 4.

If White does not respond to Black 8 or 10, Diagram 7c will result. Black 10 and 12 are absolute sente and build a wall in a third direction. White is being compressed into a tight ball of stones with no value. Black 14 threatens to turn around White again, so expect White to respond.

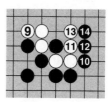

Diagram 7c

Trade Small Knight's: Diagram 8a shows an attack on a small knight's move. This is another opportunity for a sacrifice.

Diagram 8a

Diagram 8b shows Black sacrificing a single stone. While Black has built a wall, Black generally needs to go back to defend the connection with Black 12, so loses sente. Also, Black has no choice about where to build the wall. Single skips give the defender the choice as to where the wall will form. Small-knight's links give the attacker the choice.

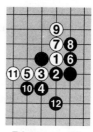

Diagram 8b

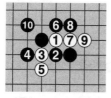

Diagram 8c

Choosing to sacrifice Black's two stones as shown in Diagram 8c is much less common because it doubles the number of stones lost. It always loses sente.

If you can foresee that you will have to sacrifice one endpoint, then you should try the sacrifice of Diagram 8d. Black, knowing that the marked stone is doomed, threatens to connect to it with Black 2. After White 3, Black can continue with *a* or *b*, depending on Black's assessment of the situation. Playing *a* has the risk of being cut to its left (being cut on the right doesn't bother Black, who was planning to sacrifice the marked stone anyway).

Diagram 8d

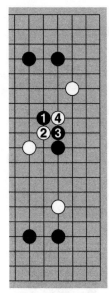

In Diagram 9a, White 2 tries to cut Black apart. If Black can do any reading, Black will see that after White cuts, there is no obvious sequence to capture the cutting stones and rejoin Black's two strings. They will have to fight separately. This can be done, but since two things need defending, the first thing that should come to mind is can Black sacrifice one of them? If Black realizes this soon enough, Black won't respond with Black 3.

Instead Black will decide to sacrifice the side handicap stone immediately, as shown in Diagram 9b. Each Black move except Black 9 threatens to reconnect, so White's moves are forced. After Black 9, White will be worried about a cut at *a* and Black has *b* & *c* to defend the main cluster of stones. Black has sacrificed a stone, but it looks like White also has a stone nearly dead. Black's sacrifice has given Black security regardless of whether White can save White's isolated stone or not.

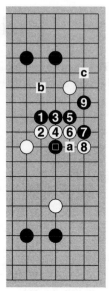

Diagram 9a   **Diagram 9b**

Trade Territory for Territory

The usual trade is some of your territory for some of your opponent's. Trading territories is a typical endgame maneuver (see *Quibbling*). "Don't answer in the endgame" is a reflex of the strong player, but the only way to avoid answering is to find an equivalent move against the opponent's territory and offer to trade damage for damage.

Sometimes trading territories is done repeatedly on a big scale and results in much of the board changing ownership but not affecting the score particularly. Games like this are spectacular to watch.

Trade Influence for Control

The purpose of a big sphere of influence is not the territory. It is, by the sheer size of the influence, to force your opponent to invade it. You then sacrifice most of your influence in exchange for smaller profits (about 1/3 of your influence) and control. You attack and attack the invader for turn after turn, making bits of profit here and there and generally controlling all play. (See *Fools Rush In*).

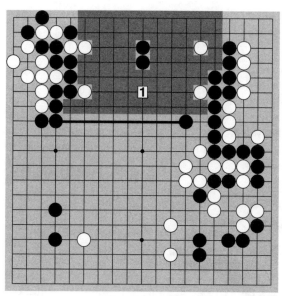

Diagram 10a

In Diagram 10a, Black has a large potential territory of about 68 points. White at 1 would aim to reduce this area. What should Black do if White plays at 1? White's move is deep inside Black's sector-line, making it an invasion.

In Diagram 10b, Black wants to make influence into territory. Black ends up with roughly 30 points. This is not trading. This is Black keeping what Black can.

The way to handle an invasion is to attack and trade away much of the potential for some territory and lots of control.

In Diagram 10c, Black trades potential for control of the game by attacking White. It is an amazing struggle, but true to form White manages to live. While White was actually killable, Black lacked the skill to do it.

So what? Black ends up with 30 points of territory anyway, sente, and outside thickness. The game is almost 40 moves closer to being done and Black hasn't lost any ground.

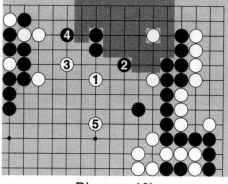

Diagram 10b

In a handicap game, control is an important benefit. Potential territories are built to provide control, not territory. Control prevents the opponent from having time for mischief.

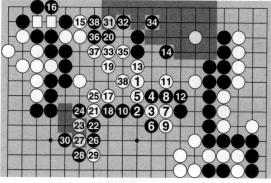

Diagram 10c

Trade Stability for Chaos

If you are losing significantly toward the end of the midgame, you do not want to play out the endgame. If you do, you will merely confirm your loss. On such occasions you need your opponent to make a mistake, and the best way to help that along is to induce confusion. Do that by destabilizing your groups, and tempting your opponent into attacks. You may lose by more, but you are already losing and it's your best chance to recover. To destabilize your groups, just answer some incidental threat abnormally, or don't answer it at all and take sente.

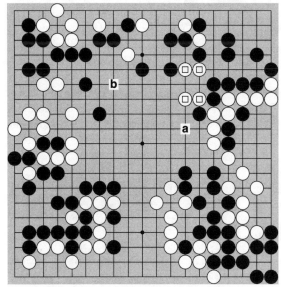

Diagram 11a

In Diagram 11a, White is losing by at least 10 points, and it is White's turn to play. All groups on the board are secure or dead, except for White's marked stones. The sensible move for White is at *a*. This saves the marked stones. Unfortunately, this also means that the endgame begins, and it is Black's turn to play.

Instead of starting the endgame, White should play at *b*. This is clearly a "foolish" move, inside Black's sector-lines and leaving the marked stones weak. This is a 6-stone handicap game, however, and White at *b* creates an opportunity for confusion.

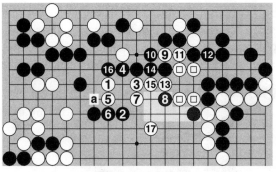

Diagram 11b

Diagram 11b shows the resulting confusion. Black begins an attack with 2, but gets confused along the way. The result is that White not only saves the marked stones, but also acquires the White shaded area as probable territory. Black now has a defect near *a* that may become a problem. Black loses this game by 10 points.

Curios

The Road Less Traveled
Go Sharping
Variations on a Theme

Fantasy Liars' Dice

*" Let everything be allowed to do
what it naturally does,
so that its nature will be satisfied. "*

The Road Less Travelled

*I*t was a deeply shaded road at that difficult time of evening when it's hard to judge distances or be sure just what is coming toward you. Why can't other drivers turn their headlights on so I can see them coming? I wish I knew what was around the next bend. These hills are so unpredictable at night. Suddenly, with a roar, a truck appeared out of nowhere. I had to swerve right over to the shoulder, but on this strange road I didn't know a ditch was there. It was over seemingly before it had begun. I was hanging upside down in my upended vehicle — what had happened? If you've been wiped out in a vicious ko fight, you know the feeling.

Some roads are avoided because of their potholes or traffic. Others are avoided for their roundabout route. Still more are avoided because of dangerous rock slides, flooding, ice, wild animals, etc. Those same roads avoided by many are sought out by a few just because they are off the beaten track, are more scenic, provide a shortcut, or have a dash of dangerous spice. The stronger Go player travels the roads of ko and seki confident of abilities to navigate and survive. Beginners avoid the ko road because it drives them crazy and makes them feel stupid, forgetful, silly, and utterly confused. They usually have the seki road chosen for them and this leaves them infuriated or frustrated.

Ko

For a game with such simple rules, it is remarkable how intricate Go can become. Ko was initially described in *The Dinosaur's Hind Brain* as a rule preventing board repetition. Ko is much more than that, however. It is a way of life in hard times and a major opportunity for unexpected gain. A ko is a fight over a false eye. Usually ko is also a fight to sustain a cut, where loss of the ko stone implies the opponent rejoining stones.

Perceiving Ko

Setting Up a Ko: Ko revolves around the capture of a single stone whose sole liberty is a false eye. The liberty isn't an eye because it is not bounded by a single string, but it has the eyeish property that it must be filled last. Diagram 1 shows the ko shapes for corner, side, and center. In each shape, Black has one or more single stones touching what looks to be an eye. With eyes control of the diagonals is critical. With ko it doesn't matter. It doesn't even matter if a stone is in atari. After all, when the opponent captures, it will be ko.

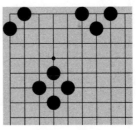

Diagram 1

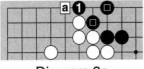

Diagram 2a

Diagram 2a is a classic ko danger during the endgame. Black has just played Black 1, creating the false eye shape in conjunction with the two marked stones. White's normal response is to play at *a*, blocking Black and placing it in atari. But because of the ko shape, Black doesn't care about being placed in atari.

Assuming Black will win the ko later by connecting on the false eye point, the board really looks like Diagram 2b. In Diagram 2b, White would never consider playing *a*, knowing that Black would cut and capture the blocking move. So White would back down to *b* or *c* and reform the doorway farther away.

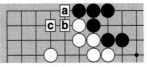

Diagram 2b

The protection offered in a ko by an eye shape is only offered to single stone-strings. If more than one stone is captured, then there can be, at most, one subsequent immediate recapture, and so no series of infinite captures (ko) are possible.

In Diagram 3a, White has responded to Black 1 by falling back with White 2. Black keeps going with Black 3, creating a two-stone string bounding the eye shape. Now White can safely block with White 4.

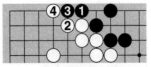

Diagram 3a

If Black dares to cut with 5, as in Diagram 3b, White will capture two stones with 6. Black can recapture one stone, after which White cannot immediately recapture, so the ko ends, Black's cut at 5 was futile, since White's capture of two stones will provide alternate connectivity for White's stones.

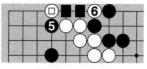

Diagram 3b

Seeing ko when the shape is complete and ready is one thing. What the advanced player does is see the ko shape *before* it is created.

Warning! Ko coming: Watch out for hanging connections (an almost eye). In Diagram 4a, White has just defended with the hanging connection instead of the solid connection. Why? White is aiming for a ko Black might miss. Assume Black plays elsewhere with 2, believing that there is no danger.

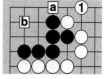

Diagram 4a

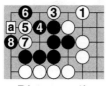

Diagram 4b

The simple-minded follow-up play for White would be to play at *a* in Diagram 4a (3 in Diagram 4b). Black would just back down and live with 4 as shown in Diagram 4b. After Black backs down with 4, White tries to drain life with 5, which threatens to connect back out to 3. Black 6 stops this. White 7 threatens to connect out the other side, which Black 8 stops. Because Black was clever in how White was stopped, White must now play at *a* to stop Black from splitting the territory into two eyes. If White does, Black is alive, but only in seki (discussed later in this chapter).

The tricky play from Diagram 4a is for White to move at *b* (1 of Diagram 4c). This move is an invasion that looks like it is not near a doorway. Wrong. The potential for ko on a doorway means *b* might connect out through that door. That is how tricky White players kill weak Black ones. The real ko is several moves away, coming at a time when it will do the most damage to Black. But the potential ko is visible now.

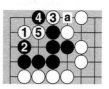

Diagram 4c

In Diagram 4c, White has played 1 in the center of Black's territory. Since Black is not aware of the impending ko, Black plays 2 from the wrong side. White 3 threatens to save White 1, so Black 4 is forced. White 5 then cuts, and a ko over *a* begins.

Black's doorway is wide open until the ko shape of White 1 in Diagram 4a is neutralized. Black could play at *a* or *b*. Playing b makes Black easily alive. Playing a is also possible if your tactics are excellent.

In Diagram 4d, Black 1 (*a* of Diagram 4a) solves the problem of ko over the doorway, so Black can now refute White's attempt to kill with 2. After White 8, Black is alive in seki.

Diagram 4d

Diagram 5a is another ko trap, this time not immediately on the edge, though the edge is still involved. When White plays 1, Black wants to play atari at *a*, but see the marked stones? They form the hanging connection. Ko danger lies here.

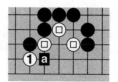

Diagram 5a

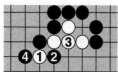

Diagram 5b

If Black plays 2 in Diagram 5b, Black is expecting White to save a stone with 3, allowing Black to capture a stone with 4. Black is in for a surprise. White won't connect with 3.

Diagram 5c

White will challenge ko as in Diagram 5c. Once again, the hanging connection shape warns you of ko potential. If the cut of Black 2 were not atari, Black would never have played it. Given the ko potential, Black still shouldn't.

By now it should be easy to see ko coming in Diagram 6. White has the hanging connection. If Black calls atari with *a*, White responds, challenging ko with *b*.

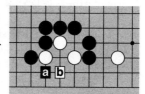

Diagram 6

Playing Ko

Don't Play Ko Against a Stronger Player: White can evaluate ko threats much better than Black. If you play ko as Black, you will surely lose, either by winning the ko and discovering White's threat was bigger, or by losing the ko. Usually you lose the ko *and* never get to carry out your threat.

There Are No Threats in the Opening: In the opening the game has the flexibility of youth and injuries are easily healed or pieces easily sacrificed. Later, positions become rigid and damage becomes more permanent. Opening game ko threats can be mitigated by subsequent sacrificial play. Winning the ko, on the other hand, generally gives profit, makes a position unassailable and leaves nearby opponent's positions weak. Playing ko in the opening is unreasonable. Creating ko usually means the creator's opponent gets to capture the ko first, requiring the creator find the first threat. Since there are no threats in the opening, the creator will lose the ko. Therefore, don't create a ko. If your opponent challenges you to one, don't even look at the ko threat. Win the ko immediately.

The classic example is from the handicap pattern shown in Diagram 7a, where Black is playing all out to kill White. This is only reasonable if Black knows that success is assured (i.e., Black knows all sequences stemming from this situation). White has options to back down up until White 15 is played. White assumes Black does not know enough and that Black will either back down shortly or mess up, If Black continues correctly, White's survival hinges on ko. And what do we know? Ko in the opening is bad!

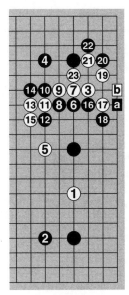

Diagram 7a

White 19 is a hanging connection, so Black must be wary about trying to atari at *a*. White can answer with ko at *b*. Not wanting to provoke that ko, Black plays 20 as shown. White 21 is another hanging connection, so after Black 22 plays atari, White 23 threatens a ko Black can't avoid. Now what? Black has many cutting points, most revolving around the ko against White 21.

If Black loses this ko, White lives in the corner and Black's side will be in trouble. Black must know this pattern to dare begin it at 10. The odds are Black doesn't know it all.

Black, having memorized this pattern, plays 24 in Diagram 7b and awaits White's ko challenge. White cuts with 25 and Black takes the ko first with 26. Black is now threatening to capture four White stones. If White makes a ko threat, Black must ignore it and capture. This will give Black a huge local profit, secure the corner and side for all time, give Black sente, and leave White's side position weak. It is almost inconceivable that any White ko threat elsewhere can have as much impact. If Black has to lose ten to twenty points elsewhere, so what? This area is worth more than that already. This is generally true of all ko fights happening early in the game. For your reference, I've never played any Black player at a handicap who knew all the right moves.

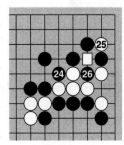

Diagram 7b

Use Local Threats First: Once you are in a ko, you need ko threats. There are two kinds of threats: distant threats and local threats. Distant threats imply damage to other positions. Local threats imply that if you win the threat, you no longer care about the ko because you have solved the problem a different way. Use local threats first.

In Diagram 8, Black is in a ko over *a*. If White wins the ko by connecting at *a*, Black will be dead because removing the three White stones leaves a shape that White can play back into and kill Black's group. If Black plays *a* (capturing the unmarked White stone) and then wins the ko by capturing White's marked stone, Black will have captured two White stones and have two eyes.

Assume White has just captured the ko. Black should not play elsewhere on the board — Black should play *b*. Why? The problem is judging the size of ko threats. If Black plays elsewhere, Black is trying to outjudge White. If Black plays *b*, Black takes no risk. It is a guaranteed ko threat. If White connects the ko, Black merely escapes containment.

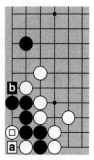

Diagram 8

Local ko threats are guaranteed in value, distant ones require judgment. Not only is there no need to test your judgment, there is no need to waste ko threats. If Black were alive in Diagram 8, *b* would never be a ko threat. It is only a threat in conjunction with the task of living in this corner.

Maximize Before Winning: If you know you are going to win the ko, try to expand the value of winning.

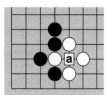

Diagram 9a

In Diagram 9a, White can end the ko by connecting stones at *a*. If White has many more threats than Black, White can widen the ko by playing as in Diagram 9b. Black must back down with 2 because Black cannot win the ko, and then must protect with Black 4. White wins the ko, gains much more, and keeps sente.

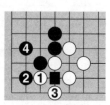

Diagram 9b

Take Ko Last in a Death Race: In a race to capture, you should take the ko last. That way, your opponent must then find a ko threat. If you take it first, at the end of the race your opponent will capture the ko and you will be stuck finding the first threat.

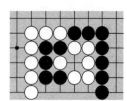

Diagram 10a

In Diagram 10a, Black appears to be behind one liberty in the death race. However, Black can get another liberty by capturing a single White stone.

If Black does this first, then Diagram 10b results. Just before dying, White retakes the ko with 4 and Black must find the first threat.

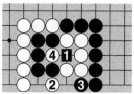

Diagram 10b

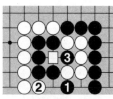

Diagram 10c

If Black waits to take the ko last, as in Diagram 10c, it will be White who has to seek the first threat. Making your opponent find the first threat is important for two reasons. First, it increases the odds that your opponent runs out of threats before you do. Second, whoever makes a threat takes the risk of misjudging the size of that threat. You don't want to take that risk if you don't have to.

Types of Ko

Ko's come in various flavors, depending upon how likely you are to win the ko and how many moves it takes.

Double Ko: A double ko involves two ko's around the same string. Normally this would be unimportant because one of the ko's could be filled in and then the other. When a liberty race is involved, however, double ko can become important. With a double ko, the defender never has to find a threat and so automatically survives. On the other hand, the attacker has an infinite source of ko threats to use in any other ko fight. The attacker just has to take back one of the two ko's during the third ko.

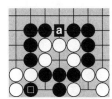

Diagram 11a

In Diagram 11a, there is a race to capture in progress. Both Black and White have big strings with two liberties. If it is Black's turn to play, Black will win by playing at *a*. The problem arises if it is White's turn. White must capture the marked ko stone to atari Black.

If White plays 1 as in Diagram 11b, Black conveniently captures with 2, relieving the atari. White cannot recapture, so White must find a ko threat.

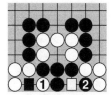

Diagram 11b

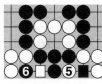

Diagram 11c

If White finds a ko threat and Black responds, then White can recapture with 5. This is of no value because Black can recapture the other ko with 6. White can never win this battle, so Black survives. During the endgame Black will have to capture White's five-stone string before trying to fill in either of the two ko's.

Multistep Ko: A multistep ko is one where you have to ignore more than one enemy ko threat to win. If you ignore ko threats, your opponent makes profit on the rest of the board to compensate for the loss of the ko.

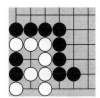

Diagram 12a

In Diagram 12a, White can live just by capturing the two Black stones. It is much harder for Black to kill White.

In Diagram 12b, after Black takes the ko with 1, White can only play 2 elsewhere as a ko threat. If Black wants to win this fight, Black must ignore the threat and pursue the attack with 3. Now White is in atari, and a direct ko develops. Whoever wins this ko now will win the fight.

Diagram 12b

Actually, Black could connect to the left of 1 and lose four stones as another way to play instead of 3. This would result in a ko again, where White has to make the first threat. Remember, however, White has made one move elsewhere already, so White will have been compensated with two plays elsewhere if Black wants to win the ko this way.

It is hard for the player who must make the extra moves to win a multistep ko. The more ko threats that must be ignored, the harder it is to win. Still, it's better than nothing as a way to kill.

Multistage Ko: In a multistage ko, winning the ko leads merely to another ko. Like a multistep ko, a multistage ko takes several moves to win. However, it is not as unbalanced as the multistep ko. After winning a stage, it is easier to win the rest of the ko. The balance of who is likely to win shifts with each stage won.

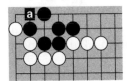

Diagram 13a

In Diagram 13a, Black can live easily by playing at *a*. If White wants to kill, White will have to play *a* directly and fight a killing ko.

In Diagram 13b, White played at 1 and Black captured it with 2. This is now a ko. If Black wins, Black lives instantly.

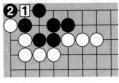

Diagram 13b

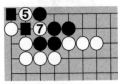

Diagram 13c

What happens if White wins? In Diagram 13c, White made a ko threat with 3 and Black responded with 4 (these are elsewhere). White then retook the ko with 5 and Black made a ko threat elsewhere with 6. White ignored this threat and won the ko by capturing at 7. Now it's a new ko to keep 7 alive. White can win this in one move. Black, however, cannot win this in one move anymore. If Black captures 7, all Black can do is play ko to try to regain the ko of Diagram 13b. The fighting can swing back and forth, with only Black at risk.

10,000-Year Ko: The 10,000-Year Ko is so named because no one wants to start it. Normally it becomes seki.

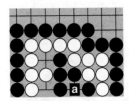

Diagram 14a

In Diagram 14a, if Black connects at *a* the result is seki. Black would much rather kill White than settle for seki.

To kill White, however, Black must play 1 as in Diagram 14b. Black 1 fills in a shared liberty, so that White can now capture the ko and put

Diagram 14b

Black in atari. Black will have to find the first threat and risks losing stones. Black will wait to launch this ko because right now Black is in no danger. Maybe Black will wait forever and decide to simply connect it instead.

Multiple-stone Repeating Ko: A multiple-stone ko does not repeat itself quickly, like a regular ko. Instead the capture moves that repeat take place over several turns.

In Diagram 15a, Black and White are stuck together. Black cannot fill at *a*, so the only thing to do is to attack with 1.

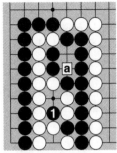

Diagram 15a

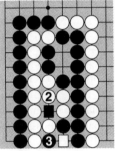

Diagram 15b

A careless White player will capture Black with 2 in Diagram 15b. Black then takes the ko with 3, and White is in atari.

White must play 2 of Diagram 15c. Now each can capture two stones. The balance of power remains unchanged. If they do this dance again, the board repeats itself and the multi-stone ko will have come full circle. Some rules make this illegal. Others declare the game aborted. It rarely happens.

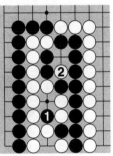

Diagram 15c

Keep Focus

Whenever you are in a ko fight, the first thing to remember is why you are there. It is easy to get sucked into playing the ko for its own sake. In Diagram 16, Black was taking a high handicap and got into a ko fight on the bottom, seeking to kill White.

When White took the ko with 1, Black bemoaned the fact that she couldn't read ahead far enough to make sense of the fight. Black wanted to evaluate ko threats on various parts of the board and could not. This misses the point.

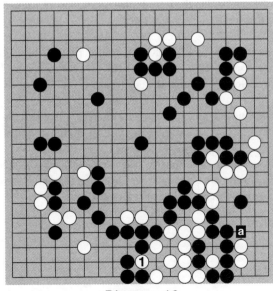

Diagram 16

Black got into this ko fight by attempting to kill White. Black thought this would be an easy way to get life for Black's enclosed lower right corner. Well, it got less easy.

Now that White 1 is played, Black must remember why Black started this fight. I asked Black, *If you knew you would lose the ko fight, what would you do?* Black knew she would play at *a*. So I said, play that as your ko threat. If White wins the ko, Black can easily live and the game goes on. But, if Black tries to make a ko threat elsewhere and White ignores it, the first thing that Black will think of is to follow through on the ko threat. White will then kill Black's lower right corner. Tricky problem for Black, judging the size of ko threats. Black will probably lose out.

Seki

Seki means stalemate. In a seki the only way to attack the opponent is to expose oneself to being killed. Since neither player will do this willingly, a stalemate or seki results.

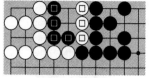

Diagram 17

In Diagram 17, neither player can play on either liberty of the marked stones without also making it possible for the opponent to kill stones. The result is seki. The shared liberties belong to neither player and are not counted in the final score.

Seki happens maybe once every twenty games or so. Whether you want to curse or shout with joy when a seki happens depends upon what the alternatives were. If you were trying to kill off an intruder into your territory, you will be upset that the intruder lives. If you were afraid of dying, you will be relieved that both of you live.

Atari Seki: A seki involving a shared pair of liberties are rare enough. Imagine a seki where several stones of both sides are already in atari! This must be inconceivable to most Go players, nonetheless, it is technically possible.

These next diagrams show how mysteriously weird Go is. They are intended as curios. Don't fret over them, they are unlikely to happen in a game you play.

Diagram 18a is a massive seki. Neither Black nor White dares play in the area, though there are nine marked stones in atari. To prove this, we must consider each case.

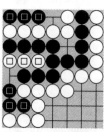

Diagram 18a

White Cannot Attack: To attack from inside, White must first capture three Black stones with 1 of Diagram 18b. Black will play 2 to prevent two eyes and then White can play atari at 3. This forces Black to capture three stones with 4 and White to play 5 to prevent two eyes. Now both sides have exactly two unshared liberties and whoever plays first will win by sacrificing a series of stones until the enemy falls into atari. Black moves first, so White dies.

Diagram 18b

If White tries to attack from outside with 1 as in Diagram 18c, White captures three Black stones but changes White's three stones in atari to four.

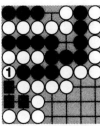

Diagram 18c

Black will naturally capture them with 2 in Diagram 18d. White plays a liberty with 3, but Black has liberties to spare. Black ataris White with 4. White captures three Black stones with 5. Now it's three liberties to three, with Black to play first (at *a*). White is doomed.

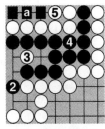

Diagram 18d

Black Cannot Attack: Black must begin by capturing three stones with 1 as in Diagram 18e to which White naturally responds with 2.

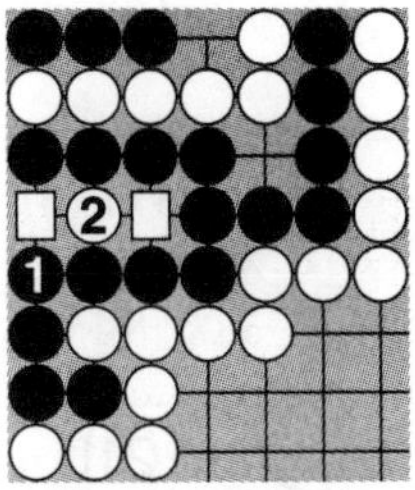

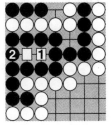

Diagram 18e

If Black then ataris White with 3 in Diagram 18f, White will capture Black's three stones with 4. The best Black can do next is play 5 to stop two eyes, but it is too late for Black. Each side has two liberties, and it is White's turn to play. Forget that. Suppose Black captures three White stones and stops? What happens if Black doesn't play 3 to atari White?

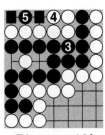

Diagram 18f

White will play inside Black with 1 in Diagram 18g. If you work it out you will find Black has to respond by capturing. Black cannot ignore White.

White sacrifices again in Diagram 18h. Now, when White captures three stones, White wins the race, four liberties to two.

Diagram 18g

Ko and seki are strange phenomena. They add a unique flavoring to an already unique game.

Diagram 18h

Hazards of the Corner

While ko and seki can happen anywhere on the board, they are most prevalent in the corners, where two edges cause all sorts of strange behavior. While there are countless corner positions one could try to memorize or read out, there is a general rule which warns you about the most common dangerous ones.

Less Than Ten, Play Again: When you have only a small amount of territory, it only takes a few opponent moves to contest it. The big danger arises when the territory is all in a single clump of empty points, with or without singleton territory points attached to the clump (bumps). If the opponent plays in the center of the clump, then all those potential eye points become contested.

Diagram 19 is an example of an eight-point corner where the six unmarked shaded points form a single clump, and the seventh and eighth points, bumps marked *a*, touch the clump. Black must play another move here.

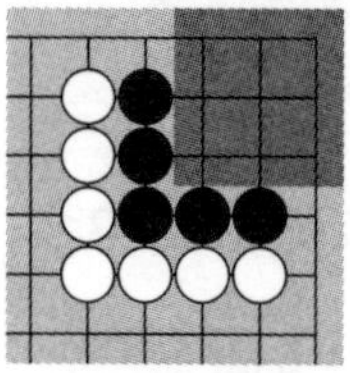

Diagram 19

Diagram 20 seems to be a big corner, but it is only nine points and they are all in a single clump. If White plays in the center of that clump, the result will be ko. This particular configuration is called the carpenter's square, and if you understand it completely likely you are of professional strength.

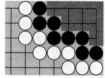

Diagram 20

Diagram 21 is an eight-point corner consisting of a clump of six points and two bumps attached to the clump. If White attacks correctly, the result will be seki. This is shown in Diagram 21b.

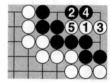

Diagram 21b

Diagram 21a

In all of these cases, the defender could be completely alive by merely placing a stone in some central location.

Go Sharping

Hit me, *I said. The dealer to my left flipped a card from the deck, which spun through the air and landed face up on my stack of cards. A two. Sitting on top of my three, four, and five, and the unexposed hole card. The dealer had 19 showing. The game is Twenty-One. Now was the critical moment.* How much should I bet? *I wondered.*

Go is a lot like that card game. At each turn you need to ask yourself:

> 1. **What do you need?**
> 2. **What do you deserve?**
> 3. **Did you mark the deck?**

The first question is answered by a global score computation to discover who is winning by how much and what the major issues are. The second question requires determining what constitutes an equitable result for both players in an area. Despite your desire to gain an advantage, you must recognize that Go is a game of sharing — you can't (usually) get it all. The third question is a reminder that you may have to try a cheat and hope your opponent doesn't catch you at it. Your opponent is not perfect. By taking account of what you know about your opponent, you may be able to shave a few more points than you deserve. Particularly if you are White in a handicap game.

What do you Need ?

A game in progress includes many local situations, each often having several choices of reasonable (and unreasonable) moves. To play good Go, you must choose a good move locally and a good locale globally.

Sometimes moves are chosen based on the global status of the game. If you are clearly winning the game, there is no reason to play too aggressively. If you are losing, you cannot afford to play conservatively. A knowledge of "how much is needed" will help you to choose both the locale of play and the type of move in that locale.

Nothing could be more disconcerting to a weak kyu player than to have some strong dan player say around move twenty that the weak player is losing the game. The kyu player is left open-mouthed. "How did the dan player do that?" It is impossible to count the final score then. The strong player has neither prescient vision nor a simple magic formula. Instead the strong player has a collection of evaluation shortcuts.

Shortcut 1 - Recognizing Bad Shape: One of the simplest evaluation techniques involves looking at the shapes of stones. Creating a bad shape when it was unnecessary is a local deficit. It is much too small a cost to use in most cases, but it is an indicator. Look for empty triangles and clumps.

Diagram 1a comes from a nine-stone handicap game. White can expect to be behind this early in the game, so what White wants to know is whether or not White is making good progress. White has made only one empty triangle (can you find it). Since it is part of an eye shape it does useful work and is not that bad. Black also has only one empty triangle (next to *a*), but it serves no eye purpose and is just inefficient. This is a minor gain for White. The real gain comes from two Black clumps. *b* participates in one of them. Before White peeped, Black must have had an empty triangle there, which has been

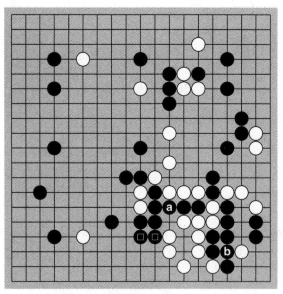

Diagram 1a

converted into a clump for Black and a weak stone for White. Again, this is only a small loss for Black. Black's big loss comes from the other clump. The two marked stones could be removed with no loss in functionality. Black has lost over two handicap stones so far, assuming all remaining stones for both sides were useful. This is certainly a good assumption about White's stones. It is optimistic for Black's.

For reference, Diagram 1b shows how Black achieved the loss. Black was attacking White. When White played 25, undercutting Black's corner, Black defended with the empty triangle of 26 instead of jumping one closer to the edge. That was the first mistake. White 27 then made good shape and undercut Black on the other side. Black ignored this and ran with 28. It developed partial shape for Black, but White rushed to ruin it with 29. Black should have pushed at 29 before running. This would have built most of a good cream puff shape that couldn't be ruined in sente. After White occupied the crucial point, Black defended six stones with 30, an empty triangle. Once

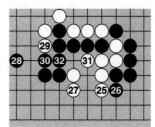

Diagram 1b

White played 29, bad shape was inevitable for Black. Unfortunately, Black should have played the solid connection at 30. When Black played 30, White played 31, threatening a snapback. White's empty triangle was useful (sealing an eye) while Black's next empty-triangle connection (32) was useless.

Shortcut 2 - Sente Wasted is Half a Stone Lost: This says that a player who wastes sente on an unnecessary small play has lost half a move. It is useful for measuring progress as White in a handicap game, where Black wastes sente frequently and scoring says White is behind.

In Diagram 2, Black 26 secured the corner and made life. Black 28, however, was an unnecessary gote move. The corner was already alive. White's group already couldn't make eyes on the side. Black's upper side group didn't need defense yet. So Black 28, while not equivalent to passing, because it does make points and adds security, was equivalent to half a pass (or half a handicap stone lost).

Shortcut 3 - Fast Scoring: Knowing the score can tell you whether to secure what you have or invade your opponent's claims, to nibble in sente or gulp in gote. That kind of knowledge is essential for long-range planning. Many

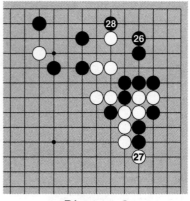

Diagram 2

players dislike counting score because it takes more work than just going ahead and playing a move. Professionals maintain some reliable count to guide their play. I recommend occasionally using a fast method that gives a rough assessment of who's winning. Your goal is solely to detect gross differences. The various mistakes I make during a game make more precise counting almost meaningless until the very end. So what I count is enclosed and potential territory. All I want to know is "If both get what they are currently claiming, who will win?" If the difference is within ten points then I treat it as a "close game".

Step 1: Draw the maximum link boundaries that will completely enclose empty points or dead stones. This is "enclosed territory" and is shown in Diagram 3a.

When I count an area, I don't count points one by one. Instead I find some convenient multiple (usually 3's) to make a rough count. Thus in the lower left corner I count Black's territory as four 3's. Counting Black's upper right corner there are eight 3's. Black thus has 11. White's left board half has nine 3's.

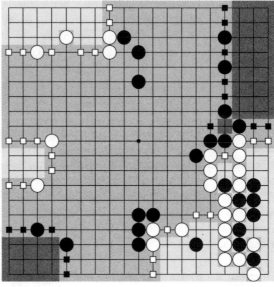

Diagram 3a

White's lower right corner has thirteen or fourteen 3's. This is a rough count, remember? White has around twenty-two 3's. I could multiply this out to 66, but I don't need to. The difference between Black and White is about nine 3's. White clearly has more territory.

Step 2: Draw the maximum sector-line boundaries and links from "pockets" of potential territory. These pockets are formed by links, stones, the edge, and a sector-line (the opening of the pocket). Diagram 3b does this.

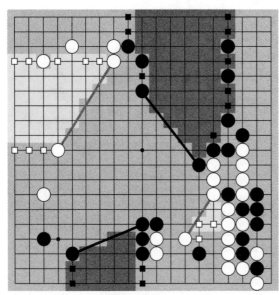

Diagram 3b

The counts for potential territory should include any link boundaries touching territory since they will no longer need to be secured. Black has about twenty-one 3's of potential (five on the bottom and sixteen on the top). White has about twelve 3's. Black has nine more than White.

Step 3: Total the differences. Black has nine more potential, but White has nine more actual, so the total difference is 0. By count, the game is close.

Fudge Factors: After I count score, I see what else might intrude to confuse the issue. Factors such as influence, group security, and territory security must be considered. For example, it is better to have actual territory than an equal amount of potential. If one side has many more stones facing the unclaimed center, that influence can be assumed to create new territory in the future. If one side has a weak group, that group is a liability that will cost something in the future. If both sides have weak groups, who knows what will happen? If one side's enclosed territory has large weak boundaries, it will be reduced much more in the endgame.

If any of the four measures (count, influence, group security, territory security) favors one player and none of the remaining measures favors the opponent, then I have a "winner" and play accordingly. Otherwise the score is ambiguous. This ambiguity can be the source of strategic planning. If you are ahead on territory but have a weak group, play to secure your group. Get rid of the ambiguity. If the measures are not ambiguous and you are behind, find one of the measures that you can change to pull ahead on. It doesn't matter which one.

If the conflict between measures later disappears, I will check the score again.

In Diagram 3b, since White is ahead on actual territory, I would prefer to be White. However, Black is ahead on stones that influence the center, so maybe I should prefer to be Black. Black's actual territory might be invaded in the upper right, whereas White's territory cannot. Maybe I would prefer White. Neither player has a weak group that needs to be saved (Black has some dead stones, but they don't matter). Obviously, the score is ambiguous. At present, since the total count is the same, but Black can acquire more territory from Black's influence, I think Black is winning, but to achieve that win, Black will have to work on using Black's influence immediately. Black does not need to take risks by invading White's potential territory. P.S., I was Black and won.

What do you Deserve?

Go is a game of sharing and cooperation. You can't just "have it all". So you need to know how much to try for.

Six Points Per Move

Each of the stones you place in the opening should be worth six points of enclosed territory.

Example 1: When Black goes first in an even game, Black is considered to have an advantage. To compensate for this, White is given initial points, called komi. In standard Japanese tournaments komi is 5.5 points. The half point insures there will be no tie games.

Example 2: A common structure seen in the opening is a corner enclosure. After occupying a corner with one move, a player frequently returns to add a second stone before placing a stone farther out along the side. The corner enclosure provides a source of profit, a safe base from which to extend, and strong influence over adjacent sides. Diagram 4 shows a corner enclosure containing twelve points of territory (six points per stone).

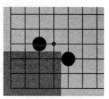
Diagram 4

Example 3: Diagram 5a shows another corner enclosure. This one contains fifteen points of territory. Doesn't it violate the six point rule? Not really. Unlike Example 2, this corner is not yet safe from invasion. White can invade at the three-three point and live with ko.

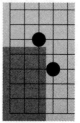
Diagram 5a

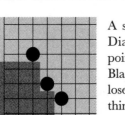
Diagram 5b

A structure safe from invasion is shown in Diagram 5b. Three stones secure eighteen points. Note that this structure is only secure if Black is a strong player. Weak players may still lose this corner to an invasion. It is this sort of thing that leads weak players to conclude that a weak player's move is worth three points, and a strong player's move is worth nine points.

In the above examples there is no reason to have the six-point rule since you can see the territory taken immediately. The rule is not normally applied to enclosed territory, since it is too late by then. The rule is used to evaluate potential territories and help you decide what to do with them.

Example 4: In Diagram 6a, Black has built a quadrant formation, extending the corner enclosure on two sides and then raising those sides into the center. It looks impressive, but what is it really worth? Will Black really get the sixty-nine

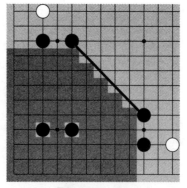
Diagram 6a

points claimed? Should White lightly reduce this or invade? These are important questions that the six-point rule addresses.

First, the nominal value of this formation is thirty-six points (six stones times six points). This implies that whatever White does, White needs to destroy almost half of it. Put that another way. Black should expect to lose almost half of it. Black shouldn't panic as that happens and think Black is being ripped off. That will just ruin Black's play.

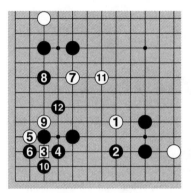

Diagram 6b

Diagram 6b is a sample reduction. Seriously invading is just too risky, so White's goal is light reduction. White 1 is inside Black's sector line, so it is an invasion, but Black will be reluctant to allow White to follow up at 2, isolating Black while simultaneously threatening to connect out to a White stone along the edge. Black therefore protects with 2. White 3 and 5 are a suicide invasion. They expect to die, but they will leave behind an aftertaste that will keep Black's attention on them later. White 7 for Black 8 is the next real reduction exchange, after which White continues the suicide group with 9. White 11 then runs away with White's main forces and Black 12 kills off the suiciders. Why do those suiciders exist? White really wants to have played a light reduction instead of an invasion. A key difference between the two is who gets sente. A light reduction ends with the attacker having sente. By creating the suicide squad, White has insured sente.

Diagram 6c shows a follow-up sequence. White 1 threatens to break into the lower side, so Black 2 defends. White 3 and Black 4 are obvious (Black doesn't want White's dead stone to escape). The resulting territory is forty-one points for Black, and four for White. This is thirty-seven points advantage for Black, which is almost exactly the six-points times the original six Black stones.

A Caveat: Big moves are moves made in isolation.

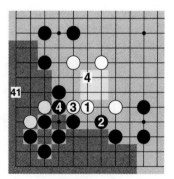

Diagram 6c

Diagram 7

In Diagram 7, White has exchanged White 1 for Black 2. This does not mean that Black now has three big moves around the corner making it worth eighteen points. It is still only worth twelve points.

Summary of par expectations: Here is a brief summary of rules about expectation, both from this chapter and from others:

1. **A big move is worth six territory points.**
2. **Invasions lose sente. Light reductions keep it.**
3. **Weak groups cost points.**
4. **Thickness is its own value**.
5. **Live in gote, die in sente.**
6. **Your opponent will get a third of his potential territory.**

Did you Mark the Deck?

Playing the player instead of the game is a Western habit supposedly much decried in the Orient. You should be honorable and only play the honest move. Nonetheless, you may just want to know some of the ways the deck can be rigged against you. You may enjoy trying these tips out in your next struggle with a stronger player and know some of the things the stronger player will be using against you. White has the psychological advantage because White is supposedly the stronger player. Even in equal games the effect persists. This is just a trick. Remember that White is the one with something to prove and that as Black you are ahead on the board because you play first. If you have handicap stones you are even further ahead.

Giving a Handicap (Being White)

1. **Don't Play the Standard Move:** Destroy whatever memorized patterns the weaker player has.

Diagram 8 is a common handicap opening against a side handicap stone. Too common. Black may have memorized some ways to handle it. If you play 5 at *a* or *b* instead, that will surely shake Black up.

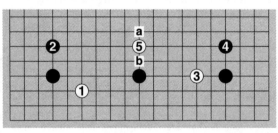

Diagram 8

2. **Attack Indirectly:** Play at an unthreatening distance from Black's weak group. The puzzlingly nebulous move is a White speciality. It seems to do nothing, but in fact is preparing for an attack by either securing a weakness of White's or building thickness from which to attack or enclosing Black within White's sector lines.

In Diagram 9, White plays 1, which is far enough from Black's stones to lull Black into a false sense of security. Had White 1 been played at *a*, any Black player would recognize it as an attack. White 1 as played is more subtle. White may slide all the way to *b*, which Black probably doesn't expect. Also, Black is not likely to notice Black's group is actually within White's newly formed sector-line. It all seems so vague and far away.

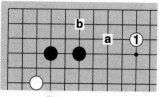

Diagram 9

3. **Make a Fake Invasion:** Black will spend extra worry moves protecting from a nonexistent threat. This kind of invasion is useful when you know that Black is capable of killing you but not of reading it out in advance. This will also generate a number of useful ko threats for later. Of course if Black protects wrongly, you may yet succeed with your invasion.

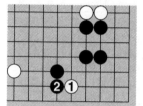

Diagram 10a

In Diagram 10a, White cannot invade and live in Black's corner, yet White plays 1 anyway. After Black blocks with 2, White plays elsewhere. This is going to prey on Black's mind forever after, and eventually Black will probably play another move in gote inside to make sure nothing goes wrong.

White welcomes this. White cannot expect to live. In Diagram 10b, White tries with 3 and 5, but Black has obvious responses and there is no room to live. Nor can White win a race to capture by trying to push and cut. Black's stones will force their way out and escape, and White will be left dead.

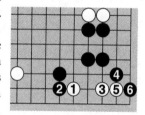

Diagram 10b

4. **Nod Sagely:** This will confuse Black about the value of Black's moves. Black looks up to you as a teacher, so will desperately want your praise. Nod sagely when Black falls into your trap so Black will think everything is OK. Nod sagely when Black sees through your trap and protects perfectly, as if you thought Black would do no less. Nod sagely after making a stupid meaningless move. It'll worry Black to death trying to puzzle out what it means. Just as Zen masters might whack their pupils across the back of the head with a stick periodically for no apparent reason, you can use your teacher status to the fullest.

5. **Create a Huge Potential Territory Quickly:** The psychological effect of looking like you own a huge potential is very useful. Black will get desperate quickly and play something foolish or Black will be so afraid to invade that Black will grant you the entire thing.

In Diagram 11, White is playing a low handicap game. With 5, White begins a bluff. If Black isn't tempted to invade immediately, White will follow up with *a* to make the potential even bigger. It looks impressive, and that's the point. Against a strong player, this potential is made of Swiss cheese, but Black won't realize this.

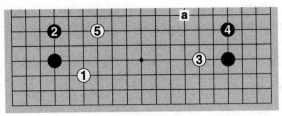

Diagram 11

6. **If it's Black, Enclose it:** No matter how weak the enclosure is, Black will either fail to get out or pay too much to get out.

In Diagram 12, Black 2 is a good move, preventing White 1 from getting easy life. Still, White can contain Black's corner rapidly, and Black will not know what to do.

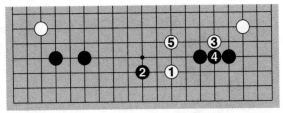

Diagram 12

7. **Play Contact to Attack:** You have superior fighting skills and can expect to get a better result out of any fight. Properly handled, a contact fight can become incredibly confusing and White stands to benefit from Black's confusion.

In Diagram 13, White wastes no time in attaching to Black and crosscutting. Instant confusion. What is White up to? How good are Black's tactics?

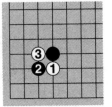

Diagram 13

8. **If *You* have to Read it, You're Safe:** If it isn't obvious to you, Black will never make the right choices because Black can't read it out. Therefore you will succeed.

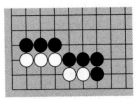

Diagram 14a

In Diagram 14a, White reads that Black can kill White. Don't bother defending. Black won't get it right.

In Diagram 14b Black makes an obvious but doomed attempt to kill White. White lives. Against a strong player, however, White is killable. I leave that unshown because it is always a mystery to the weaker player.

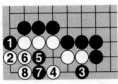

Diagram 14b

9. **Bounce Around:** Black has trouble changing focus of attention. If you play out all your moves in one area before moving to another, Black can remember what is going on, what Black wants to do, and how to do it. If you bounce around, you gain several advantages.

a. Black may become conditioned to responding to you in the obvious way.
b. Black may become irritated at being led around and may break off inappropriately.
c. Black may get tempted by something left earlier and may break off inappropriately.
d. Black may forget what Black was trying to do when you return to an area and change goals.

In the four-stone handicap game on the 13x13 board of Diagram 15a, White invades each of the corners in succession. This is too simple. Black plays out each one and knows what is happening at each moment.

Instead, White should bounce around as in Diagram 15b. After White 1 and 3 in the first corner, White switches to 5 in a new corner. Maybe Black will be hypnotized and just respond. Maybe Black will stop and wonder *why* White suddenly left. Is there a dastardly trap being set up? Is the obvious response by Black the wrong one? Maybe Black should try a different response. After Black does respond, White jumps to a new corner for the next three moves. This cannot fail to discomfort Black, even if eventually all the same moves of Diagram 15a are played. Will Black at the end of this diagram stay with White or switch to some other area in a vain attempt at displaying defiance?

10. **Memorize Joseki Traps:** These opening traps create scenarios in which the obvious naive response is dangerously wrong. Knowing a few of these is always useful. Since these are cataloged in joseki books, I won't show any here.

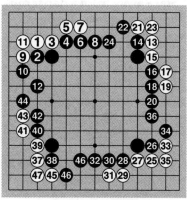

Diagram 15a

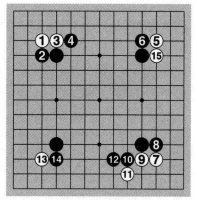

Diagram 15b

For Either Player

1. **Let your opponent fill in the last liberty:** on some opponent string so you can take it off in the next move. (Only works at real beginner stages.) Let your opponent fill in the last outside liberty on some opponent string so that a cut now works inside enemy territory (works for months, maybe even years). The way to do this is play worthless endgame fills everywhere else, and let your opponent take the dangerous liberty fill. If you played it, your opponent would examine the string to see if there was any danger. Your opponent will often play it without checking for the danger.

2. **Stare away from a dangerous move:** Let your opponent think you are going to play elsewhere. Don't pore over an intricate trap sequence. If you can find it, your opponent can, too, if you guide your opponent to look for it.

3. **Look weak:** (dangle bait). Lure your opponent into piecemealing or bad shape. If your opponent makes an outrageous overplay because you look weak, punish your opponent for it. If you are Black, don't let on that you have read this book. In a handicap game White wins by playing unreasonably. So if you can spot what White's up to and punish unreasonable moves, you will have a great advantage.

4. **Play something that looks like a ko threat but aims to do more:** In the heat of the ko your opponent may think it was just a ko threat and nothing more.

5. **Show fighting spirit:** Don't let your opponent psyche you out. A doormat is easily defeated, but so is an overly aggressive player.

6. **If you are losing, ignore your weak groups:** Keep shifting from midgame to endgame and back again.

7. **Play Mirror Go:** This minimizes thought during the opening, particularly if your opponent is better than you in opening play.

Diagram 16 shows White mirroring Black's moves. Upon seeing Black's next move, White mentally transforms the move around the center point to the opposite side of the board and plays there. Until Black plays on the center point itself, White can mimic all Black moves and no one will get an advantage.

As Black, you can even play your first move on the center point and then mirror White. White cannot stop you by playing on the center, but there is a way White can force you to stop mirroring.

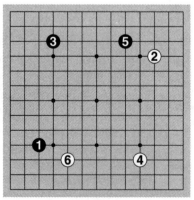

Diagram 16

If Black is blindly obedient in mirroring you, use Black's center stone as a filled-in liberty. In Diagram 17, Black mirrors each White move around the center stone (1). At the end, both Black and White are in atari because of Black 1. Without 1, both sides would still be safe. But now it seems like Black is playing 1, putting stones in self-atari. A White play at *a* will capture five Black stones. Black will be unable to mirror that, and it will be a disaster for Black. Black will have to break off earlier and give up mirroring.

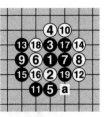

Diagram 17

8. **When winning easily, always respond to a move from a dead group:** Even spend extra moves to keep dead groups dead by removing any shape at all that they might make. This protects you from oversights.

9. **Pass to invite resignation:** It is tedious just waiting for someone to realize they are way behind. It's impolite to ask them to resign, so this is the next best thing.

10. **Play the Great Wall Opening:** If your opponent hasn't heard of it, then your opponent will go into shock, shake with hysterical laughter, or seriously underestimate you. It also ruins all joseki knowledge your opponent has studied.

11. **Always play fast and think on your opponent's time:** This induces your opponent to speed up and make mistakes.

12. **If your opponent is almost out of time, don't look at the clock:** Don't remind your opponent about the time. Play reasonably fast so your opponent can't use your time and play difficult tactical moves to tempt your opponent to read it out carefully.

13. **If your move is really good, hit the board hard:** The sound of the stone hitting the board, the "plonk", indicates the severity of your move. If you want your opponent to think you've just played an insignificant move put the stone down quietly.

14. **Play repetitious moves at a fast speed:** This will numb the opponent into doing the obvious instead of thinking.

In Diagram 18, Black 2 stopped White 1 from connecting underneath. White 3 was a Go sharp. White 3 looks like White 1 and Black 4 reacted the same way. When asked, Black readily admitted she didn't know if she could live after White 3. Also when asked, Black readily admitted she could see how to connect her five-stone string to safety by playing right of 2. But it didn't occur to Black during play. White discouraged Black from thinking about it by playing a similar move to White's previous one and playing it quickly. *Would you prefer to clearly save five of your seven stones or risk losing them all to save two more?* I asked. Black's answer did not match Black's play.

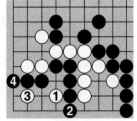

Diagram18

15. **If you are fast and your opponent is slow, walk away from the board:**
This will disrupt your opponent and slow you down enough to avoid grossly foolish reflexive plays. Your opponent can't really object to your walking away and getting a drink, going to the bathroom, etc.

Honesty, the Best Policy

Professional players would never use these sharping tricks (or very few of them). They play simple, almost ascetic moves that completely do the task at hand and will not go sour in the future. Their view is not for the greed of the moment, but for the long view of the game and their own self-training. They have perseverance and patience and focus on the ultimate result. They know the game is not usually won in a momentary flash of luck or inspiration, but instead is won in tirelessly playing good moves and constantly challenging the value of the obvious move. As long as the game is kept close, you can win as either Black or White.

In the late 1970's Atari Corporation, an American company, dominated a new market called video games. A couple of years later, the market was destroyed. All of the companies in the field went bust. Millions of game cartridges were plowed into the ground. Retailers and wholesalers wouldn't touch anyone or anything remotely connected with video games. That was when Nintendo tried to enter the market. The head of Nintendo had seen the collapse and thought the market had been mismanaged. So he tried to regenerate it against the odds.

In **Game Over**, a book about the history of Nintendo, David Sheff wrote: *If Nintendo had been an American company playing by the rules such companies follow, it would have given up long before there was any indication of success — that is, after Arakawa's original market surveys, when the AVS [the precursor to the Nintendo Entertainment System] failed, or when there was resistance at the first trade shows. Many American companies are so wedded to market research that the devastating results of focus groups have signaled death knells. Had Nintendo been American, the company would have probably retreated when retailers in New York declined to place orders or when it took more than a year for big sales numbers to appear. But commitment to an idea and pure tenacity are inherent in Japanese business philosophy, and certainly to Japanese business success.*

The head of Nintendo was a 6-dan Go player, understood the long view, and had the resources and patience to commit to it. He felt Atari hadn't played the honest move. Atari had cut corners and played for maximum immediate profit. The market crashed because anyone and everyone was making games and selling them in huge quantities. Large numbers of awful crap games made it impossible to distinguish the good games, and this destroyed the reputation of all games. Nintendo kept total control over who could make games, how many games a year they could make, and how many were produced. Nintendo kept even the best games in short supply. If the games were good and consumers couldn't pig out, the market could be built into a lasting one. Nintendo has sold over one billion video games.

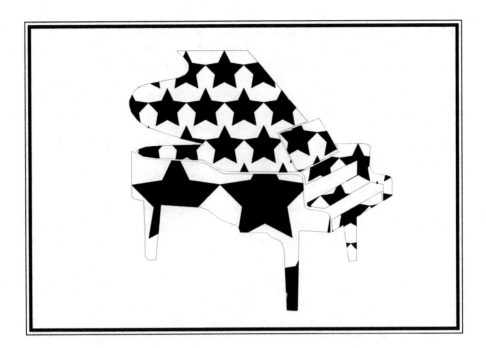

Variations on a Theme

A pianist practices scales. Over and over again walking up and down the keyboard. Is this music? No. Yet it useful as a training exercise. A volleyball player begins practice by stretching and twisting exercises, getting the muscles limber. Is this volleyball? No. Yet during a game a volleyball player will stretch and twist in various contexts. Practice a part to perfect the whole. In Go there are books and books of life and death problems, best move problems, and commented professional games. Studying these is obviously useful, but you must be a dedicated Go aficionado to do so.

The training exercises presented in this chapter are easier to enjoy for a wider audience. For example, I teach many of these to business professionals in a five-year leadship program offered by Hecht and Associates, Inc. Hecht and Associates, Inc., is an educational institution for business people who want to gain the knowledge and skills needed to design satisfying careers and successful businesses. They bring me in to teach the application of the metaphor of Go as it relates to designing powerful business alliances and structures (shapes).

In their five-year program, 150 business professionals play a Go tournament in the afternoon lasting about an hour to an hour and a half. During the tournament background music is played, candy is given out, and prizes enough for fifteen or more people are displayed on a prize table. The goal is to provide a fun but distracting environment to throw people off center so they can observe how they are triggered to go for the prizes rather than remain focused in their business conversations. Why are they playing Go? Will they get distracted? Will they be seduced into playing for the prize and lose sight of learning or respectful interaction with their opponent? How is this relevant to them and how they move in business?

One of the "tricks" I pull is to have them play a tournament under changed rules. Remember, the focus of this group is on accumulating power in a complex, rapidly changing marketplace. Changing the rules has them look at the fundamental premises to see what implications the changes have toward new strategies and tactics. Here are some of the variant games they play.

The Big Five: In regular Go each player places one stone per turn. What happens if each player gets five stones per turn? Each stone placed must still obey all rules for legal moves. You still can't capture a group with two secure eyes because when you place the first stone in an eye, it suicides. I played this once with a strong Korean professional. He knew lots more Go than I, but he didn't appreciate what changes in the rules would mean, so he lost easily. What are some of the implications?

1. A string is in atari with five liberties.
2. Sketching with links is wrong since links can be destroyed in one turn.
3. The only good connection is a solid one.

The typical mistake is to think you are given five turns in a row. From this viewpoint you recreate regular Go by the usual sketching process. Wrong. You are given one turn consisting of five stones. Play them all connected together as a fast and safe wall.

The lesson is that speeding things up does more than just change the time frame. It can change the underlying nature of the game. It used to take years to develop new products. In many industries that time is now down to six to nine months. This has implications for all aspects of the business

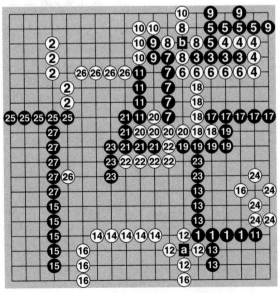

5 in a Row

including marketing, production, design teaming, etc. It is not just a speedup. The business itself may need to change.

In Diagram 5 in a Row Black played *a* with turn 1 and *b* with turn 3. Since neither stone was safe, White spent turn 8 capturing and filling *b*, and turn 12 capturing and filling *a*. After White 8 Black spent most of turn 9 insuring life for his corner. At the end of the current position, White can capture Black's turn 7 stones if he wishes. White 24 is part of a living group. If Black captures the single White 16 and then fills, Black will have only five liberties and White can recapture the five stones (a *snapback*). It is important to leave no gaps into territory. Black's two big territories still have leaks in them, whereas White has made it a point to keep White gaps to a minimum.

The Big Ten: If you've had fun with the Big Five, now try the Big Ten. Same rules, but now you have ten moves in a row. Other than the obvious continuations of implications of the Big Five, what new implications arise?

    1. You can create a living group with two eyes in one turn.

    2. Areas need to be smaller to prevent invasion (a consequence of #1).

Lightning Go: Play a regular game of Go on a 19x19 board, but use a clock set to ten minutes per player. If you run out of time, you lose. This emphasizes strategic vision and discourages tactical reading. This is particularly important since most Go books cannot teach strategy and vision and instead teach tactics. You will do well if you have mastered the sector-line running principle and contact fights. These keep your position intact with no real reading involved.

Actually, for me, ten minutes per player is not lightning Go. This is my normal time in a tournament. When I want a lightning game, I set five minutes per player. Once, on the Internet Go Server, where you suffer from transmission lags playing Go over a network, I played three minutes per player. It's like musical chairs because you know someone is going to run out of time. In that game my opponent did, but he was also losing on the board.

Most Wins: In a tournament lasting only one and half hours with no clocks, you need to find good winning criteria. If you play games on 9x9 boards, then you can play a large number of them. Most Wins encourages fast play, which is always desirable in beginners, and teaches important lessons. In new domains covering the ground rapidly with experiments is much more productive than methodically thinking about each move. In business, when a new market opens up, speed of exploitation is critical. Experiment rapidly with small things. Abandon those you appear to be losing and move on to the next experiment. Most students found this an exhilarating and liberating experience, particularly those who tended to be fearful of mistakes and so wanted to think longer. Here they could see that thinking didn't lead to winning.

Most Games: Sometimes I get a really mixed crowd of people, some who have played Go for a year and some who have just learned that day. The challenge is to find a fair contest that will still act as a training vehicle. I give them this one. The rules are normal

Go rules, but the winner is whoever plays the most games. You may only play each person once.

Think about this. You can resign at any time and that constitutes a complete game. Obviously there is an advantage to resigning early if you are losing. For those of you really wanting the tournament, you can resign at the first move, count the game as played, and move on to the next game. Some people did this. It was self-defeating. Not only do you get little of value out of it, you may not even win the tournament. The winner of this tournament did not do this.

Instant Death: I usually teach this after having given an extensive lecture on sacrifice. The game is regular Go rules but with one addition: if you capture an opponent's stone, you win instantly. Naturally all the material on sacrifice is now worthless. In addition to concentrating the mind on tactics and slow, safe development, this variation has the virtue of fast feedback. I use this game after emphasizing games with speed and spontaneity in them.

Instant Replay: This one requires a bit of trickery. On all boards in the room, I had the players set up the exact same situation I had concocted at the front. It was in the midgame and Black had a powerful position while White had a feeble one. There was no question, even for beginners, who would win this game. The only question was by how much of a slaughter. I asked them to decide who was the stronger player in advance (this game is for people who've played for a while) and have the stronger player take Black just to magnify the victory. I told them to play it out from there and that after the game they would switch sides and try it again. Each player's score would be the sum of the margins from their two games (signed for color). Therefore, White should try to minimize the loss and Black should try to maximize the win. I told them White should pay careful attention to what Black did, since then White could use information on what happened to advantage next time. The games began. (Afterwards we discussed how they felt as Black and White.)

What I didn't tell them was that I lied about the rules. When the first game finished, I announced a rule change. Instead of switching sides, they were to keep the same sides,

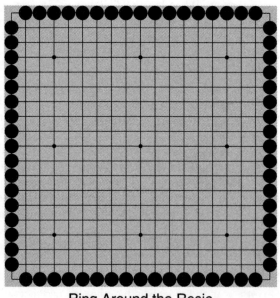

Ring Around the Rosie

and their score would be how much better they did this game than last. Now, suddenly, things were different. If they had spent the first game planning how they would play when they switched, their planning was wasted. A Black player who had crushed White in the first game had a much harder time improving on the score. A Black player who hadn't been as successful the first time had a much better chance of winning the tournament by showing the most improvement. White had a good chance too. White would still lose the game, but if White could reduce the margin of loss enough, he might win the tournament. You can have lots of postgame discussion on how rules change unexpectedly and how people behave who geared up for the previous universe.

Ring Around the Rosie: In the Ring-Around-the-Rosie diagram, it is White to play and live. Black's stones around the edge are safe and White must try to make shape without using the edge. This is an excellent training device for learning shape development, shape attack, and the intermingling of shape and contact needed to gain life.

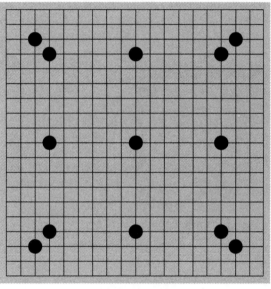

Unlucky 13: White to play and live in Diagram Unlucky 13. This 13-stone handicap doesn't leave room for White in the corners, but the edges are open. Where is the best invasion point? How should each side play?

Unlucky 13

The best invasion is at the fulcrum between two areas and in contact. White 1 of the Diagram Unlucky 13: Invade is optimal. Black's highest priority is to keep White off the edge, and avoid being involved in a contact fight, so Black 2 is good (better than one to the right of it). White 3 dare not extend far. Black 4 blocks further edge expansion while threatening to steal territory. It can connect back to the lower right corner for safety.

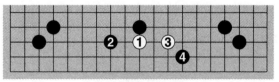

Unlucky 13: Invade

Kriegspiel Go: This is played on three boards, one color of stone on each player's board plus a referee board with both players' stones. The players sit back to back and cannot look at each other's boards. The referee arbitrates constantly by comparing both boards and announcing if a proposed move is legal or not. Effectively, your opponent's stones are invisible to you but still have their usual effects. You are told if an intersection you attempt to play on is occupied, and if you are surrounded by invisible stones your stone is taken off the board. This game requires a great memory and is full of crazy constructions of vast amusement to the onlookers, exercising the skills of prediction and the traps of the unexpected.

Death Room: In the diagram at right, it is White to play and live. This game teaches life and death tactics and principles. Most Go players think there is no challenge in it. They think that a 3-3 corner under a handicap stone can always be invaded. Here, there isn't a Black stone within miles of the 3-3 point. However, with reasonable play (no great sophistication), Black can generally kill White.

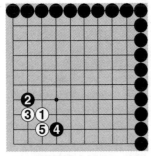

Death Room

The key is that there are no weaknesses in Black's wall. Diagram Death Room: Attack shows a typi-

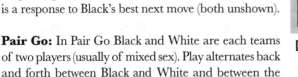

Death Room: Attack

cal beginning. White invades and Black immediately threatens each of White's doors. After White 5 White has a single eye in the corner. Black's stones can fall back and join safely to the wall, and with good play White will not get an eye in the open region. Because of this, professional players had long been believed when they claimed that White could not live.

Eventually, Maeda, a professional known for his life and death problems, found the two trick moves needed by White to insure life. Diagram Death Room: Defend shows the first of the two trick moves. Rather than defending, White 3 puts severe pressure on Black. Though the pressure can not kill Black, it distracts Black long enough for White to get life. The second trick move is a response to Black's best next move (both unshown).

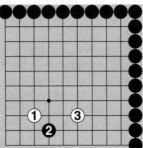

Death Room: Defend

Pair Go: In Pair Go Black and White are each teams of two players (usually of mixed sex). Play alternates back and forth between Black and White and between the two players on each team *without consultation*. This is particularly interesting when the two players on a team have wildly different skill levels. The weaker player must hold up his or her end by learning to play noncommittal global moves. The stronger player must avoid moves likely to confuse the weaker partner as to their intent. Together the strong and weak player must learn to combine their best strengths without conversation.

Fantasy Liar's Dice

This is not Go but is a mental exercise useful to Go players and a popular pastime of British Go players. It encourages memory, flexibility, and inventiveness. It is a variant on a game using poker dice known as Liar's Dice. The dice faces are: ace, king, queen, jack, ten, and nine.

In the 'straight forward' version, a concealed hand of dice is passed from player to player seated around a table. After each pass, the player holding the dice can choose to roll any number of them to improve the value. How many are rolled is declared, but no one else gets to see the result of the roll. The holder then declares a poker hand value that he claims is being passed on.

The next player has the option of believing or disbelieving the description of the hand as conveyed to him by its current holder. Depending on this belief, the next player chooses whether to accept or refuse the hand. If challenged to prove the contents of the hand, the holder must reveal it. If it is of lesser value than declared, the declarer has to lose one of the three 'lives' the declarer started the game with. If the hand is at least as strong as declared (or stronger), then the recipient loses a life. In either case, all five dice are thrown by the next player and the declaring of value starts over.

Actually, the decision on whether to challenge often depends a lot on whether you think that the person following can be persuaded to accept the hand you will pass them. Only if one is convinced that

the following person will challenge will one make a precise judgement as to whether the dice are there or not. Hence the stratagem of calling easy-to-improve-hands to encourage people to accept (four nines and a ten is likely to be improved upon rolling the ten) and calling hard-to-improve-hands to try to make people challenge (three aces and two kings). The real skill comes in bluffing with these stratagems when facing experienced players.

The value of a hand ascends from a random jumble of dice, usually described as "rubbish" through one pair of matching number or court symbols, two pairs, a full house, then series of symbols such as three nines, four jacks up to the maximum call: five aces. (To be precise, the value of a hand ascends from nine, ten, jack, queen, king through five other non-matched hands (e.g., nine, ten jack, queen, ace) to two nines, ten, jack, queen), etc.

A full house is three of a kind plus two of a kind — all dice used, hence full. The sequence is one pair, two pairs, three of a kind, full house, four of a kind, and five of a kind. It is also important to point out that the largest part dominates, i.e. three aces and two nines is better than three kings and two aces, that three aces and two nines is better than three kings and two queens. It is also worth stating that unspecified dice default to the lowest value consistent with the call, thus "full house" is three nines and two tens; "better" is three nines and two jacks. Four of a kind would beat a full house, higher cards beat lower-card combinations, and descriptions of the hand can be precise or vague. There are no runs or flushes.

"Better" is an allowed call but is permitted on the understanding that a calculation of the contents of the hand can be made based on its original call. For example, imagine starting with a call of two pairs followed by "Better" three times. The original hand would be presumed to be two nines, two tens and a jack. The new hand would have improved to two nines, two tens and an ace.

An original unspecified call is always assumed to be as low as possible. It is illegal to make a call lower than a preceding call; it must be an improvement on the hand. It is not required that one roll the dice each time, just that the call be changed. Any number of the dice can be rolled each time but the number must be declared and is an important factor in assessing the veracity of the subsequent call.

Being caught out in a lie results in paying a forfeit of a life. Catching someone out results in being allowed to roll a new hand of dice and starting a fresh round of the game. The game continues until there is only one person still with a life. The first person to lose all three of their lives is given the "dog's life" (an extra life) but must stand on a chair and bark. After that the loss of all lives just means that person is out of the game. (It's not a New Age game!)

If you are passed a call of five aces, there is no way you can improve on it. Instead you are given three complete rolls of all five dice in which to get five aces yourself. If you fail (most likely), you lose your life. If you succeed, the passer loses one.

Fantasy Liar's Dice permits a more flavorful description of the contents of the hand. The relative merits of the symbols must be preserved, but the descriptions of them may be obscure or fanciful. Each call must embroider or continue a story or theme started by the first call of a round. Careful attention is needed to assess what the call is based on in the normal liar's dice world, in case of a challenge. An example of a call could be three fighter pilots in the company of two shady ladies — clearly a full house which could be as low as three jacks and two queens. The story could continue with the fighter pilots receiving top promotions because they shot down many enemy planes (The hand becomes three "aces" plus two queens.) Of course none of this has to be true, it may be better or worse, depending on one's lying and fantasy skills.

You may wonder how this relates to Go. Go has its own culture in the West. At tournaments there are traditions as to what else goes on as well as playing Go and its mutations. One of these traditions involves playing Liar's Dice (preferably in a bar), but some of the most successful games have been played in restaurants. As with Go, the rules are simple, but to play the game skillfully is a matter of practice. Other traditions involve the singing of Go songs — many of which require a knowledge of Japanese Go terms or Go historical figures — hence their restricted appearance here.

You Rang?

Who Was That Masked Man?
How to Form a Go Club
Want More?
What Does It Mean?
A Repast of Books
Where Was That Bit About?

*" To know oneself,
one should assert oneself."*

Who Was That Masked Man?

Before we say a hearty "Hi-Ho Silver" and ride off into the sunset, the reader may well ask "who were those masked authors?"

Bruce Wilcox, 5-Dan

EZ-GO's metaphoric affliction is merely a manifestation of my fascination with words and meanings. Words define the world, how it is perceived and acted upon. When I was in my late twenties and early thirties, I used to try to learn about people by asking questions like: *Summarize your life in three words or less.* This was my parody of those essay questions that asked you in 25 words or less to describe whatever. What is interesting is how much can be covered in a mere three words. How people answered the question, if they were willing to be constrained to three words, and how long they took to come up with them were as revealing as the answer itself. Here is my current answer:

playful, program, Go.

My words are eclectic; an adjective, a verb, and a noun, as I am a mixture of science and psychology and art.

I am and have always been **playful**. I played and designed games in high school and programmed games in college. I design games for 3DO. I mangle words for fun. I bring entertainment into the workplace. I have been known to "drop in" on secretaries (falling flat on the floor in front of them), "beat eggs in a bowl" using my fists. My wife and kids are careful to ask for cereal in a bowl, with a spoon and milk, lest I neglect one of them. Being a programmer, I interpret words literally, for fun.

My career has always been to **program** software. I started programming for money during a summer in late high school and have been doing it ever since. My specialities are Artificial Intelligence (AI), system software and compilers, and Go. After graduating with a Bachelor's from the University of Michigan, I worked as an AI researcher. Shortly into my job, I was asked to program the computer to play Go. I didn't know how to play, and this led to my acquiring a unique perspective on the game. I was the first, in 4,000 years, to learn the game not to play it, but to program it. People who learn for the sake of playing, soon incorporate what they have learned into reflexes and forget how and why they make moves. I learned as I was programming the game, so I developed a conscious theory of play that can be taught. This book is a distillation of much of that. My theories were first published starting in the late '70s as a series called "Instant Go" in the *American Go Journal*. This book expresses and vastly expands on those early ideas.

My calling is **Go**. Since 1972 I have been programing, playing, teaching, and writing about the game. I expect to continue doing so until I die. I have been called the "Father of Computer Go" for creating the first successful program and writing enough about it to encourage others to try their hand. I am also the only recognized Western Go theorist and am paid to lecture on Go at the US and European Go Congresses and to teach the interaction of Go theory and business to an ongoing business seminar.

Bruce and Sue Wilcox playing Go in Hawaii.

Sue Wilcox, 10-Kyu

I am only an egg. Maybe an egghead. I love Go but perhaps from a different perspective from most Go players — I like to understand people by what they reveal of themselves as they play. One of my beginnings was as a psychologist. The habit of asking questions and looking for odd answers between the lines persists. Words define the reality we agree on, so I am inevitably entangled in words. Whether this means this book is too wordy is up to you to decide. Certainly I feel it is time someone tried to demystify Go for the Western world. Having been a talked-down-to kyu player for far too long, explanation has become a cause of mine, explanation with humor and oddity, because structure is only part of how we remember.

I am a writer with a background in art, science, computing, and psychology. I currently do free-lance writing for hi-tech magazines and am the VRML Pro at *www.inquiry.com*: specializing in Virtual Reality Modeling Language, 3D worlds, and other such esoterica. My three words are:

create, change, chance.

Three verbs: to create, to change, to chance. Verbs because they describe movement — energy and travel have characterized my life. I have always been a creator: of art, writings, designs, food, music, clothes, jewelry, ceramics, gardens, and houses. To create is to cause change and I thrive on variety. Perhaps what I create most often is myself. But to change is to take chances and to trust that the universe knows I am going in a good direction. My rate of change seems to be accelerating, so who knows where I will be next. The field of computing communications is where I am most at home. The pace is frenetic, and I can use all my skills at once. Visit our Website (**www.slip.net/ ~wilcox**) and see what I mean.

Creating interactive multimedia on the World Wide Web is the thing that brings work closest to being play. I once described myself in print as a steam buff into synthesizers — now I'm more of a Sci-Fi buff into Go. I've been reading science fiction since I could read and playing Go since 1985. The technological high frontier is waiting for Go to reach it. I hope this book is the last old tech before cyberGo. See you in the future...

EZ

How to form a Go club

Seek out local Go players and find a time when you are all free to get together. Organize a place to meet. Find a way to pay for the club. Travel there, argue about the smoking rules, membership fees, who locks up, who cleans up, where to get Go sets, what rules to play by, whether to affiliate with the AGA, who is in charge, then see if there is time left to get a game — if the person nearest your strength isn't already playing. OR

Buy

EGO

Choose among nine congenial personalities to play on an opulent Go board in the comfort of your own home whenever you choose. Approximate strength: twelve kyu depending on whom you play. Particularly recommended for teaching beginners (no Ego problems with letting them win games.) Animated icons give you insight into the program's thought processes. Enjoy watching it change to a defensive watery strategy when you have it on the run. See the flicker of its fiery temper when its being aggressive. Every personality has an animation to show when its in control of Ego.

Psycho: a player obsessed with the Great Wall opening.
Leaper: a believer in the power of tenuki.
Pirate: what's yours is mine
Earthy: it takes lots of points to win
Watery: a strong defense is the best attack.
Airy: influence is all
Fiery: blind fury incarnate
Schizo: there's a lot to be said for all these approaches
Samurai: balance is the secret of true aggression

EGO is a DOS product that can run under Windows. Its is written by Bruce Wilcox, author of such famous antiques as Nemesis Go Master and Instant Go.

Preview EGO by downloading EZ-GO from ftp://bsdserver.ucsf.edu/Go/comp/ez-go.zip and see if you can handle a Psycho or a Leaper.

Order EGO from:

Bruce & Sue Wilcox
P.O. Box 5558,
Redwood City, CA 94063- 0558

$25 or 18 pounds sterling (no plastic) or address questions to
wilcox@slip.net

260

Want More?

In the above photo, Bruce is playing with his traveling Go set. If you aren't as strong as Bruce, you may prefer a computer Go program. Bruce has written commercial computer Go software since 1984. Originally, it was NEMESIS Go Master in the US and Taikyoku Igo (by BPS) and AI Igo (by Something Good) in Japan. Now EGO (EZ-Go in shareware) is his current software product.

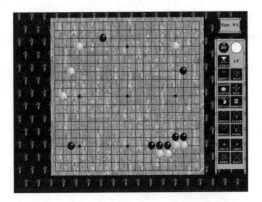

Screen Shot of EGO Program

Some of Bruce's writings on Go theory were originally published under the name Instant Go. This book is the current revision of those theories. It concentrates on the theory. We have further vaporware works planned for release in the new millennia:

EZ-GO — Oriental Strategy Dissected: a volume of game commentaries explicating EZ-GO theory applied in real game contexts.

EZ-GO — Oriental Strategic Enigmata: a volume of EZ-GO illustrational problems to improve your mastery of the theory.

We both think multimedia is great. Paper lacks a lot of flavor. We hope to have multimedia products to offer you someday. Stay tuned.

How to keep in touch with our new products: the easiest way is to join our mailing list; then you'll hear when we have a new book coming out, a new Go program upgrade, a new intelligent IGS client or a multimedia Go product ready. We have been known to move a lot and even e-mail addresses change (with no forwarding arrangements possible as yet). The Go FAQ on the Internet will always be a source of our latest address. As of the beginning of 1996, our e-mail address is **wilcox@slip.net**. A posting on the Go newsgroup will also find us rapidly. The American Go Association always has a good idea where all its members are, and the American Go Federation, who supported the production of this book, can also help you contact us.

Big news we would always post on the newsgroup (rec.games.go), which is the pulse of the Go community worldwide.

Look out for the EZ-GO lectures at Go Congresses — Bruce hopes to appear as time and sponsorship permit, both at big events and at local clubs.

For further information about Hecht and Associates, Inc., contact Theresa Allen, VP of Sales and Marketing, at: (408) 730-2234.

Contact American Go Association to find local Go clubs and members.
PO Box 397, Old Chelsea Station, New York, NY 10113-0397

What Does It Mean?
Some Japanese Terms in Western Go

If you should happen to find some old English-language Go books lying around, they may use terms from the original Japanese instead of English substitutes. Here is a translation guide:

Aji: Potential, options, possibilities, lingering flavor.
Aji-keshi: A move that destroys one's own aji in a situation.
Atari: The threat to capture a stone or group because it has only one liberty.
Atekomi: A tesuji that wedges onto a diagonal link.
Atsumi: Thickness.
Boshi: A capping move.
Byo-yomi: Overtime; extra time given a player when his clock has run out.
Chuban: The middle game.
Dame: A liberty; or a neutral point.
Dame-zumari: Shortage of liberties.
Dan: A strong player's rank. Amateur dan ranks go from 1-Dan (shodan) to 7-Dan
Dango: A clump of stones with no eye shape. Also called a dumpling.
De: Cut.
De-giri: Push and cut.

Furikawari: A trade.
Fuseki: The opening moves of the game.
Geta: A way of capturing stones by using a net formation.
Goban: The Go board.
Go ishi: Go stones.
Goki: Go-stone bowls.
Gote: A move that does not require an answer; it loses the initiative.
Guzumi: An empty triangle that is necessary.
Hamete: A trick move or trap.
Hanami-ko: A ko where only one player is at risk.
Hane: To bend around enemy stones with a diagonal move. Played from a friendly stone in contact with an enemy stone, leaving a cutting point.
Hasami: A squeeze play.
Hazama tobi: A diagonal skip move, leaving an empty point diagonally between.
Hiriki: An extension.
Honte: The proper or honest move.
Horikomi: A sacrifice move to create a false eye.
Hoshi: A star point. One of nine places where a handicap stone may be placed.
Igo: The Japanese word for Go.
Ikken tobi: A one-point jump move (leaves a single empty space between).
Insei: An apprenticed professional student.
Ishi-no-shita: Meaning "under the stones", it involves visualizing making moves where stones are presently existing, but which will be captured in the future.
Jigo: A drawn game.
Joseki: A classical sequence of moves said to produce a fair result for both sides.
Kakari: An attacking approach move against a corner.
Katachi: Shape (usually good shape).
Kata tsuke: Shoulder hit move (diagonal and toward the center against foe stone).
Keima: A knight's move, large or small.
Keshi: A reducing move.
Ki: The old name for Go.
Kiai: Fighting spirit.
Ki-in: Go association.
Kido: The way of Go.
Kikashi: A forcing move or threat.
Kiri: A cut.
Ko: Literally means a very long time. A situation of repeated captures interspersed with threats. Without the ko rule the game could go on forever.
Kogeima: A small knight's move.
Komi: Points given to White in an even game as compensation for playing second.
Kosumi: A diagonal move.
Kyu: A player's rank below dan level. Kyu grades run from 35 (weakest) to 1-kyu.
Magari: To bend around enemy stones with an in-line move. Played from a friendly stone in contact with an enemy stone.
Mane-Go: Mirror Go.

Miai: Alternative moves; if your opponent takes one, you must take the other.

Mochikomi: A failed invasion.

Moyo: A large area of potential territory.

Nakade: Playing inside a large unsettled eye shape to reduce it to one eye.

Nidan: 2-dan.

Nigiri: A way of deciding which side, in an even game, will play Black. One player takes a few White stones from the bowl, the other player guesses if there is an odd or even number of stones. If the guess is correct, that player takes Black.

Nikken tobi: A two point jump move (leaves two empty spaces between).

Nobi: A solid extension.

Nozoki: To peep a connection.

Oba: A big point in the opening or early midgame.

Ogeima: A large knight's move.

Oki: A placement move inside an enemy territory.

Ponnuki: The shape of capturing a single stone.

Rengo: Team Go.

Sabaki: Playing lightly, without commitment to specific stones.

Sagari: To descend towards the edge.

Sangen tobi: A three-point jump move (leaving three empty points between).

San-san: The 3-3 point.

Sanren-sei: An opening involving playing on three starpoint stones in a row.

Seki: A stalemate position where two opposing groups each lack two eyes and neither can attack the other without losing his stones.

Semeai: A capturing race which must end in death or seki.

Sente: Keeping the initiative by forcing the opponent to reply.

Shibori: To squeeze stones, forcing them to fill in a false eye.

Shicho: A ladder sequence or zigzag pursuit, in which one side keeps putting the other into atari until the stones are driven to the edge of the board or into the opponent's stones and captured.

Shicho-atari: A ladder-breaking move, played in the path of the ladder, to rescue the enclosed stones.

Shimari: A corner enclosure.

Shodan: The first dan level of player.

Suberu: A slide.

Takefu: A bamboo joint formation.

Tenuki: To play elsewhere, ignoring your opponent's last move.

Tesuji: A skillful tactical move.

Tetchu: A third-line in-line extension from a fourth-line side handicap stone.

Tobi: A jump.

Tsuke: A contact play or attachment.

Tsume-go: A life and death problem.

Watari: A move that links up two friendly groups of stones.

Yose: Endgame.

Appetizers

Learn to Play Go by Janice Kim
Lessons in the Fundamentals of Go by Toshiro Kageyama
In the Beginning by Ikuro Ishigure
Graded Go Problems for Beginners (Volumes 1-4) by Kano Yoshinori

Main Courses

All about Life and Death by Cho Chikun
Tesuji by James Davies
Attack and Kill by Masao Kato
Appreciating Famous Games by Shuzo Ohira
Basic Techniques of Go by Haruyama Isamu and Nagahara Yoshiaki

Desserts

How Would Confucius Ask for a Raise? by Carol Orsborn
The Way of the Peaceful Warrior by Dan Millman
The Treasure Chest Enigma by Noriyuki Nakayama
Healing Our World by Dr. Mary Ruwart
Psychotrends by Shervert H. Frazier
The Official British Go Association Song Book collected and edited by T. Mark Hall
Powershift by Alvin Toffler
Game Over by David Sheff

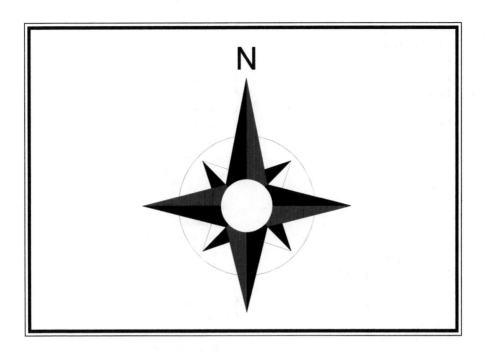

Where Was That Bit About...?

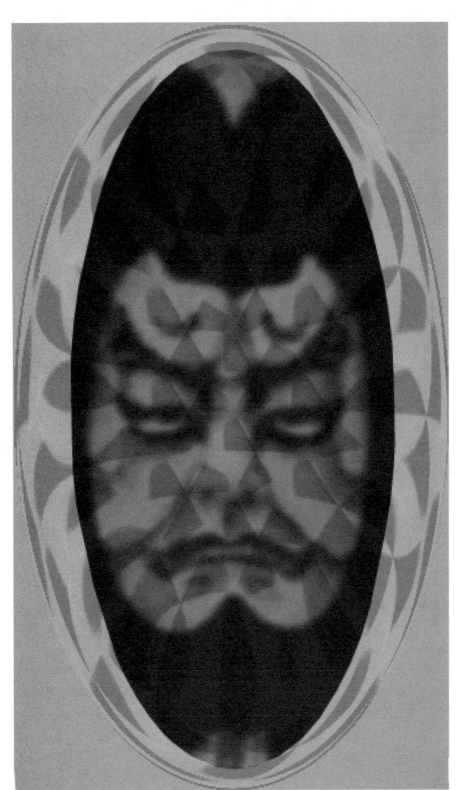